Todd Alexander has been writing for as long as he can remember. His work has been published in magazines and periodicals, and he is the author two novels and two memoirs. His first novel, *Pictures of Us*, was published in 2006, followed by *Tom Houghton* in 2015. In 2019 Todd released his bestselling memoir *Thirty Thousand Bottles of Wine and a Pig Called Helga*. It was long-listed for three industry prizes for best non-fiction book.

In 2012 Todd, his partner Jeff and their black alley cat Leroy left their busy city lives for a tree change in the Hunter Valley wine region of NSW. Today, Todd spends as much time as he can with his pig Helga, six goats, two sheep, chooks, ducks and peafowl. He writes whenever he gets the chance.

Web: toddalexander.com.au
Instagram: @toddalexanderwriter
FB: @toddalexanderauthor
Twitter: @Todd_Alexander

CW00551297

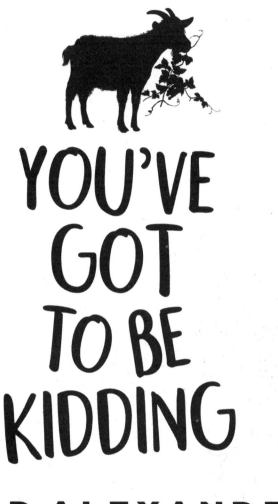

YOU'VE GOT TO BE KIDDING

TODD ALEXANDER

HarperCollins*Publishers*

HarperCollins*Publishers*
Australia • Brazil • Canada • France • Germany • Holland • Hungary
India • Italy • Japan • Mexico • New Zealand • Poland • Spain • Sweden
Switzerland • United Kingdom • United States of America

First published in Australia in 2021
by HarperCollins*Publishers* Australia Pty Limited
Level 13, 201 Elizabeth Street, Sydney NSW 2000
ABN 36 009 913 517
harpercollins.com.au

A catalogue record for this book is available from the National Library of Australia

ISBN 978 1 4607 5928 8 (paperback)
ISBN 978 1 4607 1298 6 (ebook)

Cover design by HarperCollins Design Studio
Cover images by shutterstock.com
Photographs by Work of Heart Photographic Studios
Typeset in Bembo Std by Kirby Jones
Printed and bound in Australia by McPherson's Printing Group
The papers used by HarperCollins in the manufacture of this book are a natural, recyclable
product made from wood grown in sustainable plantation forests. The fibre source and
manufacturing processes meet recognised international environmental standards, and carry
certification.

For my kids, Lucy & Charlie
I love you *just as much* as your four-legged siblings,
I swear

Contents

LIST OF RECIPES

There is no point at which you can say,
'Well, I'm successful now. I might as well take a nap.'
– Carrie Fisher

One

The Beginning of
the End

'That's it,' I said to Jeff. 'I'm out.'

'I'm out too,' Jeff said glumly. 'This isn't what we signed up for.'

After almost seven years of pretending to be farmers, you would have thought we'd have got our shit together. But I was feeling just as out of my depth as I had the day we'd moved in to one hundred acres of vineyards and olive groves with our dream of opening boutique accommodation. Back then, I'd pondered just how big one hundred acres was, but that was only after signing the contract for the purchase of 'Block Eight' (a name we'd once been determined to change).

Though to most people we might have looked successful, in reality we were constantly worrying where our next bit of income would be coming from, praying that it'd arrive before our next bill did. Day to day, we were barely scraping through and it felt like Jeff was checking the bank balance as often as I checked myself on the scales – every few minutes. And only one of those numbers was steadily on the rise.

We weren't being greedy. I'd have been happy to win second prize in a beauty contest the next go around the board, but instead the card I was being dealt was 'Assessed for street repairs'.

Enough was enough. I told Jeff I would give Shelly, the local real estate agent, a call and ask her to come and chat to us about putting Block Eight on the market. She'd been the one to sell us the property in the beginning, and we'd stayed in touch with her over the years.

'Good, because I'm so ready,' Jeff said and opened up the laptop to begin searching for a new property to buy. You know, with that million dollars in cash we had buried in an old barrel beneath the olive tree in row twenty eight.

'I just want somewhere quieter,' I said dreamily.

'And we need something that's more financially manageable,' Jeff added. 'Let's face it, we really need to be mortgage-free.'

This meant we had a strict budget but also wanted a parcel of land large enough that no other person could ever disturb us – we would be the masters of our own noise-making. Oh, and I definitely needed commanding views. In many respects we were firmly back to square one: two city idiots – one with a vision of becoming the Hunter's version of Maggie Beer, the other with a desire to use his hands to build stuff. No prizes for guessing which one was me.

Turns out, thousand-acre properties with beautiful views for under a million bucks don't exist. Who'd have thought?

'What about this one?' Jeff asked, turning the computer around to show me a bush block of about two hundred acres.

I thought: bushfires, snakes, hemmed-in, no views, too remote, too much hard work all over again and ... where would our animals live?

'Hmm, looks promising,' I said instead.

In truth, I was in mourning. My dream to become the next Maggie Beer hadn't been realised. Sure, I made jams that sold well at a local cellar door, and our wine and olive oil managed to sell out most years – until recently, at least – but no one had yet snapped me up for a cooking show. And where were the hordes of people coming to our property to eat our food or buy our produce, as they did at Maggie's? Is this how Maggie felt when she made the decision to shut down her restaurant and sell the last stake in her food business?

All of that aside, could we really consider going out on a low? The sense of relief I felt at the prospect of no longer needing to manage Block Eight was tinged with a dull ache of sadness that I knew would probably never go away.

Shelly agreed to come and see us the following week. I suppose I wanted her to do cartwheels at the prospect of selling the property as it was, and quote us a price way beyond the bounds of reality. *You're ready to list and you'll get four million for it*, she'd say before spreading a sold sticker over a sign down on the road. I'd prepared a list for her of the various tasks I thought we should consider doing before putting the property on the market in the coming spring. I went through the list and asked Shelly to prioritise which of those she thought were most crucial to getting the property sold.

'Well, I'd do all of those,' she said bluntly. 'It's a slowing market and you don't want anyone to think of hard work; just that they can move in and start making money from the business right away.'

When I mentally tallied all that the two of us had to do, it probably amounted to four to six months of constant work at the cost of the best part of one hundred thousand dollars. But then, what was the point of putting the property on the market only to have someone deduct money for jobs we could do at a fraction of the cost?

Then, as we walked around the property that Jeff and I had put so much of ourselves into for almost a decade, Shelly highlighted a few other jobs that would never have appeared on my list. It was eye-opening, to say the least. Walking around your property with a real estate agent is always going to give you a cold, hard reality slap. In truth, it helped us see the property more objectively, perhaps for the first time in a couple of years.

That needs a re-paint. Floors need some attention. I'd paint the roof of the house while I was at it. Need to tidy up the internal roads. The list went on. We were like two hapless dimwits on *Selling Houses Australia*, wondering why on earth no one wanted to pay top dollar for our property. At least Shelly delivered her pointers as gently as possible, because both of us were rapidly deflating.

We'd worked incredibly hard to tidy things up for the arrival of Jeff's mum, Millie, but there was still a shitload of heavy lifting to do. Now we had to decide if we would put a substandard property on the market and, if not, where the fuck we were going to find one hundred grand. My international modelling career just wasn't bringing in the cash like it used to.

'So what are you guys thinking of doing next?' Shelly asked after we'd driven her around the property trying to show off its best points.

'We want something a bit more remote; something quieter, so probably larger.'

'Just be mindful of moving further out to a larger property,' she said sagely. 'You might have more land, but in my experience that doesn't necessarily buy you privacy. People tend to roam onto larger blocks, or ride dirt bikes, because there isn't much of a concept of boundaries and, if it's too big for you to see the fence line, then you may never know who's on your land.'

'Or a bush block,' I suggested. 'Something that gives lots of privacy and we could just build a villa or two. Offer the whole bush-retreat type of experience?' I was seeking her approval.

'And be careful of bush blocks,' she continued her warning, 'because it's really tough to get permissions through council because of bushfires and other regulations.'

'Do you think we're crazy for selling?' I asked. 'I mean, I know you're our agent and it's not like you're going to say yes to me, but really …?' *Please, just wave your wand and make everything okay for us.*

'I think if you've decided the time is up at Block Eight then you've already made your mind up. You've got a beautiful property and you will walk away with the amount of cash you want for your next step.'

'But that's just it, isn't it?' Jeff said, sounding defeated. 'What is the next step?' He repeated Shelly's question – one we'd been pondering ourselves with no answer.

* * *

After we'd seen Shelly to her car and waved her off, Jeff sighed heavily.

'What?' I urged out of him.

'I'm so fucking confused.'

'About what?'

'It just feels like there's nothing else out there for us.'

'A week ago we both agreed we wanted out and now suddenly options for the future are too scary?'

'I'm so confused,' he said again, but I knew that wasn't the sum of it.

No two ways about it, we were both shit-scared that we were making the wrong decision. So much had happened to us since we'd decided on a rural tree change. In some respects, we *are* Block Eight and I'd tell anyone who'd listen that it was bliss and we loved it and we wouldn't change a thing. These two useless city boys had taken their complete lack of country knowledge and had mastered the tough times, ridden out their losses and were now high on success. But was any of that actually true?

* * *

Four Cs had originally inspired our tree change: curtains, cookbooks, cardiac arrest and cushions.

In 2010, we'd gone on a holiday to the Barossa Valley with our best friends Mel and Jesus (say it with a Spanish accent: *hey-Zeus*) and had paid a fortune to stay in some hovel with net curtains. Net curtains are like torture to Jeff's design sensibilities. He thinks they should be a capital offence. But despite how *bad* that place was (Tuscan hillside charm? More like a fibro garage converted into what could barely be termed a 'villa'), it was booked solid for the foreseeable future. We came back to Sydney relaxed and ready to undertake the biggest, longest, most expensive renovation known to humankind on our Annandale home, while hitting that familiar 'going nowhere' corporate treadmill.

By the end of the build, my only solace from the stressful job was collecting cookbooks, which I never cooked from. I had, on occasion, bought the same cookbook three times, having forgotten I already had two copies on the shelf. Jeff's parallel obsession was buying every single decorative cushion for sale in greater Sydney and placing them in questionable positions in our home. Like on a bookshelf from where he'd just removed some of my rare first editions and piled them on the floor. For Jeff, cushions are the equivalent of your nanna's afternoon sherry tipple; cushions just calm him, soothe him. And one is never enough.

The real clincher that something had to change in our lives was when Jeff ran the Sydney Marathon so fast that he collapsed at the finish line and had to be rushed to hospital in an ambulance (with me in the front very excited by the sirens as the driver ran red lights). There had to be more to life.

'Let's move out of the city and open our own accommodation,' I said to Jeff, who was still over the moon with his 3:18 marathon time (there'd been no cardiac arrest, thankfully). 'We'll blow net-curtain-clad cottages out of the water with your eye for soft furnishings and my marketing prowess.'

Then, after nearly eighteen months of inane and fruitless searching, we finally found our dream property – one that would allow me to transform into the Hunter Valley version of Maggie Beer. Okay, that may have been a stretch – I just wanted a nice kitchen garden and to make a few jams for family and friends, but there's no harm in aiming high.

We bought the property: one hundred acres in the wine region of the Hunter Valley in New South Wales, along with its twelve and a half thousand grapevines and one thousand olive trees. It wasn't until after we'd signed the deed on the property and driven away that I turned to Jeff and asked, 'Just how big is one hundred acres anyway?' For the record you can fit almost twenty-five Sydney Opera Houses or about thirteen Federation Squares on it.

Before Block Eight, the largest outdoor space we'd had was in our newly renovated house in Annandale in Sydney's Inner West, with its three-by-three-metre courtyard and a few herbs in pots ... and they were usually dead. And that was fine – we weren't buying the property to become farmers. We wanted to build accommodation. Our carefully considered plan was to eventually bulldoze the grapes and olives.

Things took an unexpected turn the first night we moved in, with our sometimes-feral black alley-cat Leroy aka Bertie aka Roy (only a few people have required antibiotics over the years after one of his Satanic switches into attack mode). That night, we tried a bottle of wine made by Brokenwood from our (*our!*) grapes and it blew our minds. It was quite possibly the nicest wine I'd ever tried.

'Shit,' I said to Jeff. 'We're going to become farmers now, aren't we?'

'How hard can it be?' he asked.

We raised our glasses to an easy, profitable, manageable, predictable and rosy future of living and working on the land. If they made a film about our lives (where naturally I'd be played by a Hemsworth … and any Hemsworth will do, thank you), the audience would erupt into laughter at this scene. Nevertheless, being us, one thing was certain – we would be giving it all we could. Jeff and I had thrown in our successful corporate careers in the city to jump together from a very steep, very high cliff. To hell with where we were going to land. We just figured we'd work out a strategy once we hit the bottom. And we have hit rock bottom – more times than we can count or care to remember.

You know the theory that says if you spend ten thousand hours doing something you're probably going to become an expert at it? Well, I bet you a million dollars the guy who invented that theory never set foot on a farm.

We'd been 'farmers' for almost seven years, or 61,320 hours, when we called Shelly to get her views on selling. I include sleep time in those hours, because most of the night I'm either dreaming about something to do with the farm, waking myself up panicked that I forgot to do something, or inventing ways to do something better.

Over those seven years, we have worked harder than we ever have in our lives. It is frigging backbreaking, muscle-tearing, skin-splitting labour. This whole farming lark cost us every single cent of our savings from Sydney, and then some. Just buying a tractor set us back over seventy grand. Who knew just how expensive it was to make your own wine and olive oil?

Hell, who knew it took the best part of six days just to mow the property? We'd be up for a twenty grand ride-on after we discovered the task couldn't be accomplished with just a pair of rusty garden shears and an Aldi electric lawnmower lent to us by my dad. (Before the ride-on, Jeff would mow around the house in a tight little circumference using three extension cords end to end.)

We sure did learn a hell of a lot over those years though. In fact, by our fifth anniversary on the property, together with help from countless friends, locals and hours of watching YouTube videos, we'd somehow, miraculously managed to land on our (now callused) country feet. Sure, we'd nearly gone broke about thirty times and, if you stopped Jeff any day on the street and asked him to tell you our bank balance, it would rarely, if ever, be more than a few hundred dollars. But by then we were used to living skint, having curbed most of our Sydney addictions and more frivolous materialistic purchases. There'd been no holidays, but that was okay too, because our pace of life in the country was just that much more chilled, genuinely less stressful and wonderfully healthy, with fresh air, vast open spaces and flavour-packed vegies plucked straight from our organic kitchen garden.

Our wine won awards – a wholly unexpected development but a thrill; a real pat on the back for some of that hard work, and for choosing one of the best winemakers in the Valley, Dan Binet. We sold out of our wine most years, selling it to a combination of wholesale buyers, friends, family and our accommodation guests, and we even sold out of our first olive oil too.

After living through building sites for most of it (flushing toilets were a city luxury I soon learnt to live without and, of course, Jeff never heard a single complaint from me), we could finally feel some satisfaction. We'd completed four tourist cabins and each was renting well. On the whole, we had a predictable income and were self-sufficient, living within our means. For the first time, we were paying GST to the government and at the end of the year had actually turned a bona fide profit. Our business was finally a few hundred dollars in the black, after accruing losses of hundreds of thousands.

Just like Maggie Beer, we even raised our own animals. Though ours weren't for eating, and had what most people would consider luxurious lives.

We could now be considered serious, *actual* farmers and country folk, couldn't we? (In fact, by then we no longer enjoyed the city at all and we'd made a nice little circle of local friends.) Country life? Totally nailed it!

At that five year point, we'd toasted to our life on the land and made more plans for our future. And that's just how stupid we were.

You see … you really shouldn't bother making plans when you live in the country. We were, after all, just tiny dots on the surface of the earth, and Mother Nature is one hell of a formidable, stubborn, strong-willed force. She really gets the giggles when you tell her you're making plans, and we were walking straight into her sticky web.

Two

Cushioning the Blows

Mother Nature broke into fits of laughter when she sent a storm to blow the metal roof off our close-to-finished, hand-built wine room in our fifth year at the property while we (Jeff, me, Winston and Wesley the goats, and Helga the pig) tried to take cover beneath it. Inspecting the damage was heartbreaking, infuriating and gut-wrenching. It was also, of course, all Jeff's fault.

Jeff is our self-appointed chief builder. After getting all the on-the-job training he could with our initial builder, Pete, he goes online for any additional building knowledge he requires. I thank all those people with nothing better to do with their time than make how-to videos on YouTube. As a result, Jeff *did* know that roofs need to be strapped down (hell, even I knew that). He *also* knew the winds on our property were sometimes gale-force, and he'd even been reminded by another builder mate, Richard, that strapping the roof down is essential. It's downright dangerous not to.

But, like me scrubbing the villas' toilets, there are just some jobs you prefer to put off until you've mentally prepared yourself for the shitty reality of them.

A less sensitive partner might have yelled at Jeff. A less sensitive partner might have questioned why Jeff had delayed the roof strapping for so long; might have cried over the loss of thousands of dollars in materials and countless hours in our labour. Yes, a less sensitive partner would have gone on and on (and on) about what a waste it was, what a setback, how it was all needless and avoidable. But lucky for Jeff I'm not like that! In the moment, I'm all sugar and spice and 'of course I'll help you build it twice'.

'It's completely ruined.' Jeff sounded like a man whose dreams had just been shattered. Maybe not quite as shattered as my confidence in him as a builder. On the field in front of us was a mess of twisted metal, wood, nails, screws … but no strapping, I noted.

'More like utterly fucked,' I added for a little dramatic effect.

When I looked at the sheer mass of the roof before us, it truly was mind-blowing that things hadn't ended more tragically. The wind had been strong enough to push the entire roof clear of the room, back about fifty metres. If it hadn't, it without a doubt would have crushed all five of us who'd been cowering inside, slicing our heads off with one swift blow. Phase three power also runs down to the room – three heavy wires of electricity that could have been yanked from their poles to whip about in the pouring rain, looking for some flesh to sizzle. An instant human, goat and pork barbecue.

Once we were all inside again and safe from the storm, I focused my mind on more positive things. Like the fact that the only personal injury had been a messing-up of Wesley's now-towel-dried, once-snow-white fur.

'Jeffy,' I said softly, 'it's just time and money. We will make both of them up, and we'll build an even better roof. Just you wait and see.'

'You know, it's funny,' he said, though without a hint of a smile. 'I was never satisfied with that stupid roof anyway. It just didn't sit right on the building.'

'Well, there you go. It was meant to be. Everyone's safe; no real harm done,' I said, a bastion of positivity. 'We get to rejig the design any way you want. But for now you deserve a little treat, so come on, let's go buy some cushions.'

* * *

'Oh hello, Jeff!' Deb, the shop assistant beamed when we entered one of the home furnishing stores he regularly visits. They've become quite friendly over the years. Apparently I was invisible. Jeff's mute design assistant, perhaps, or minimum wage trolley pusher.

'We've got some great new releases in this week. Have you seen the latest catalogue?' she asked excitedly. It was all she could do to keep from rubbing her hands together. I mean when would she get another Designer Gay in the shop in Rutherford?

'Yes, I downloaded it online,' he said. Well, of course he had.

Snippets of Jeff's conversation with a ridiculously enthusiastic Deb drifted past me as I made my way to the back of the store where the specials are kept. You never know when a turkey-shaped soap holder or a framed print of a half-eaten apple is going to be reduced in price, after all. It was a shame they didn't sell cookbooks because I've been known to buy one or two in my time.

'... al fresco,' I overheard Jeff saying.

'But within your usual style ethos?'

Jeff has a style *ethos*?

Sometimes I like to test this and bring home the ugliest piece of shit I can find. 'I thought this might look nice in a villa,' I'll say, then watch him try to find the most delicate way of telling me he'd rather die than display it to our guests. Once I brought home a pink ceramic animal – Deb and I had debated for fifteen minutes whether it was a rabbit or a kangaroo. It was kind of art deco, but one hundred per cent naff. He doesn't know I do this on purpose, just one of the little games I play with him. Well not until he reads it here.

That day, it was close to an hour later, after I'd browsed through both the pet *and* baby shops for something slightly less inane to do, when Jeff emerged with two massive bags of rather unremarkable flowery blue-and-white cushions.

'I decided I wasn't ready to buy any for the Wine Room yet,' he explained. 'But I thought these would look nice in our guest house.'

'Oh, okay,' I said, resigned.

'But I did buy a lovely bench seat for the Wine Room ...'

'*Okay ...*'

'And I got you this.'

He rifled around inside one of the bags and pulled out a large black statue of a piglet. The shape of this ceramic, at least, was unmistakable.

'Oh Jeffy, thank you,' I said, genuinely touched by the gesture.

'Well, I know you miss living with Helgy in the house, so I thought we could put this in our bathroom to remind us that's where she used to hang out.'

'I love it.'

Little did I know this would begin a small trend of people giving me pig paraphernalia. I wouldn't say I'm a hoarder, but I have dabbled in a few *collections* over the years. Largest of all was my Meryl Streep media clippings collection, which got to over two thousand pages long before I simply threw them all away and watched as the garbage truck struggled to lift its load the following morning. Then, of course, I have my cookbooks. There was a Joe Dallesandro movie poster phase; every CD Cyndi Lauper has ever produced; every book certain authors have ever written (Carrie Fisher, Ian McEwan, Anne Tyler and Maggie O'Farrell) and ... did I mention cookbooks? So what harm is there in keeping a few piggy statues around the house?

While cushions still and always will light up his dial, I think I have done poor old Jeff a disservice. I so often take the piss out of his predilection for cushions that I think people have come to our property expecting to find the villas literally overflowing with the things – you open the door and a tidal wave of cotton and fluff knocks you over. In place of grapevines, there are fields of cushions growing in the hot Hunter sun.

17

In actual fact, since opening our accommodation, Jeff quickly came to realise that an abundance of cushions isn't practical in our line of business. They mean more cleaning, more clutter, and more things to worry about. For their part, guests don't really want to shuffle around two hundred of them before getting into bed or sitting down on the couch. Instead, Jeff has very meticulously chosen just a couple of accent poufs, an umlaut to the 'o' in accommödation, if you will.

When our neighbour redesigned her own house to let to tourists, she definitely took several leaves out of Jeff's design manifesto (most notably his love of wainscoting, which adorns every single wall at hers, much like recycled wooden palings do at ours). But one thing she utterly ignored was his sage advice to keep cushions to a 'statement piece minimum' (Jeff's SPM theory). Jeff is in pure heaven every time he goes to take a peek at what she's done next, drool visibly collecting at the corners of his mouth. At ours, however, cushions naturally require regular updating and the poor outdated ones are simply discarded, left to rot in a far corner of the Singleton dump. Jeff has to stay 'on trend' so he'll never quite kick the addiction. He has a style ethos to maintain, after all.

'Guess what I did today?' he asked me after returning from one of his must-do shopping trips.

'Hmm, I dunno,' I said. 'Ran another marathon, though without nearly dying this time?'

'Yes, very good. At least I finished! No, today I did something that will make you very proud!'

'Go on …'

'Well, after I bought the new dining table at that furniture place going out of business' – *and coffee table and lamp and vase and mirror and armchair,* I silently added – 'the guy said "don't forget all of our cushions are reduced to ten dollars" and he pointed to this massive pile – and, I mean it, Toddy, they were stacked up over my head. There were kids literally hiding in there' – his face was beaming, he just couldn't hide his joy – 'and I didn't even stop. I just walked straight past them all,' he added surprisingly.

Yes, why pay ten dollars for one when you can get them online for eighty dollars apiece?

While I was scrubbing toilets and washing kiddie fingerprints off windows, he got to go out and buy homeware? It hardly seemed fair. What would be the equivalent for me, I wondered? *I'm going to my brother's holiday house for five days to write a book?* Oh, wait … never mind – forget I even mentioned it.

Could Jeff actually have kicked the habit? I needn't have worried. A few weeks later, while watching a people-with-no-experience-renovate-a-down-on-their-luck-person's-home-for-them program, Jeff's face came over all dreamy. He'd been transported to that design corner of his brain, the one I don't possess … or even remotely understand.

'I like that cushion,' he said, to which I chuckled knowingly. 'No I mean it; I really am going to buy one with a rabbit on it for this villa.'

* * *

We arrived back home and placed my new black piglet on the marble vanity Jeff had recently installed inside the fifth and as-yet-unfinished absolutely bloody final villa. After two years living in there, we still didn't have flooring, a kitchen or painted walls ... but we now had a lovely statue of a pig.

For all the time we've lived in renovation sites on the property, I swear I really never have complained about progress – unless you ask Jeff. I prefer to consider my 'I wonder if we shouldn't prioritise ...' conversation starters as helpful organisational aids, without which he'd definitely become lost in the detail.

Over the following months, we *did* prioritise getting the Wine Room to the point at which we could host wine tastings for our guests. We won a small victory over Mother Nature and even got a new roof on before she could take it away again ... complete with strapping this time. As I fell behind in my role as chief vine-pruner, I served instead as Jeff's labourer, cutting pieces of wood in mostly straight lengths, drilling what felt like 14,347 screws, carting Jeff's precious structural pine from one side of the property to the other, and getting shitty at having to move the same crap somewhere else (though of course keeping my tongue firmly bit).

Before becoming a country bloke, the only power tool I had ever used was a cake mixer (mine is such a lovely sage green colour) and the hardest work I'd ever done was typing. True, my help saved thousands of dollars in builders' labourers, but it also meant that time ran out for me to finish pruning the vines, forcing us to bring in casual workers to get that done before the spring. But that's just the way Block Eight works – save a penny here, spend an absolute fortune there.

At least building the Wine Room gave us countless hours of quality time together. One of my purest joys of working on a serious building site with Jeff happened when I was up a ladder, having him pass me this nail or that. *Safety should always come first*, I often reminded him.

'Can I please have the hammer?' I asked.

And off he'd go to fetch the tool.

'Sorry, I can't quite reach it. Would you mind climbing up the ladder a bit?'

He'd do all of this without really looking up and only when it was too late for him to back down quickly, he'd finally see that a very particular tool was poking out of my tight builder's shorts.

'Oh my god, that is so disgusting. Put it away!' he cried. 'What if one of the guests can see?'

That look of shock he got gave me the giggles. 'Well I'm flattered,' I said, 'but the villas are about five hundred metres away.'

Or I would hand him pieces of structural pine, each with their measurement carefully scribed in Roman numerals, or with each number spelled out ... whatever to break the monotony. Sometimes the wood just had doodles of doodles next to the number. There are countless knob pictures buried behind the walls of the Wine Room.

Jeff's vertigo is different to mine. Unlike him, I'm not afraid of breaking a leg or an arm, so ladders or roofs (while not my favourite places on the planet) don't send me into hyperventilating fits of anxiety. Put me in a skyscraper, a plane or a very high amusement park ride, on the other hand, where falling means unquestionable, non-negotiable, why-bother-hoping-for-anything-other-than-instant-irreversible death, and my stomach becomes a regular tumble-dryer for all the things I've consumed in the past several days.

In Jeff's design of the new roof, part of the structure would overhang the dam – admittedly a beautiful design feature, but a ridiculously difficult thing to complete. It is a corner that can't easily be reached by ladder, scaffold or tractor – and guess whose job it was to hang off the building by a solitary fingernail to get that done? But that's okay, I'm not afraid of survivable heights.

I was leaning over the roof trusses at an awkward angle while doing so, hammering in nails, and I put all of my weight on that lean … and it just happened to be my rib cage against the structural pine beam. *Crack!* I felt one snap. I've cracked ribs before but this was my lucky day – only one! *Just keep hammering and you'll be fine*, I thought.

The next day we started to go for a run, but about ten metres into it I thought my insides were going to burst out of my navel. It took several weeks for that little setback to heal.

Sure I'll climb up so you don't have to feel scared, Jeff! Why don't I pop on a foil hat when there's lightning? Pull up a huge chunk of structural pine with a broken rib? No problem!

It was usually me up on the roof – not to sing Carole King love songs, but to be passed various building materials by a safely-on-the-ground Jeff. Among my least favourite of these were the six-metre lengths of corrugated tin for the new roof, the perfect sail to send me up like *The Flying Nun* if the wind was strong enough, metal flapping about in the air just inches away from those heavy electrical wires.

It reminded me of when I used to work with my parents back in the 1990s. Their office had a little window at about head height looking out onto the car park. I carefully folded one of the cardboard boxes we sold, stuck it to my head and then 'angled' it into the wind like Sally Field used to do in her '60s TV show. Mum and Dad still laugh about it to this day: 'Remember when Toddy went sailing past the window like Sister Bertrille?' I'm not sure what the butch truck drivers thought of it, but I was the boss's son so I never heard.

I've lost count of the number of times Jeff or I have been dangling from some homemade contraption, just inches from death. We're not stupid, or fond of taking risks, but sometimes we just have to make do with the equipment we have. If a ladder isn't tall enough, we stick a pallet onto the forks of the tractor and one of us lifts the other up as high as it can go – about four metres or so. There are no safety harnesses, of course, just a lot of wobbles and one of us very unsteady on our feet, one hand holding on to the frame of the tractor for dear life, the other hand holding some bloody heavy power tool completing this or that task.

Occasionally we hire a scaffold, which we climb about like well-practised monkeys, but the stability of those things really does depend on how flat the ground underneath them is.

We knew we did things a little riskily but it wasn't until we asked our electrician, Pete (not to be confused with our builder Pete, our tiler Pete, our neighbour Pete, or our previous plumber Pete), to come and change a light fitting in one of the villas – with its four-metre-high ceilings – that we realised not everyone did the same. Whenever we needed to get up to the ceiling there, we'd simply place an old rusty ladder atop a three-legged table and do whatever needed to get done.

'You don't really think I'm going to be climbing up that, do you?' Pete said when he saw what we'd thoughtfully set up for him.

'What? Why?'

'Boys … come on.'

So off Jeff went to buy a brand spanking new four-metre-high safety ladder with a fancy stable platform on top.

* * *

One of the things on the property that simply had to change after we moved in was the bright green shed at its centre. Whoever thought green Colorbond would blend seamlessly into a bush environment sure lacked Jeff's style ethos. As it fades, it turns into a dull kind of aqua – and there aren't exactly an abundance of trees and trunks in the Australian bush matching that hue.

I got it into my stupid stubborn head that I would take on the task of painting the entire shed – about twenty by eight metres, and about five metres high at its peak. I think they should abolish prisons and the only punishment we should be handing out is painting exterior walls. Our crime rate would drop to almost nothing. I'm sure there are worse jobs in the world but, if they exist, I haven't done them.

We went back and forth on the best colour for the shed and finally settled on one that clearly highlighted we'd both lost our minds. Imagine if a baby spent two hours eating every kind of curry known, chased that down with a gallon of breast milk, then spent the next three days wearing the same nappy. That's the colour we chose. I think Dulux call it 'This One's For You, Daddy'. We paid a few hundred bucks to buy litres and litres of the stuff.

I knew the second I brushed the first stroke that it was the wrong colour but it was one of those I-can't–bear-to-raise-this-with-Jeff moments and he was similarly thinking, *I can't break Toddy's heart by saying he has to start all over again.* And so on it went.

There I was, up a scaffold four metres off the ground, painting with a brush too small for the job, when I got the excellent idea of buying one of those electric paint sprayers. Then, hey presto, the job would be over in a couple of hours and I could get back to my life – and to pondering where it had all gone wrong and why I was being punished so severely. The thing no one ever really tells you about those sprayers is that they need to be constantly cleaned. Every time *I* paint, I emerge looking like the biggest loser from a game of Skirmish. Clean painting and I simply do not mix, so I certainly wasn't about to faff around washing the sprayer's nozzle every couple of minutes.

The *other* thing they don't tell you about those sprayers is that if you don't clean them, they get clogged up. And, as paint runs down your arm and down the sprayer, it tends to find its way down the electrical cord … and then on to the point where you've connected it to an extension cord. Electricity doesn't really like liquid.

Four metres high isn't the best place to be when an electric shock runs out along your arm and zaps your fingers. I jumped, but thankfully I'm not the most graceful of characters, so that wasn't very high or far. I placed the sprayer down carefully and went to turn the electricity off at the source, and then picked up my brush and kept toiling away.

All in all, it took me about three months to finish the two coats on the shed. That wasn't constant work, but mostly fighting back the dead weight of the dread that filled me whenever I found myself with spare time and knowing the shed desperately needed to be finished. And once it was done, it sure did look better ... just not the best.

Friends of ours bought a vineyard down the road and immediately painted their shed black. We knew then that we'd well and truly made a mistake. Jeff bought me some black paint (another few hundred dollars later) and I waited patiently for my brain to empty of all sense before I got back up that ladder and started the job all over again.

Those two coats of black took me four years. A four-year sentence for a crime I didn't commit. Netflix is currently filming a documentary about my unlawful incarceration.

At least Jeff's brand new safety ladder came in handy. Admittedly it still took me another six months after he bought it to find the courage/stupidity to get on with the shed-painting job, but I tell you the ladder transformed the experience. I'd been taken out of general population and put into protective custody.

I swear I won't go so much as one kilometre over the speed limit ever again if I never have to see a paintbrush for the rest of my life.

* * *

Painting wasn't the only task requiring a shortcut and sometimes our mates suggested that big expensive tractor should be put to more use. While we were finishing our fourth villa, Mel and Jesus came up for the weekend to help us out. Aside from net curtains and Colorbond, Jeff also has a life-threatening aversion to metal doors. He says he hates anything that looks and feels cheap, though that never stopped him from falling in love with me. All of our villas contain tall and heavy wooden-and-glass doors and, to save money, Jeff bought all ten of them at once, and they remained in our shed until we were ready to install each one. Jesus is a big unit of a man, so the three of us decided to carry three sets of doors from the shed to the new villa, about one hundred metres. It was hard, but not impossible, and a few stops for breathers saw us get the first one there safely.

'There's got to be an easier way,' Jesus said after the first door was safely in place.

'Nah, I reckon we'll be just as efficient carrying the next two. It wasn't that hard,' I said.

'But you've got a tractor. Why not make it do all of the heavy lifting?'

It had taken us about six minutes to walk the first set of doors down to the villa, maybe less. Well, for the next forty-eight minutes, I watched Tweedle Dumb and Tweedle Even Stupider stuff around with the tractor and pallets and mattresses and rope and blankets, and eventually the two remaining doors were 'safely' tied to the tractor. The road between the shed and the villa is bumpy, so it took us another twelve minutes to ever-so-slowly drive down to the villa, to prevent the doors from knocking against each other, as much as was humanly possible.

Finally, the tractor arrived at the villa and we lifted off the second set of doors and took them inside. As we were in there however, the wind picked up – and *wham*! The last remaining set of doors blew over and their glass smashed into a thousand tiny pieces, gone forever, along with the thousands of dollars they cost us. Another win for Mother Nature.

'One of us should have stayed to hold onto it,' Jesus said, ever so helpfully.

Jeff took a very deep breath and held it in.

I love Jesus like a brother … but that day I just had to walk away. Very quickly.

'How's it going?' Mel asked when I walked back inside the house to be with her and Sophia and Amelie, their daughters.

'I had to walk away,' I said.

'Why? Toddy? What's happened?'

'Oh, Melanie,' I said with a sigh. 'Let's just say your husband can't perform miracles like his namesake.'

* * *

Aside from the broken rib and near-decapitation, the Wine Room building site was treating us well, with no further mishaps. Sure, it came in about ten grand over budget, but as we were just *made* of money we somehow found a way to pay off the credit cards and invoices. Often we'd take the animals down there to see the progress. Leroy the cat hated it and hissed to be returned back to the shed and the twenty-three beds he has there, thank you all the same. Helga loved exploring under the deck and wallowing in the mud, to then come plastering her dirty trotter prints all over the floor. Wesley's favourite thing to do was to walk out to the far edges of the deck and eat the water reeds that grew through the gaps, but for Winston, his mind was on one thing only: dancing. Once he heard the sound his hooves made on that deck, he was in heaven, doing his Fred Astaire impressions from one side to the other, tilting his head as he did so (a sign of goat euphoria), showing how altogether pleased he was with his moves. He'd bleat away and race back and forth, clip-clopping to imaginary music, putting on a show for the invisible crowd sitting in the water of the dam, gazing up to marvel at his mastery. Winnie never grew tired of this act, often asking Jeff to join in as his dance partner, a Baby to Winston's Johnny Castle.

In time, the Wine Room took its beautiful shape and it just bewildered Jeff and me that we'd managed to create such a lovely yet enormous structure with only our two sets of hands. Aside from a couple of hours of electrical work by Pete's two brilliant employees, Ryan and Mitch, we assembled every single tiny component of that building ourselves.

My cousin Faith launched a company called The Rusty Garden that makes rusted metal statues, ornaments and signs, so we commissioned one in the Block Eight font to place on the top edge of the building. It says simply, The Wine Room.

I had gone from (self-appointed) poster boy for corporate success (note: no posters were ever printed), to bona fide builder's labourer, capable of erecting sturdy structures. Never in a million years could I have seen that one coming.

* * *

We don't do it often enough, but every once in a while Jeff and I will grab a few beers or a bottle of our wine and sit out on the deck just to watch the world go by. The birds frolicking in the water, the roos bounding across our fields, our guests coming and going … some nights the sunsets are so magical you feel like you're dreaming colours of pink and orange, black and grey. Sometimes it's even easy to pretend we don't have a worry in the world.

'This is the life,' I say to Jeff when we chink our beer bottles.

'We'll never ever find another property as beautiful as this,' he says, his gaze far off in the distance, towards the olive grove.

The question of how long we'll stay at Block Eight and whether we'd be better off living mortgage-free somewhere else has a habit of niggling away in the background. It's not that we hate it, but sometimes it would feel nice to have more than those few hundred dollars in the bank.

'You know when I die –'

'Yes, Toddy, I know. Your ashes set off in fireworks over the dam while Barbra sings "Don't Rain On My Parade". I know.'

'Just as well. We're so lucky to be here aren't we? And to think in Annandale we could barely see any sky at all,' I say.

'I just wish we could do this more often. I wish we had more time just to relax … and enjoy,' he says wistfully.

'Maybe one day. Who knows?' I say. 'But right now I have to go and feed Helga and the boys, and I know Winnie would love you to ask him to dance …'

'Oh, Winnie,' he says and we pack up our things and walk away together to do another chore, though that hardly feels like the right terminology.

The Wine Room has become our default venue for entertaining family and friends, and every time we invite guests to enjoy it they are speechless. There is something about the beauty of the building, with its stone and timber façade, Jeff's requisite recycled fence palings and internal wainscoting, its tastefully and elegantly selected cushions and throws, its strong and formidable roof (the next big storm was a bit of a pooey pants moment, but the roof stood its ground as though actual, professional builders had built it). It juts out over our huge dam, which we ensure remains full to overflowing, providing a view that affords a real sense of the scale of our property. But it's the peace and quiet that impresses people most, I think. It is the perfect place to sip wine as the sun sets.

Three

Todd's Tours A-Go-Go

Some days, the thought of cleaning another villa is about all I can take. On those days, I'd prefer to have every single hair on my body plucked out with blunt rusty pliers rather than head into a villa and scrub away at a toilet, or wipe up liquefied animal remains from somebody's couldn't-be-bothered-to-clean-it barbecue.

I suppose I feel this way about twenty times a year, which by my reckoning isn't all that bad, about a five per cent dreading of work when I know most of my friends in the city would probably be sitting at about eighty to ninety per cent workday dread.

When I was part of that corporate machine, another cog in its wheel, I used to absolutely hate Sunday nights – that sinking feeling my freedom was coming to an end. I suppose it harks back to when I was a kid, and Mum, Dad, my brothers Grant and Glen, would be watching the footy. From another room I would overhear Ray

Warren's booming voice, and Mum would serve what she'd affectionately call SOT for dinner (shit on toast). Monday mornings would mean facing schoolyard taunts again, another five days until Friday was Happy Night.

At least at Block Eight I never have the Sunday/Monday blues and I never wake up thinking, *I really don't want to do this any more*, which is more or less how I had felt for the last two or three years of my career in the city.

While I might wish I didn't have to clean a toilet, I can't say that it alone is enough to make me feel like I have to be somewhere else. One of the jobs I definitely do *not* hate doing, on the other hand, is mowing the lawns at Block Eight, which I've insisted to Jeff is now my job, and mine alone. After being banned from a number of hire places around the Valley because I constantly damaged equipment, we finally took the plunge and bought ourselves a zero-turn ride-on mower for the price of a small car (in fact, my first three cars combined). As Jeff is in charge of the finances, I neither asked nor wanted to know how we could afford the repayments.

Using Dad's electric mower, it would've taken Jeff twelve weeks and fifty extension cords to mow the whole property, but with the brand new, fast ride-on, the job takes around thirty hours all up if I mow every spot on the property we like to keep short.

Most days I don't listen to music or any podcasts or anything; just switch off from everyday stresses and think. Our son, Charlie, on his visits to Block Eight, says I'm like Kel Knight in *Kath & Kim* with his ideas for sausages: *Toddy's Mowing Idea Number 205: Do camels live well with goats? Toddy's Mowing Idea Number 206: Why don't we start doing wine tours ourselves?*

Now that *was a winning idea!* The wine tour idea came to me on the mower on one of those very days I just couldn't face cleaning. It wasn't that I *wanted* to be a tour guide, per se; it was just that I saw it as instant extra income without really outlaying a cent. About one in five of our guests asks for a recommendation for a wine tour, so it seemed like low-hanging fruit.

After the considerable expense of rebuilding the Wine Room, I delicately suggested the idea to the sensible-with-money Jeff. (Well, at least he shows 'sense' any time *I* want to spend money.) Jeff's a real financial pragmatist, and by that I mean, pessimist. I talked through the whole idea: we buy a mini bus on lease, we drive our guests around for one hundred dollars per person, we just need twelve people per week and bingo, we're looking at a cool sixty grand per year.

'Well, that's gross, not net,' Jeff said sombrely.

'Yes, didn't I say that?'

'No.'

'Well I meant to …'

'Okay, well it makes financial sense, so I think we should look into it and see if we can get financing. But you need to know, Toddy, that I will never ever drive wine tours – that's not something I want to do, just to be clear. This one is *your* baby.'

'Yes, of course!' I said, though I wasn't really listening because I just couldn't believe he'd agreed to *my* idea. Maybe it was time I stopped bringing home art deco rabbit-kangaroos.

'We'd get roughly the amount of income we get from a villa,' I continued, rabbiting on excitedly, 'but we don't have to find the hundred grand we'd need to build another one. We'd just pay off the bus lease as we go. And plus, we have a captive audience, so we won't even need to advertise our tours. We'll just promote it to our own guests.'

'Yes Toddy, I understand. Now you'd better start teeing up bus inspections.'

That was one part of the process I wasn't looking forward to. It was time for me to channel my inner country bloke again, just like we'd done when we negotiated for the tractor and, later, the ride-on mower. But this time, I reasoned, things were different. I wasn't pretending to be a farmer, buying expensive machinery I had no idea what to call (or what it did). I was just a businessman wanting another vehicle to add to his fleet.

Maybe it's just me, but gone are the days of haggling with car salespeople. I'd long held the belief that the price quoted was the *starting* price and we'd both happily work back from there – me with a stupidly lowball counteroffer, them with stubbornly small reductions, before we eventually had our *let's get serious now* chat and agreed on a price that neither of us was particularly happy with. But dammit, when we got there the guy at Toyota had coincidentally just sold a Hi-Ace to a woman the day before, so he simply pulled up her price, printed it off and said, '... and that's the best I can do.'

We'll see about that, I thought.

I called another Toyota dealer and pretended to be Jeff, just in case they'd entered my details (and quote) on a centralised database that all fellow Toyota dealers could tap into.

'I've got a quote from a local guy up here and I'm not happy. I'd much prefer to go with you because I grew up near your dealership,' I ventured.

'Okay Jeff,' he said to me, 'let's see what we can do for you.'

I had considered trying Jeff's Brummie accent to help seal the deal, but the only word I've ever mastered with his twang is 'Penelope' – not exactly one you need often when negotiating for a car. It did occur to me to find a dealer in Australia named Penelope, but that was probably taking my method acting a step too far.

Weirdly enough, the guy came back with a quote that was almost identical to the one I'd already received. Dammit, they must have a database capable of attaching your partner's name and number to you – it just couldn't be coincidence, or that a price was *the* price.

So I went to another company. 'You know, I've got quotes from Toyota and I'm really not happy with them or their vehicles ...' I began, and it was as if I had just rocked up carrying a suitcase of unmarked bills.

'Yes Todd, sure Todd, come for a test drive, Todd ...' and then I was introduced to the guy with the slicked-back hair and way-too-liberally-sprayed French cologne and then the Manager Guy and then some other guy. I was told they had only one vehicle left in stock in Australia, it was bright orange and if I *signed today* I would get an extra five hundred dollar discount. They were hovering like vultures.

I considered it for a minute or two but decided not to give in to their suffocating tactics.

'Fuck it,' I said to Jeff as we walked away. 'Maybe this is a stupid idea altogether and I should just get over myself.'

'What happened to your inner bloke in there?' he asked.

'I think he shat himself under all that pressure. God, weren't they vile?'

'Yup.' Jeff had gotten out his phone and was looking up something. Clearly he was staying true to his word and this venture sat squarely on my shoulders, and mine alone.

'I think we should drive down to Mercedes-Benz while we're here in Newcastle,' he said instead. 'They're only about twenty minutes down the road.'

'We can't afford them,' I said resignedly. 'Let's just go home.'

'Come on, it can't hurt just going for a look,' he insisted. 'But you'll be doing all the talking, of course.'

Now I've been labelled a snob once or twice in my life, but I have to say, sometimes a gay guy scared of being belittled by car industry 'professionals' just responds to the pleasantness of a luxury-brand experience. We walked onto the lot and were greeted with warm smiles by a woman (yes, a *woman!*) and when I told her we were interested in taking a look at a Sprinter bus she said one of the guys would be out to see us soon.

'Can I get you a tea or coffee while you wait? Bottled water?'

Now *this* was how to buy a car. Finances be damned, I would be getting me one of them there Benzes!

Lucas came out to greet us. A guy in his thirties, I guessed, unassuming and dressed in a smart black suit. There wasn't a hint of dickhead to him, not even a whiff.

He expressed his surprise that we'd just walked onto the lot without making an appointment but took us out to the bus and then took us for a little drive in it. I have (another) real phobia of driving in the presence of sales staff, so suggested that Lucas do the driving 'so I can feel what it's like for our passengers because the smoothness of the ride is what this is all about, not how it is to drive.'

We chatted some more about the vehicle, I told him it was between him and another, and that we'd go away and think about it some more. I suspect he thought he would never hear from us again, but the truth of the matter was that the Mercedes-Benz was only a few thousand dollars more expensive than the other brands and it was a far, *far* superior vehicle for passenger comfort. When you were paying off a lease, those few grand stretched out over four years of payments really didn't add up to much. I guess that's also why there's not a lot of wiggle room for haggling when you finance a vehicle, because even a few grand is ten or twenty dollars extra a week.

It was time to negotiate so I played Lucas off against the smarmy guys. The smarmy guys wanted *me* to make them an offer and I said *no, that's not how we're playing this* and every price they came back with was literally one hundred dollars less than the previous one, with a list of excuses for why they couldn't go any further. Lucas came down quite a bit and then I told him he was very close.

What price would get me the sale? he emailed back.

'He wants me to state a price,' I relayed to Jeff.

'So just do it. You know you want that bus and it doesn't make all that much difference to us. Saying your tours are in a Mercedes-Benz will probably get you more bookings than any other car too.'

Seventy, I emailed Lucas back.

Within a few minutes, the phone rang. It was Lucas, calling to congratulate me. So just like that, in one day, we'd bought a vehicle that was the second-most expensive thing we'd ever purchased at Block Eight.

The next day I went in to apply for financing and within another day it was all approved. No reams of financial statements – just a simple form – and in a few weeks you could drive that seventy-grand vehicle off the lot after paying a mere few-hundred-dollar holding deposit (put on credit card). If it was all this easy, why wasn't everyone buying mini buses? They were practically a licence to print money, after all. As soon as I got this baby back to Block Eight, our guests would be falling over each other to climb aboard and pay us the income that was going to get me out of cleaning forever. But first we had our designer Chris at Pixel Eight create a branded decal for us, and within another week our white bus came back all flowery and Block Eightified and hot damn if we didn't have the prettiest, most remarkable looking wine tour bus in all of the Hunter Valley.

I put brochures in each of the villas. I updated our website, and every single person who booked to stay with us received a link to also book their very own bespoke wine tour with me, your host, driver and guide. The cash was about to start avalanching in! But … nothing happened.

There were no bookings. Meanwhile, the bus's bills came flooding in: repayments, vehicle insurance, public liability insurance, fuel, updates to our driving licences, registration, CTP insurance, government fees, cleaning supplies ... and all of this without taking a single cent of tour income.

* * *

My first booking came via my second cousin, an adorable girl named Michelle who lives about forty minutes from us. I was to drive some of her workmates around for a pre-Christmas get-together, which happened to fall on my birthday. On the actual day of the tour, it was like my first day at a new school ... something inside me flicked a switch and I became absolutely determined to uphold an extreme (and unhealthy) level of professionalism. I'm sure Michelle wondered what boring nerd had come to consume her once-fun-loving, wisecracking cousin. But, this being my first ever tour, I wanted everything to run smoothly, the classic 'swan paddling beneath the surface' analogy, and one thing I didn't want my passengers to see, was that I was human.

They were running long at their last stop, a winery where the toilet can only be accessed by walking through the tasting area. They were twenty minutes later than the agreed departure time and I didn't want to walk past them to make them think that a) it was a hint that they needed to wind it up or b) I urinated. *It's just a twenty minute drive to Singleton*, I told myself. *I can wait that long and then duck into the pub toilet when I drop off half the group.*

I listened to them tell each other hilarious stories about their workmates. Like the old guy who's been in the company for decades, and still hasn't learnt how to use a computer. *Fuck! Fuck!* he'd yell across the office. *My work! It's gone! Fuck!* And then anyone who was new and hadn't been trapped with him before would rush over to help him, and show him how to ... maximise a window he's accidentally minimised.

As we got close to Singleton, my pained bladder grew very excited at the prospect of being relieved. *I'll just duck in to the loo while you guys say goodbye*, I'd carefully rehearsed. But, dammit, when we pulled up, three people ran inside to the toilet and the others stayed behind and insisted on asking me about a thousand questions. The farewell lasted fifteen minutes and it seemed unreasonable for me to delay my remaining passengers any further. *It's only another twenty minutes to the next drop-off at Branxton. You can use the pub's toilet there*, I told myself.

But at Branxton the goodbyes to the next group dragged on and they suggested it'd be fun to finish the day with a beer in the pub. I couldn't go in there after them to use the loo! As it was my·birthday, I was due at Mum and Dad's house for dinner. And they were just four minutes down the road. *Easy as.*

The second I shut the bus door and was alone however, my body had other plans. My bladder now knew there was absolutely no excuse for not being relieved. I was in extreme pain. I hadn't even noticed there was an empty water canteen next to me (this wouldn't occur to me until three weeks later).

I was approaching McDonald's. *That won't work!* I told myself. *You won't make it from the car park into the restaurant. And what if you let go in front of everyone eating a burger and fries? Avert your eyes, children! That grown man is pissing himself!* My only option was to try to make it to Mum and Dad's house. I had never felt pain like it. I started losing all sensation between my legs and, in a panic, convinced myself I was partway towards being permanently paralysed.

Then, on Mum and Dad's street, just one hundred metres from their house, as my body knew relief was ridiculously imminent, a telling, small, wet patch (well okay, it spoke volumes) appeared on the front my pants. I was so ashamed. So bewildered. *How could this actually happen to me?* But I managed to hold back the floodgates and just kept up my inner chant: *You can make it. You can make it. You can make it.*

I parked outside their house. It just wasn't going to happen. *Come on, Toddy, you can do it!* There were two equally unappealing options. Let go inside the brand new Mercedes-Benz, or burst out that door like a paratrooper and make it just clear of the upholstery. When you're a forty-four-year-old man standing on the side of a quiet suburban street pissing your pants, you realise you've finally made it in life. It's the point you accept you're no longer young and, without you even realising it, fucking middle age has crept into your room to possess you overnight, and things you once took for granted – like being able to make it to a toilet – are now simply beyond your control. And then it dawned on me … I needed to face my parents.

I sloshed in my wet shoes to their front door and stripped down to my underwear, unconcerned what the neighbours thought. *Oh, I see Jude has ordered another of her regular strip-o-grams.* As fate would have it, the two miracles on my side were that Mum and Dad don't lock their front door when they're expecting me, and the en suite is within two metres of it, my parents a safe distance away in their living room.

'Only me,' I called out. 'Just ducking to the loo.' *I can still get away with this!* I thought excitedly. *You're actually going to do this! No one need ever know!* But then reality slapped me on the face. How on earth would I explain why I needed to borrow a pair of my father's pants?

'Mum? Can you come in here a minute?' I called out.

'Happy B–!' she said as she came into the room but stopped when she saw my face, and the towel around my waist.

'I've ah … well, I've just pissed my pants,' I said. 'Can you grab me a pair of dad's shorts while I take a shower? No undies, thanks, I can't bear the thought of wearing a pair of his.'

'– Birthday!' she finished. And we both got the giggles.

The final icing on my yet-to-be-received birthday cake was that while I was showering Mum had gone out to the porch, collected together my piss-soaked clothes and had placed them, subtly, into the washing machine.

'And here I was thinking I'd be changing *your* nappies by now,' I said as I finally entered their living room. 'Forty four years ago today you changed my first one and now hopefully you've changed my last.'

'No big deal, love,' Mum said with a smile. 'There's plenty more time for you to be changing mine.'

But the trauma of the event scarred me. Now as I drive tours, I know where practically every single toilet in the entire Hunter Valley is. I still try to restrict evidence that I'm human ... by keeping it to venues where bathrooms aren't in the middle of a wine tasting area.

* * *

While I kept my personal setback a secret, I still thought our guests would scramble to get a seat on our bus. But week after week, they showed little interest in our service. I had it open for public tours and did a number of those, but often found myself working seven- or eight-hour days for $160 gross, and Jeff was very quick to remind me of the costs involved in running the bus. It just wasn't profitable, so I switched to doing private tours only – a base rate to hire the bus regardless of how many passengers you booked for. I experimented with restaurant transfers, concert transfers and other ad hoc jobs but eventually realised that being on call as a taxi driver meant I was effectively working twenty-four hours a day. With so few bookings coming in from our guests, I had no choice but to start advertising online and gradually the bus got some bookings. One of the unexpected benefits of driving around non-guests was that in ending each wine tour back at Block Eight for a casual tasting, we were introducing our offering to a whole new audience, and accommodation bookings and wine sales trickled in as a result.

I was driving around a lively family of four a few months later and, as usual, ended at Block Eight. It hadn't rained much overnight or during the day but, by the end of the tour, the clouds were massing and they were black and heavy.

The approach to our Wine Room is across the grass at the edge of our main dam – more like a large lake, really, with water full to the edge. In torrential rain, the channel behind the dam can overflow, so there's no point in putting in a roadway. In heavy rains, it too would just get washed away.

During the tasting in the Wine Room, the clouds opened up and the rains came down thick and fast, but even in this kind of weather the Wine Room is lovely and we all enjoyed watching the atmosphere change, and then change again. It started getting dark, and was time to drive the family back to their accommodation.

I got everyone back onto the bus and then, as I'd done countless times, reversed back past the close inlet of the dam to then turn the bus around on a large grassed area between the channel and the dam's edge. But this time, as I was reversing back, because the grass was slippery from the rain, the bus started sliding.

You know when you're in those situations and you can foresee the entire disaster unfolding, but you're just plain stubborn (or stupid) and you continue on with blind hope assuming that nothing that bad can ever happen to you? Well, I put the bus in forward and managed to creep up a few metres and then tried again to reverse.

Though I'd started off close to the ridge, by now the bus had slid back towards the inlet and was teetering very close to the edge. The inlet is the one part of the dam where there is a small drop between the grass and the water, about a metre or so. It was like I was driving on ice and I had no control whatsoever over the bus. The brand new, seventy-thousand-dollar machine was determined to end up in the drink – not to mention the harm I could have caused to my passengers (and our entire livelihood). I pretended like it was fine, but knew the more I attempted my little daredevil stunt, the more slippery the ground beneath us became. When we were about fifty centimetres from the drop, I finally decided to change plans.

I put the bus into drive, determined to use the grassed area adjacent to the Wine Room to complete a three-point turn and drive us straight past the inlet to safety. But that grassed area is on a slight incline and, once again, the bus was having no part of it – I was seriously, joyously bogged.

I ushered the guests (who were drunk enough to find the whole scenario absolutely hilarious) back into the Wine Room for complimentary wines (they couldn't have cared less about my predicament) and called Jeff to see if he could help me out of what was now a very muddy mess.

Jeff brought down some wooden boards (not his precious palings, don't worry) to try to give me traction, but after several attempts and another heavy downpour, it was clear this was going to be a mammoth task and not one we could achieve in front of a tipsy audience. The father of the group was trying his best to help, giving instructions, doubting Jeff's, et cetera, and as the last light of the day disappeared I called it – I would drive them back to their accommodation in our car, a shedload of our wine given with our compliments as an apology. They kept insisting it was fine – a memorable and enjoyable end to the day – and they eventually came back to stay with us and book me for another (drier) tour.

But at this time, I was still taking restaurant transfer bookings; so, once I'd dropped them home, Jeff and I had about two hours before I was due to drive some of our guests to their dinner. Back and forth and back and forth we went on those boards, edging inch by painful inch away from the dam and onto what felt like more stable ground.

'It's not working!' I cried all dramatic and defeated.

'It is!' Jeff yelled.

'Forget it! Let's just leave the stupid bus here for days and wait for the ground to dry out.'

'Forward! I said "forward"!' he yelled back at me.

'I *am* driving forward! The bus is slipping. I have no control! Don't you think I'm trying to drive forward?'

'Slower! Slower! Why are you going so fast?'

'I just thought …'

'Stop thinking! Just do as I say.'

'Stop yelling at me! What are you yelling at me for?'

'Well there's no one else here!'

'This isn't working either!' I huffed.

'Hold your nerve! Just hold your nerve!' Jeff used the phrase Pete the builder had taught him whenever it looked like Jeff was about to throw in the towel on a building site.

We were wet, exhausted, hungry and mutually pissed off. My levels of frustration were at breaking point and I wanted to set the fucking bus on fire.

After another one and a half hours we finally managed to get the bus free and it was then just a one-hundred-metre drive to our roadway with its reliable stony traction. I eased on cautiously but, in the moment, you forget the tiny details – like the twenty-five-degree ridge the bus needed to ascend in order to reach the road. Getting up was fine and with it came the euphoria that I was finally out, but then at its peak, the bus decided it had no traction and I lost all power in the accelerator. The wheels simply stopped turning and I slid back down the hill. The more I did this (I tried four times), the further back the bus slid, so that I ended up back towards the inlet where I'd begun in the first place, only closer now to that drop into the water.

When we moved in, I'd asked the previous owners how deep the dam was and they said, 'About five metres at its deepest point.'

'How do you know that?' I'd asked.

'Because one of our contractors forgot to put the brake on our tractor and it went down the hill, straight into the dam and completely disappeared.'

And here we were, doing exactly the same thing.

'Stop!' Jeff yelled at me. 'This isn't working. We need a new plan.'

He decided the only way out was to go get our tractor. We found it perplexing that nowhere on the bus was there a hook for a winch or anything of the sort, so the only option for us was to push the bus up the hill with the tractor, using a Jeff-devised safety device of a pallet wrapped in two mattresses and about every blanket we owned (but strictly no cushions). I saw visions of smashed glass, just like Jesus's miraculous door-carrying solution.

Jeff worked meticulously to place the pallet in exactly the right position and I stood dangerously between the tractor and the bus to keep the mattress and blankets from falling down. Then once the tension was right, I climbed back onto the bus and he pushed with the tractor. But of course I pressed too hard on the accelerator so the pallet fell to the ground. Over and over and over again we tried.

After multiple pushing attempts, I was finally back on our roadway. I was so deflated I could have crawled into bed and stayed there for three days. But I had a group of six to happily drive to dinner, and we were due to leave in fifteen minutes.

By the time we got back to the house, I had five minutes to scrub out all of the mud the bogged guests had trampled through the bus, and about twenty seconds to put on my 'hello, how are you?' happy face and get my next passengers to their destination.

Much like my photographic memory of Hunter Valley toilet stops, I am now forever conscious of any road – any surface, in fact. Whenever we've had more than twenty spots of rain, I think I am going to get the bus bogged again.

Getting older does that for you; plants a scare into the deepest recesses of your mind and forever holds you hostage.

I remember saying to Mum once when she was in her late fifties, 'You used to love rollercoasters and rides when you were younger. What suddenly made you start being scared of them?'

'I don't know why,' she said, 'but it just happens when you get older.'

I shrugged, because I didn't understand.

'You'll see.' Mum smiled knowingly.

Shouldn't it be that the closer we are to death, the more we stick our middle fingers up in its face? Otherwise, it's like we're surrendering to it before it even arrives. I still go on (most) rides; I just don't want to risk pissing my pants in public.

* * *

It can be a very lonely job, driving the bus. And as fun as many of the groups are, this is my job and our business and it's crucial I keep things professional. Most of my groups are self-sufficient, so I find myself driving and answering questions whenever they're asked. I do believe that is my role – to be largely invisible, like the best waiters who are always at your table when you need them, yet never hover; and it's only at the end of the experience that you realise just how integral they have been to your overall enjoyment.

Some days I pretend I'm on a road trip, exploring the beautiful Hunter wine country for the first time. Its natural beauty still has a habit of creeping up on me, and I often find myself marvelling at views as though I am seeing them for the first time. I find a nice quiet spot to eat my packed lunch, just soaking in the surrounds, being warmed by the sun. And then I get out my laptop and plug away at the latest book. It's where I generally do all of my writing.

Some days I overhear conversations that really tickle my fancy and I can't help but laugh out loud – like the woman who went skinny dipping in the dark with her workmates but, as she was swimming past her boss, her hand accidentally 'brushed bush'. Though I've often meant to write down the funny things I've heard, I never have.

Most days, I love driving the bus. It makes a very welcome change to the internal-facing chores at Block Eight and gives me a chance to interact with people in a more social, lively environment. And sometimes passengers really want me to be a part of their day – it's fun and interactive. By the third or fourth wine tasting, I'm generally referred to as Toddy, and the music increases in volume and the sing-alongs begin … and sometimes I even join in.

I've never once driven twelve people within one week, so my plucked-from-mid-air financial modelling hasn't yet been achieved. There are benefits to having the bus, but as a bold money-making idea, even I have to admit that it's still overwhelmingly in the red. And did I mention that I still scrub toilets?

Four

Goodbye, Barry

Buoyed by how easy it was to get financing for both the ride-on mower and bus, we knew the time had come to replace Barry the Barina. We'd brought Barry with us from the city, not realising that – maybe like us – he had no place in the country. In all honesty, country folk used to laugh at us when we rocked up in Barry.

In fact, we'd brought all of our stuff from our renovated house in Annandale – and kept it in storage in the shed at Block Eight for four years. There was art, knickknacks, keepsakes, Meryl Streep movie magazines, movie posters, a Cyndi Lauper doll, furniture … a whole mezzanine full of stuff that we assumed we'd need, or want, one day. But then during one of his notorious tidy-ups, Jeff cracked the shits and went through it all, and we ended up filling a skip full of crap from our old life – stuff we knew simply had no place in this one. Two carloads were taken to the local charity and yet more stuff was given to local friends.

Another of Jeff's talents is throwing away stuff we *do* need, but of course you only realise it months after the event and needless to say, he never can quite bear to part with one of his precious cushions.

I've come to dread Jeff's marathon tidy-ups because anything that's kept is moved to the least likely of places.

'Jeff? Where's my passport? I need it for that RSA police check.'

'I put both of ours under the toothpaste in the bathroom so we'd always know where they were.'

'Jeff? I can't find my wallet.'

'Open your eyes ...' he waves a hand around the kitchen. 'Have you even looked for it?'

He also has shocking short-term memory loss, or at least that's my professional medical diagnosis. So if he's not answering my questions it could also be because he simply doesn't remember where he put it.

'Jeff, you're the kind of person who wouldn't remember the name of someone you've been married to for seven years,' I joked with him once.

'Can you just tell me, please?' I asked again about my wallet.

'Right there between the plain and self-raising flour. You could have at least looked before asking!'

Barry had transported three houses' worth of building materials, several zoos' worth of animals and animal food, had dropped an entire city's worth of rubbish to the local tip (Jeff's second-favourite place on the planet ... after Bunnings) and had kept me linked back to Sydney those years I'd commuted from Block Eight to my part-time job in the city. By the time he was edging close to two hundred thousand kilometres on the odometer ... he was a mere shell of his former self. The cigarette lighter cover was lost months previous, part of his front bumper just decided to fall off one day, various other knobs and buttons had long since disappeared, and despite having been regassed several times, the air conditioning no longer worked ... which made for really pleasant family car rides when the kids were in town and we were suffering through a string of forty-plus-degree days. Lucy and Charlie would literally have their heads out their windows with their tongues panting like the farm dogs we've never had.

Like many of us, I'm guilty of giving my parents the shitty jobs I hate, just to 'keep them occupied' in their retirement. So it was that Dad had ended up with any job that was car related – especially anything mechanical. Not that this is his forte, by a very long shot, but he knows a mechanic on the Central Coast and so I gave him Barry to take for servicing on his bingo-calling days so I didn't have to deal with being charged more for being gay.

Incidentally, Mum's job is our washing and ironing. She insists on doing it (really!) and, like her mother before her, takes great care in ironing things just so. Shirtsleeves have a very precise crease and everything is folded as if brand new. If ever I do a load of washing myself, she gets this look on her face like I'm questioning her abilities or taking the job away from her. She calls herself 'Iron and Whine' and after 3pm, the 'h' is discarded. I sometimes leave things in my pockets to test her honesty like a highly regarded and hard-hitting journalist on *A Current Affair*.

I've left the two-dollar coin I found in your pocket on top of the washing, she texted one day.

Congratulations, you've passed another test, I texted back. *Pop it in the pokies.*

While Dad is off calling bingo (and sometimes taking Barry to his service) on Mondays, Jeff and I have christened them 'Mumdays'. I think we could count on one hand the number of Mumdays we've been unable to go and visit her, usually staying for a cup of tea or taking her lunch. It's a lovely, quiet and often laugh-filled respite from our inevitably busy weeks and if I am too busy to go or on a book promotion tour, I love that Jeff still finds the time to see my mum.

The visits mean the world to Mum. Without fail, she makes sure she has non-dairy milk for us in the fridge and a vegan biscuit to have with our cup of tea, taking her time to read the ingredients in the supermarket to make sure she gets it right. We often stroll through the garden that Jeff and I created for her, marvelling at how healthy it looks, sometimes picking fresh leaves from her vegetable patch to feed Winston, Wesley and Helga. And, without fail, we depart with massive bags of freshly laundered clothes, and mountains of perfectly folded robes for our guests to use.

On one of these Mumdays, Dad returned from Barry's last service with grim news.

'The [insert mechanical detail here] is on its last legs,' Dad said like a doctor at a hospice. 'The mechanic said Barry's just gonna give out on you one day and that could be very dangerous.'

It was time to turn off Barry's life support.

We asked our friend Merv to find us a new car, and resolved to embrace the country life with a utility vehicle. *You won't know yourselves once you get a ute,* about four thousand five hundred and twelve people said to us repeatedly. Nearly every local we knew owned a ute because it's the most practical vehicle to have when you live in the country. In fact, I can't think of a single one of our friends who doesn't own one. *But really?* we still thought. *It's hardly going to revolutionise the way* we *live!*

Merv is a fastidious researcher and we knew he'd painstakingly trawled through every piece of information on the internet about every single utility vehicle there was to buy, so we knew that if he'd chosen a Mazda BT-50 as Barry's replacement it *had* to be good. That took the most laborious part out of purchasing a car; now all we had to do was go and buy it.

'I'm tired of being the hard-core negotiation guy,' I said to Jeff one day. 'I think you should buy this one.'

'Me? What do I know about negotiating?'

'Well, you've been negotiating around my mood for thirteen years ...'

'True, but that's different. That's just me having to work out which Todd I'm seeing that day. *You're* the self-proclaimed negotiation expert.'

'Yes, but I'm worried about financing. The bus is in my name and the ute needs to be in yours, so we need to have clearly defined roles from the outset.'

'Yeah but you know I'm crap at this stuff,' he complained.

'Well, I think it's about time you tried a little harder. You can do it, Jeff. Do it for Barry. It's the least you owe him before he ends up on a scrap heap.'

Much to my surprise, Jeff actually set up a meeting at a local dealer and we went over to chat about a ute. Car dealerships are just unnatural environments for a pair of gays, kind of like footy players doing ballet. In my paranoid-about-being-gay delusions, however, I knew our Block Eight uniforms were a godsend. At the outset, we'd just be considered workmates. (In my most paranoid state, I like to think those uniforms have saved us from being served shandies instead of beers at the local pub.)

The salesman was unremarkable in just about every single way. Darren, Paul, Jim …? I don't recall his name, what he wore, what his cologne was or what he said to us. I just knew he was desperate for a sale, as evidenced by the oversized cheque he'd had printed up for us to sign, made out to him for the sum of forty grand and with photographers on standby in front of an arch of balloons. At least that's how it felt.

I let Jeff do most of the talking, interjecting at crucial moments to add serious car terms into the mix like 'tray', 'four wheel drive', 'tow bar' and 'rear cab' – all terms I'd had to conduct significant online research to identify and rehearse.

The test drive was as unremarkable as the salesman – it was a ute, it smelled new, it felt smooth. A few days later (necessary thinking time as negotiation tactic), after we'd agreed on a final price, it came time for us to take Barry for the trade-in, and sign all the financial paperwork.

'I swear if we don't get two grand for Barry we're just going to walk away from the whole thing. I mean, he didn't even come down a token five dollars in your negotiation with him. Nothing!'

'But we need a ute.'

'So we'll go find someone who's actually prepared to negotiate, at least give us *something*!'

'But Merv did all the research and ...'

'Oh Jeff, come on!' I snapped. 'Don't worry, I'll do all the talking – you just be prepared to walk, okay? Don't be embarrassed. We'll just calmly walk away and then he'll call you and come grovelling for the sale.'

'Okay ...' Jeff sounded less certain than I'd ever heard him before. 'Should we clean Barry at least?'

We never washed Barry – maybe once or twice through a car wash in six years. Sometimes Dad would take his car duties that extra mile and surprise us by making Barry gleam, usually using a hard-bristled broom so that the Barina's black shiny exterior looked more scratched than a stainless steel bench in the busiest restaurant kitchen in the world.

This was not one of those times. Barry had seen better days. In fact it's probably safer to say this was the worst day of Barry's life. He was filthy. The back seat was stained so badly it looked like several people had been murdered there. Two wheel hubs had fallen off. Several of the blades in the air vents had fallen out. He had rust spots and windscreen chips. His floor was more farm than carpet and if you looked closely there were probably two full cans of plain Pringles in crumb form.

'Nah,' I said, 'no point polishing a turd, they can see straight through that tactic.' This being the very first car I'd traded in, I of course knew so much about the topic.

'Morning, Todd,' Whatshisname said to Jeff. 'Morning Jeff,' he said to me.

'Other way around,' I corrected him.

'Oh sorry,' he said half-heartedly.

'Don't worry – happens all the time. I mean, we look identical.'

'How was your weekend?' he asked the real Jeff, choosing to ignore me.

'Yeah, good.'

'I spent mine with my sister and her partner up the coast.'

'Okay …'

'Yeah, my sister's partner, Valerie, loves fishing, so we went out on the boat together and had a great time.'

It was just like how any statement that begins 'I'm not being racist but …' is bound to offend every sensibility in your body and usually ends with '… and because our neighbour happens to be an Oriental chappie.'

I handed the now-impossible-to-call-homophobic Whatshisname the keys to Barry and mentally practised my walkout if the trade-in price was so much as one cent below two grand.

After a short while, he came back into the room chuckling.

'My reseller guy just said, "And what do you expect me to do with *that*?"'

'Mmm hmmm,' I muttered. I'd practically gotten up off my seat already. Jeff's eyes were on the ground.

The guy continued, 'So really the best we can do is five hundred dollars.'

'We'll take it!' I snapped his hand off.

I didn't have to look at Jeff; I could *feel* what he was thinking. *Old Mister Negotiation Expert strikes again ...*

We sat with the finance guy (who could very well have been the same man as the sales guy, I couldn't be sure) and answered a string of questions about our business. Then we signed all the paperwork and walked out of there, much like with the bus, having never showed a single piece of evidence about our income. Why is it that you have to hand over the life of your firstborn child in order to get a one thousand dollar credit card from your bank, but if you want a thirty (or seventy!) thousand dollar vehicle all you have to do is talk about what your business earns, list a few of your outgoings and, hey presto, you're in more debt than a kid fresh out of uni? Now we just had to work out how we were going to afford the repayments each month. More money to conjure out of thin air.

A few weeks passed while they got the car ready for us, adding a tow bar and replacing the tray with a more practical one for Jeff's endless visits to Bunnings for building supplies, and for my endless visits to the local shelter for yet-to-be-rescued animals.

'Just you watch. Barry is going to explode on us the day before we have to drop him off,' Jeff prophesied, but fortunately for us we got him there minus just a few more knobs and buttons.

It's silly, isn't it, that a piece of metal and rubber can come to represent so much of your life? Barry had been there with us for our whole tree change, from the night we moved in and our cat Leroy had shat himself on the backseat, to flat tyres in the Barrington Tops (where Jeff had learnt that painting a rural fence black *really lifted it*). He'd transported more in his life than just about any other sedan in Australia and, despite the broken odometer and speedometer when we'd first gotten him, and his lack of cool air, old Barry had never once actually broken down on us.

'See ya, Barry,' I said as I got out of him for the very last time. 'Thanks for everything.'

Whatshisname at the dealership took us through all the controls and buttons inside a perfectly new-smelling ute. Then, just to confirm my paranoia over the whole Todd/ Jeff mix up, he showed us how to connect our phones via Bluetooth. Helpfully, someone's iPhone was already connected.

The name of the phone was: 'Boys Fucking'.

'I see the boys in the garage have had a bit of fun,' he said with a chuckle, before moving on to explaining the next feature.

Had it not taken us weeks to get to this point, I would have jumped out of that car and stormed off the lot yelling something about where he could shove his ute. But it was one thing being called Jeff; we certainly couldn't risk me being labelled a hysterical queen too now, could we?

'Can I grab a photo of you both for the socials?' he finally finished. And out came a bright pink bow, I kid you not.

* * *

When I was young, Dad bringing home a brand-new car was huge. It was one of the most exciting, momentous and amazing things I could ever imagine – the smell of it, the comfort of the back seat, the proud look in Dad's eyes of *I've really made it.* My brother Glen loved one of them so much he used to sit in the front driveway listening to his mix tapes, and I remember once he came inside and left the door of the car wide open overnight. We were amazed that no one stole it, though thieves did come back a few weeks later to take it for a joy ride. But getting a new car on the business, one you didn't actually hand over any hard-earned cash for, was not quite as momentous. It had a few cool features that made us realise just how out of his depth Barry had been. One of our favourites soon became Car Play, and its ability to read and send text messages by voice.

Jeff, this is the car speaking. You are a complete and utter knob.

Todd, this is the car speaking. Put down the Pringles, fatty! I repeat: put down the chips.

In time we came to christen him Daryl, after the letters on the number plate, though the R is in fact a W so you have to say it with a slight speech impediment: Dawyl.

And, wouldn't you know, those people who insisted having a ute would transform our lives were right. We just couldn't believe how convenient it was – not only in transporting Jeff's precious homewares and building materials, but all the animal food for my furred and feathered kids. On the property, transporting one heavy thing or another got a hell of a lot easier. There's barely a week that passes that one of us does not remark to the other, *this ute has changed my life.*

* * *

'Have you checked the water in the tanks lately?' Jeff asked shortly after we got Dawyl.

Of course I hadn't. 'Yep, it's on my to-do list today, don't worry.' I tried my hardest to sound convincing.

Two days later Jeff prompted me again. 'The water must be really low by now ...'

'Yes Jeff!' I snapped, as I usually do when he is right and I am wrong.

There are three main reasons I hate managing our water so much. First, it is crucial to the smooth running of our business. If we run out of water in one of our villas we'll have to cancel bookings and probably also pay for an expensive last-minute room elsewhere to send our guests to. Most city folk have no idea how precious water is in the country – we learnt the hard way not long after we moved in when we couldn't find 'the mains' and realised instead we had to rely on 'the rains' or expensive truck deliveries.

It's a lot of pressure and should be enough to outweigh my two other grudges against the task. But no. I also hate carrying the long, heavy ladder down to each villa to climb up the tanks to check the water level because – without fail – it contorts my back into strange angles and takes days for the kinks to sort themselves out again. It's hard to get the ladder stable against a rounded tank and on uneven bushy ground, so the possibility that I will one day break my neck is currently at 4 to 1 odds at Sportsbet. (If you're a punter, you may be interested to know the odds of us running out of water are at even.) To avoid carrying the ladder, I spent three hundred dollars on electronic water-depth readers that are capable of sending me text messages when the water's low. But for whatever reason they remain in the shed somewhere – probably next to the eight hundred dollar electric fence that's never been used, or the five hundred dollar bar fridge I bought for the bus but, after trying it once, it didn't seem to work so I never looked at it again.

But if I'm being completely honest, the main reason I hated the job so much was Phil the water guy. He's a nice enough bloke, on the whole, but he has this perverse way of lauding his water-carting power over you, and most days I spoke with him I ended up feeling like a useless loser … like someone who'd moved from the city without knowing a thing about country life. It's just the *way* he speaks to me. Some days, he'd answer my calls like we were long-lost poker-playing buddies and he'd chat on and on about his plans for the future while I made appropriate sounds of awe and admiration. Then, other days, he would be so gruff it felt like calling to pay him money for water was the greatest insult he'd ever known.

So after Jeff prompted me twice to check the water, I knew the situation in the tanks wasn't going to be pretty, but I also had blind hope that somehow I'd scrape through by the skin of my teeth. Sure enough, every tank was drastically low. Drought low. Jeff was going to have several cows.

'Hi Phil, it's Todd from Block Eight.'

'Yep,' he said brusquely. Okay, so it was one of *those* days.

'Can you bring me three loads?'

'When?'

'As soon as you can, please?'

'Huh!' he chuckled. 'Best I can do is some time after Anzac Day.' That was in eight days' time.

'Okay great, thank you so much, Phil. Any chance you can do it earlier? For me?' There was so much grovelling in the last two words that even gruff, cold, and holier-than-thou Phil would've been at pains to miss it.

'No.'

'Okay, thanks so much, Phil. See you then.'

And then he hung up the phone without a goodbye.

I went back to report to Jeff. 'I'm sorry, I've fucked up ...'

'What? I told you to check the water three days ago!'

I tuned out. Whatever rant Jeff was on sure wasn't going to bring about more water, aside from the tears of frustration I was desperately holding back.

'Okay!' I yelled. 'I already said I fucked up. It's done. I can't change that now.'

'Call Phil back and tell him we need it now.'

'Jeff, that's not the —'

'We've been loyal to him for over four years,' he interrupted me. 'Tell him he owes it to us.'

As Jeff had never actually had a conversation with Phil, I knew he was ridiculously off the mark, but sometimes I do as Jeff says because it's easier to fail at his idea than trying to convince him it won't work.

''lo.' Phil was driving by the sounds.

'Phil, it's Todd from Block Eight again.'

'Yep.'

'Look, I've fucked up. I'm so low on water I'm calling to ask you a favour.'

'Yeah …'

'Is there any way at all you can bring me just one load sooner? I am so fucking stupid, and I know that, but I'm just begging you to bring me some now.'

'Nutt.'

'I will pay you anything you want. I can give you cash.'

'We're booked up.'

'You could do it after hours as a special favour. Name your price.'

'Doesn't work that way. Union rules. Insurance.'

'So there's nothing at all you can do for me after I've been loyal to you for four years?' (Bam! Jeff's line. A real clanger). 'I've never, ever ordered water off anyone else. Only you.'

'Mate, not my problem you don't check your tanks. I'm booked up, I told you that. I've got lots of customers. You think it's fair I bring you one of their loads and then they're in the shit? Just doesn't work that way.'

I thought about challenging him on this. That surely there was one customer who wanted more than one load, and one load would be enough to get them out of trouble, that we could take their second load and then in a few days' time he could go back and give them more.

'So there's nothing at all you can do for me, even though I'm desperate and literally begging you …?'

'Four days,' he practically spat through the phone.

'Thanks Phil, you're so great. I really appreciate it.'

But we were still in major shit. I called four more companies but they all had excuses for why they wouldn't come. I'm convinced the water mafia was against me that day, and they all had a list of each other's customers and were in a pact never to deliver to someone else's. One guy said he never did the dirt road leading up to ours and, without a word of a lie, THAT AFTERNOON I saw him driving down our road to deliver water to our neighbours Derice and Ross, three doors down. I went back to report to Jeff.

'So keep calling,' he said, beyond pissed off with me. 'Call Newcastle or Central Coast companies. Tell them you will pay whatever it takes.'

I was on the internet for the best part of an hour researching, then calling and calling, and then I came across another company in Singleton. It was a *big* operation. Lots of trucks. They mostly delivered to mine sites but, what the hell, I was so desperate I would have called people on mains water in Cessnock and offered them ten bucks a pop to bring me buckets of the stuff.

'Would I be able to order about forty thousand litres of water, please?'

'Of course, where's it going to?'

I gave our address.

'And when would you like it?'

I laughed. 'I guess today would be out of the question?'

She laughed back. But her laugh wasn't quite as sinister as Phil's. She ruffled through some papers. 'No, I think we can do that.'

'Are you serious?' I leapt through the phone to hug her.

'Yep, no problem.'

Old Tank-failure Toddy strikes again! So, on paper, they appeared more expensive than Phil. But when I drilled down into the numbers, their trucks carried more water and Phil had just last month called to lecture me that his drivers hated coming to our place because they had to split their loads into several tanks and from now on he was charging me more, and why couldn't I just spend three grand with my plumber to get all the tanks linked together underground?

I texted Phil, *Don't worry about the load in a few days. I got some.* It was a horrible break-up and I was cowardly enough to do it by text. Our four-year relationship had come to an end. He never wrote back, and I never heard from him again.

Our new water company is so efficient that they get me water next-day every single time. And that's a *very* dangerous precedent for me to rely on. Which, inevitably I do. I have only called in desperation once and their response?

'Todd, you're a regular. And looking after regulars is what we do. You'll have it today.'

So now I only hate two things about checking the tanks.

* * *

Though Dawyl the ute couldn't solve our water issues, he had other surprising uses – like the night we took him to the local drive-in with Lucy and Charlie. Being late autumn, it was bloody cold, but we laid a mattress on the tray, reversed back to face the screen and rugged up tight against the evening air watching two of the worst movies I have ever seen. But for me it wasn't actually about the films, it was about being with our kids and giving them memories like this – ones I hope will live on.

Five

Child Labour

When I'd decided, on my thirtieth birthday, to donate my sperm, I never would have envisaged how my relationship with Lucy and Charlie would pan out. I'd decided I never wanted kids for myself and I made the decision more to help out friends than for any personal gain. At least, that's what I thought at the time.

When they were about five and six years old, Lucy and Charlie visited us in our inner city terrace in Sydney. Together with their mums, we all crammed into our tiny courtyard and sat around having adult conversations. There was never really any thought of doing something specifically to entertain the kids because the four of us adults didn't see each other very often and it was more about us catching up than doing something to keep the kids amused.

When Jeff and I moved to Block Eight, Lucy was seven and Charlie six. We took it upon ourselves to ensure that, whenever they visited, their time (as much as possible) would be filled with fun and memorable things.

It began with a tradition of making short films each school holidays. This started with a silly and low-quality horror film (really just a collection of scenes) but they loved making it and liked to watch it back – always getting the giggles. Then as they continued to visit, our production values increased and I taught myself to master editing on iMovie so before long we had actual movies to film, though never with a script.

Inevitably, our animals played roles. Firstly it was Rodney and Billy, who'd been my first pigs. When they grew too large and aggressive for us to handle, I had to find them a new job: they became studs impregnating sows around the Hunter Valley. Then Winston and Helga took starring roles in the films.

Visiting their dads in the Hunter would often be pre-empted with lots of long phone calls to discuss the upcoming film shoot – mostly Lucy sinking her teeth into the ideas, Charlie always just happy to go with the flow.

When Lucy was learning about war at school, she came up with the entire storyline for their longest movie, a fifteen-minute love story called *War Flowers*. It wouldn't be out of place at Tropfest, but then I'm probably a little too close to it to make that call, having taken on a minor role as the evil Nazi. Charlie was the hero, a famous rugby-player-cum-spy, and Lucy was the beautiful-yet-tragic love interest. It borrowed heavily from classic Hepburn/Tracy quips, but unfortunately it did signify the beginning of the end of the kids' enthusiasm for making movies. After one final film called *Feral* – co-starring Helga, and with a scene where Lucy wallowed in the pig's muddy, pissy toilet all in the name of 'method acting' – it sort of dropped out of the kids' consciousness.

So what do you do with two kids who are fast approaching their teens and would rather obsess over Instagram messages (Lucy) or watch back-to-back Marvel movies (Charlie)? One of the little games we used to play with them was called 'Prize Time' and we'd test their powers of observation during drives, et cetera. Anyone who buzzed first and got the correct answer would win a gold coin to take home with them. As Jeff got carried away, this could sometimes result in forty or fifty dollars.

This all went swimmingly until the day I offered Lucy 'double or nothing'. She took the challenge and saw her forty dollars rise to eighty and, always one to push the kids' tolerance to the limit, I offered her double or nothing again.

'Can you tell me the question first?' she asked cheekily.

'No, that's not how it works. But I promise you nothing I ever ask you will be impossible. It will always be a test of your levels of observation, that's all.'

'Okay, I'll do it.'

We were on our way to the airport and time was running short.

'Are you absolutely sure?'

'Yes, Dad. What's the question?'

'So, just to be clear, you currently have eighty dollars. If you get the question right, you will receive one hundred and sixty dollars. But if you get it wrong, you will walk away with nothing.'

'Yes, Dad, I understand. What is the question?'

The previous night we'd watched the film *Miss You Already*. In it, the R.E.M. song 'Losing My Religion' featured heavily. It was both on the soundtrack, and there was a scene where the two lead characters sang it.

'Can you name fifteen words in the lyrics to the song?' I asked.

Bless her, Lucy thought and thought and she squirmed and proclaimed unfairness, then she took a stab citing lyrics from some song that still hasn't been written. She had until we got to the airport to say the words and, as we pulled up, it was clear she wasn't going to get there.

'I'm so sorry, sweetheart, but you've lost.'

I don't think I've ever seen Lucy more disappointed, or angry. I neglected to say that Charlie had also played a round of double or nothing but sensibly stopped at fifty dollars, and no amount of teasing or coercing from me could tempt him to play again.

They were running late for their plane so I hurriedly said goodbye to them and their mum, Jane, and drove away. In my mind, I thought it was very important that Lucy learnt a lesson about being satisfied with your lot in life, about not being greedy, and about the power of gambling to draw you in and ultimately disappoint. I mean, we didn't want her to turn into the best friend of the one-armed bandits like my mother!

I drove away feeling stupid. Yes, it was a lesson ... but did I really have to teach it to her in such a way?

Two minutes later my phone rang. It was Lucy. She was bawling. 'Dad, I didn't even say goodbye to you. I didn't get to say goodbye …' She was inconsolable.

'You did, *bella*, you did! You hugged me and you kissed me and you said goodbye.'

'But I don't remember, Dad. I don't think I did.'

No amount of reassuring could convince her otherwise. We eventually said goodbye and said we loved each other, and I drove home feeling like the most miserable, fucked-up, arsehole father on the planet.

As they got older, the kids started responding to the concept of receiving money for chores they completed on the property. It was nothing too strenuous (not like the time Jeff made them stack four thousand fence palings neatly), just things like vacuuming, tidying, stripping beds and such. We always tried to get our work done as fast as possible, to free us up to take them go-karting, bowling, swimming, to the movies or whatever, or just for a stroll to explore more of the property. Finally we arrived at a solution that appealed to them way more than making movies – they became our first proper employees, receiving fifteen dollars cash an hour for any work they completed. Aside from the odd squabble over who was working hardest, they absolutely loved it.

* * *

I'd known Jane for years and one thing she wanted more than anything else in life was kids. When she met Vicky that complicated things somewhat. I mentioned to her off the cuff that I was happy to help out. After original discussions of me being merely a donor, the agreement between Jane and Vicky and me was that I would be known as the kids' dad so they could gain a sense of their paternal identity, but there was to be zero financial contribution from me and I wouldn't be taking on a parenting role.

Before saying yes, I'd thought through what I considered to be every single eventuation and asked a lot of friends their counsel. I started with Kirsti, the hardest hitting of them.

Kirsti and I met the first day of uni in 1992 and instantly hit it off, despite the fact she was wearing leggings and I was wearing slacks and boating loafers. To say she is the most pragmatic of my friends would be like saying some people consider George Clooney to be sexy. She's very much the yin to my yang, providing the ground beneath my feet when my head has a tendency to be up in the clouds, and on occasion she's even been the wind beneath my wings.

We were sharing a beer at some dive of a pub in Newtown when I brought it up again.

'So, I've thought about it,' she said, having received a heads-up from me the day before. 'I think there are three scenarios you need to consider. One: what happens if the girls break up? Two: what happens when they ask you for money? And three: what the hell is going to happen if you decide you don't want anything to do with the kids? So, one?'

'Hmm, I have thought about this one too, obviously. The way I see it, if the whole world worried about what would happen if parents might split up in the future then no one would ever have children, would they? And you can't tell me you're of the school of thought that considers a lesbian relationship less or more likely to break up?'

'Of course not ...'

'Then I'd deal with it if it ever happened. Billions of kids around the world survive broken families, so that's not really a concern. I suppose it just depends whether it's an acrimonious or a bitter break-up and whether I'd be expected to take sides.'

'Which you never could!' Sometimes she speaks to me like she's found me out, is calling my bluff or telling me something I could never in a million years work out for myself. It's one of the many reasons I'm drawn to her. It's just that some days our same magnetic ends touch and we each recoil in shock.

'No, Kirsti, of course not,' I said drolly.

'What if in the break-up they wanted to split up the kids?'

'Again, not a death sentence. Kids can be robust and, if not, maybe I'd need to play more of a role in helping them cope.'

'And number two?'

'I told you we've already agreed there's no financial expectation of me.'

'Oh come on, you can't be that naïve. You studied law, you know what money can do to people.'

'Yeah, and I know I've said no, and I will always say no when it comes to money.'

'What if the kids needed operations and the girls couldn't afford it?'

'What if I asked you for a lung?'

'You wouldn't want mine; it's got girl germs.'

'Well, you know, there's about a billion what-ifs. If they asked for money I'd consider the circumstances ... then probably say no.'

'What if they sued you for it?'

'Ah, but I won't be on the birth certificate!' I said, Perry Mason-like. It was my turn to be cleverer than her.

'So what? A DNA test would soon fix that. Don't delude yourself – if they ever want money, you'll have to pay.'

'I disagree. I think it would be very complicated and they'd have to drag it through courts and none of us can afford to do that. But I get it. Money is a potential issue. But, so what? If at the end of the day the worst thing that happens is I lose my house and the kids get a better life, well then that's not the end of the world.'

'But at this point in time you don't even have a house. You might feel differently about it if you've been slaving your guts out paying off a mortgage for ten years and then they want a piece of it.'

'So I'll put the house in Mum's and Dad's names. There are ways around paying a bill. I could declare myself bankrupt.' I could see there was no way I was going to come up with a satisfactory argument against this one and chose to let Kirsti win, which was rather magnanimous of me.

'And number three? What if you decide you don't want to have anything to do with the kids?'

'Why would I do that?'

'I don't know. But it's not impossible, is it? You don't have a partner at the moment. What if he wanted nothing to do with your kids? What if you decided you wanted to have kids with him?'

'Ain't gonna happen. I told you I don't want to be a full-time parent.'

'Well, whatever the reason. Let's say the kids know you as Dad and you decide you don't want that any more?'

'I can't imagine a scenario where that's ever likely but, okay, say it does happen. I have two angry kids who want to blame me for all their woes in life and two angry lesbians who never speak to me again. Maybe the kids will blame a distant dad figure for stuff anyway. So ... what if it's the opposite and I fall in love with them and I want to see more of them?' I asked rather prophetically.

'You tell me ...'

'I have absolutely no fucking idea how I'll deal with that.'

'Indeed.'

'So it's a no, then? Based on all these what-ifs?'

'I never said that. Ultimately the decision is yours alone to make. And if it all falls apart, after telling you I told you so, I will be here to pick up the pieces just like the time you called me crying because Ben's brother dumped you!'

'You're such a bitch.'

'Takes one to know one.'

'Come on, imbecile. Let's do Thai. My shout.'

'Good, because after you have kids, you'll never have any money ever again.'

* * *

My next port of call was to my friend Mel. Mel and I met while working at eBay in the early 2000s. In a move completely unlike me, I rocked up to her birthday party just after I'd started the job, not knowing a single person and, as I'd got the times wrong, and she got there early to secure a table at the popular bar where it was being held, we found ourselves alone together and developed an instant rapport. Though she left eBay a year or so after I started, we'd had enough time to become firm friends and our relationship grew in strength and love as the years passed. Mel is perhaps the most conservative of my friends and I knew her perspective would be unique.

We were sharing a bottle of wine at a funky garden bar in Kings Cross, the same bar in which she'd introduce me to her future husband, Jesus, in some years' time.

'I completely understand the agreement you have with the girls,' Mel began. 'It sounds very sensible and well thought through. But I just question whether life is like that; whether things can be so black and white?'

'But if we all go into it agreeing this is how it's going to be, then no one can really argue for it to be otherwise, can they?'

'I think not having your name on the birth certificate is both a godsend and a curse.'

'How so?'

'On one hand you will have some ... not total, but *some*, protection financially. You won't be recognised as a natural legal guardian, that would have to be proven by tests or whatever and it's a good buffer. But by the same token, what if you fall in love with these kids and their mums deny you access? "Sorry, you're not their dad, it says so right here on their birth certificates!"'

'I think about this all the time, Mellie. I'm confident that I'll be able to keep my distance from them. I know I'm a sperm donor known as Dad, not the kids' father. I am going into this whole thing knowing, in my heart, that's the reality.'

'Honey, I'm just not so sure you can make it so logical and unemotional. I know you. I know your heart and how much love there is in it. Do you really think you can look into the eyes of your kids, knowing they're yours, then walk out of the room telling yourself you don't want to know them better and you're fine with all the parenting decisions the girls are making? What if they're making decisions you think are really crap?'

'I have to tell myself to step out of the picture; that that's not my role.'

'Again, I know you think you can do that, but I don't think anyone could. They're your children, Toddy. Whether you put another name to it or not doesn't change a thing. Whether they were created out of a mutual love shared with their mother or in a laboratory somewhere doesn't change that. I just know if I ever get the chance to have children they will become such a deep part of me I could never ...'

Both of us had tears in our eyes. We forced out a laugh.

'I know, Mellie. I get what you're saying. Really, I do. But, without stating the obvious, I am a man, you know?'

'Really?'

'True. And I do think it's different for women.'

80

'But you're sensitive; more than most men. I just worry for you, that's all.'

'Well let's say you're right and this does happen. Let's say I want to see the kids more. I know it's not part of the agreement now, but what if I have to earn that trust and respect from the girls? If I have to work hard for it, and it's what I want, then I will.'

'But they could still say no. They could stop you from seeing them altogether if you got too close.'

'They could. But like you said about the birth certificate, if I was desperate I could prove I'm the dad and seek some sort of legal decision on seeing them.'

'And be hated by the girls. It'd be so ugly – a family full of hate – and nobody wants that.'

'You're right. But anyway, it's another of those what-if scenarios. I know I'll be able to control my feelings and emotions because, as much as I might love those kids, I absolutely know for certain that I do not want to be a full-time dad. If I did, I don't think I would even consider saying yes.'

'Yes, that makes sense. I guess the other thing I wanted you to consider was having such little control over the future of the children. I know you love Jane and Vicky and you all get along well, but I wonder how you might feel if they make decisions you fundamentally disagree with – big decisions like religion, schooling, ethical and moral issues ... I worry you wouldn't be able to help yourself and you'd want your opinion to be heard.'

'You know, that isn't really something I've thought much about. Do I trust them to always make the right decision on everything?'

'See how passionately you feel about it when the time comes, I suppose. But you'll need to pick your battles very carefully. I'd be letting all the small things go through to the keeper, myself, and only try to have my voice heard on the really big-ticket items.'

'You know, Mellie, you always have a way of helping me see things more clearly. I hadn't really thought through that I'm giving two lives to two women to mould and shape as they see fit. I'm going on blind faith that they will create two human beings of whom I can be proud, when it's inevitable, somewhere along the line, that I'll be sitting in a room somewhere and think to myself, "Oh, I'd never raise the kids like that."'

'Precisely!'

'So I guess at the end of the day I need to say over and over again, "They are not my children."'

'And that, my friend, is the biggest challenge of them all.'

* * *

At the time, I genuinely thought I would be able to accept that I would have zero input in the raising of the children. I had no interest in clouding their understanding of who was in charge. Together, the mothers would make good decisions for the kids. There would never be any reason or need for me to step in. At least, that's what I firmly felt at the time.

I've never asked another man how he felt on finding out he was going to be a dad, or on making the decision that he was going to try to have a child. I can only assume that for most of us it doesn't feel like the strangest or grandest notion on the planet. It just feels like it's the next step in our personal evolution – what we are here to do. The fact that none of my counsellors (I ended up asking four friends for their thoughts) had children at the time is significant. Now all four of them have had children of their own. While the content of the conversations, had we had them today, would probably be more or less the same, I can't help but feel their views would be shaped by their own experiences as parents and the joys they've each felt would probably reduce some of the what-if scenario testing.

* * *

I telephoned Jane and Vicky early February 2004. We said our hellos but there was no point pretending this phone conversation was about anything else.

I asked them about some of the outlying concerns I had, a few of the topics raised by some of my friends. *What would happen if you two ever broke up? What will we do if one day I realise I'm not cut out for this and don't want the kids to call me Dad? What if the kids take a dislike to me because I haven't been in their lives and they resent that? What happens if you both lose your jobs and you need money to help raise the kids? What if the kids needed an expensive operation?* It was a job interview and the girls were passing with flying colours. It seemed that just about every scenario I'd considered was one they had too.

'Okay, last question. What if I fall in love with the kids and want to spend more time with them?'

Jane was taken aback. 'Do you think that's going to happen?' The last syllable rose in her tell-tale way. It has an unmistakable gasp of *you can't do that!*

'Honestly, I doubt it very much. Not with the way I'm feeling about it right now. But it's not impossible and I want to know what you would do if it did happen.'

'Can you ever see yourself wanting them to live with you?' Vicky asked. She is as pragmatic as the guy I would eventually end up with.

'Never.'

'Can you ever see yourself wanting to move to Brisbane?'

'Highly unlikely.'

'So what you're saying is there's a small chance you might want to come and visit the kids every once in a while?'

I hadn't really thought through the practicalities of this what-if. 'Yeah, I guess that's it.'

'Well I can't really see there being a problem with that,' Vicky said, matter-of-fact. 'Can you, Jane?'

'We want the kids to know who you are,' she said. 'That's the whole point of choosing you. Otherwise we would have gone with an anonymous donor. Now if you're talking about flying up here every weekend and asking for visitation rights, that's a slightly different matter!' She laughed awkwardly, uncomfortably, and again I heard that gasp in her voice.

'Let me say it again: I will never want custody of the kids. I will never want the kids to live with me. I'm not saying I *will* feel the need to see them often, I'm just asking that if I do want to see them occasionally whether you'd be open to that.'

'We will work together on the how and when,' Vicky said. 'We see you, what? Three or four times a year at the moment? You visit us in Brisbane, we visit you in Sydney. Neither of us sees that changing, so the kids will have face time with their dad whenever we see you.'

'Okay good, thank you. I guess it would be nice to have them call me every once in a while when they're older, just to see how I'm going.'

'Good.' Jane said. There were a few moments of silence. 'So ...?'

'Oh yeah! Well you've probably guessed it already, but the answer is yes!'

'Really?' Jane said excitedly, the glee in her voice was hard to ignore.

'No, I'm kidding; the answer's no. Of course it's yes, silly! I think it's always been a yes from the minute you asked me, but I just needed to be sure.'

* * *

In the end, except for the bits about me not wanting the kids in my life at all, most of it happened – nearly every single what-if became an it-is. The girls broke up in 2016 and from there, everything changed. Yes of course I was in love with our children, and had been since they were born, though my deep-seated respect, heartfelt love and desire to see them be the best they could be came a little later, particularly after they started visiting Block Eight without Jane and Vicky. Like most parents, I consider our children remarkable, irresistibly compelling and, on the odd occasion, just a wee bit annoying! But above all else, they both have this uncanny ability to make me laugh – genuine hearty belly laughs and almost every time Jeff and I are with them I silently thank their mothers for this incredible gift, for which I will be eternally grateful.

Much like moving to Block Eight, I suppose it was utterly naïve and foolish for any of us to assume things would pan out as we imagined they would. But sharing Block Eight with Lucy and Charlie is one of the most uplifting triumphs of Jeff and my tree change. We know, for their whole lives, that random farm memories will bubble back to the surface and we hope they will always be received warmly and affectionately by the kids.

Like the night Mel, Jesus, Sophia and Amelie visited the four of us, and we spent hour after hour making up jokes about peoples' names.

Jesus: What do you call a retired artist? Drew.

Me: What do you call a woman who sets her mortgage on fire? Bernadette.

Now that our kids are grown, and are less excited by the more trivial things, Jeff and I turn our attention to the children of our closest friends.

I loved the weekend Kirsti brought her daughter Xanthe to the property and I taught the four-year-old a song about poo, which she loved so much she couldn't stop laughing. Years later, during a heat wave, we took time off the property to hire a little shed with a pool and we played Marco Polo until our skin turned to prunes.

Whenever Andy and Ali visit with their son Sam it's down tools and we take him on adventures like wheelbarrow tours, or we just sit and play or read with him because we've come to appreciate these moments are rare and worth savouring. And of course when our friend Pet and her partner Simon brought most of their family up for a joint birthday/ Christmas celebration, we had one of the most festive nights of our lives, revelling long into the night and wishing it could become something we did every single year.

We host regular get-togethers with my old eBay crew and their partners and kids. Our laughter echoes out across the property – genuine, affectionate, 'these are my people' laughs. And recently we introduced my cousin Wendy's son Theo to the property and we had such a great time we still call each other often (mostly so the ten-year-old can take the piss out of me being vegan, or for me to try to trick him about something, like my Uncle Brian used to do to me).

We know we would have socialised with all of our friends in Sydney too, but in being in the Hunter Valley anyone who visits is instantly in holiday mode and we embrace the feeling fully, momentarily ignoring the demands of running the business.

Our annual visit from our English friend Sheena is one of the things we look forward to most. She has a warmth that envelops you like a yearned-for hug. On one memorable visit, I'd been contacted by Stewart and Evelyn down the road – they'd read my book and wanted to catch up. So we took Sheena to their cellar door for a wine tasting. Within two minutes of our arrival, Sheena and Stewart worked out they all used to live in the same building in London. Small world coincidences like that are one of the things I love most about life.

We particularly enjoy time with our honorary nieces, Sophia and Amelie. We've taken them to what we would have previously dismissed as pointless tourist attractions like Snow in July and the Christmas lights in the Hunter Valley Gardens. Holding Sophia's hand as we climbed the big slippery dip again and again, her never tiring of the bumpy ride, is a memory I'll cherish forever. I replicated that for both girls back at Block Eight by taking them on lawnmower rides down the steepest slope we have, their hearing protected by Jeff's ear muffs, and when I motioned for whether to continue or not, Amelie's little thumbs-up just melted my heart. And neither of them can believe we have such a famous pig, whose image appeared in bookshops all over the country!

'See that pig there?' six-year-old Sophia asked her little friend Beau one day. 'That's my Uncle Todd and Uncle Jeff's pig ... she's pretty famous,' she said, bursting with pride.

Six

Snakes Alive!

Publishers started showing interest in my *Helga* manuscript towards the end of 2017.

'If I get a deal for this, I want to put every cent of it towards building a proper place for the animals,' I said to Jeff.

Where the animals lived was always meant to be temporary. It was a smallish five-metre-square pen we'd originally built to house about eight chooks. Then our male pigs, Rodney and Billy, moved in, cramping quarters somewhat, so we tacked on another five-metre-square waist-high pen for them. Then when Winston the goat followed me home one day, we added a third pen hastily built out of star pickets and concrete reinforcing mesh (or 'reo', as us blokes call it). Over time, and after Rodney and Billy took up duties elsewhere, the three structures were opened into each other and became one large pen to house Winston, Wesley and then Helga, and our chooks became open-range.

But the pen had its limitations. One of Rodney and Billy's legacies was how they'd ringbarked all of the eucalyptus trees within the animal enclosure. The trees all died as a result, and on occasion dropped their heavy limbs to the ground. Wesley was scared of the sound of the wind or moving branches and I didn't think it was much of a problem until the day I heard a small branch fall to the ground and watched him race to hide his head under the climbing frame for protection. My only explanation was that a falling limb must have hit him before. It took me ages to coax him out from under his hidey-hole, convincing him everything would be okay. But that one of our animals could be killed by a Widow Maker brought tears to my eyes and every day when I approached the pen I feared one of them would be dead on the ground – like the time I thought baby Wesley was a goner.

Jeff had thought it a bloody brilliant idea to buy a black plastic crate, fill it with hay, and then screw part of a cheap plastic garden screen to the front. It was Jeff's very own hay feeder invention and Wesley would have to work out how to retrieve the food (poor Winston's fat head wouldn't fit in). It was part feeder, part brainteaser. I had to admit I thought it was pretty nifty. Most days, Wes could be found with his face deep inside it, gobbling up as much delicious lucerne hay as his body would allow. That was until the day I heard his muffled bleats from a distance.

I ran to him like Meryl Streep ran to the tent screaming for a torch in *Evil Angels* and found him lying there bleating, his head stuck inside, horns caught by one of the screen's patterns. How long had he been there waiting for someone to free him? Winston just stood on the sidelines sniggering, *Dumb kid. Anyone could see that was gonna happen.*

I freed Wesley, expecting him to be shell-shocked, but he got right up and started eating the hay again so I reefed that feeder over the fence and he was never allowed near it again.

The goats (unlike Helga) also hate rain, and especially mud. As the pen was located in the bush behind our main shed, there was nothing on the ground except dirt and leaf debris. When it rained, the whole thing turned into a slushy pit and the goats refused to leave their sleeping hut for days on end. Placing pallets as stepping stones helped a bit, but wasn't the ideal solution as the boys often found them slippery when wet. And though Helga loved the mud, she didn't enjoy wallowing in the small bath Rodney had previously excavated, and generally used it as her toilet.

None of these were major issues in themselves, but the size of the pen wasn't enough for proper exercise, so every day I'd take my three mates on a walk to get their heart rates up and to provide them access to limitless supplies of fresh grass and huge dams for Helga to wallow in. We'd gotten into the habit of walking the three of them from their pen down to the dam between the two olive groves and, as Helga wallowed and the boys ate grass to their hearts' content, we'd sip a few beers and watch the sun go down.

'They really love it down here, don't they?' Jeff asked after getting back from one of his Winston play-fights.

I love watching Winston get excited battling Jeff – the way he pushes his horns into Jeff's legs, which he does without force or malice, it's more like a goat vs human arm-wrestle. Winnie gets so excited that he ends up dancing and rising up on his hind legs, and Jeff gets all out of breath from having to continually push him back. The only way to end the game is to crouch down to goat height and scratch him under the chin while making the 'boosza boosza boosza' sound I invented to calm him (Winston, not Jeff).

'I think this is Helga's favourite dam,' I said in agreement as she turned herself over like a rotisserie chook to ensure the mud covered both sides of her body.

'So why would we put the fence up there' – he pointed to the top paddock – 'where we would have to build her a new dam and there's not enough shade, when down here they have everything they need?'

'You know, it's usually me coming up with all the brilliant ideas on this property but, hot diggety, that sure is a good'un.'

Sometimes I think Jeff pooh-poohs my ideas just because they came out of my mouth. To combat this, lately I've been trialling a new strategy with mixed success, though at least that's better than my usual strike rate. I'll put my head down close to Helga's snout then turn to Jeff to say, 'Helga would like to know if you could maybe ...' and then whatever Jeff's response is, I'll relay it to my clever pig.

One day I bent down close to Leroy (we mostly call him by his nicknames of Roy, Bert or Bertie) and turned to Jeff. 'Bertie would like to know if it's possible to have his cage moved to the other side of the house.' (He uses a cage for outdoor time when we have guests because we can't risk one of them losing a limb.)

'Yeah, okay, that's a great idea,' Jeff said.

'What's that, Bert?' I asked and leant in towards his face again and pretended to listen to him. 'Okay Bert, that's enough!' I snapped. 'You're just being nasty about Jeff now.'

Even though the location of the new animal enclosure had been Jeff's idea, we did agree on the overall plan. Over the next few weeks we got some quotes to fence in the entire area around the small dam between the olives. And naturally, this wasn't just a simple four-by-four area for my beloveds; we decided to make it about an acre in size. The quotes came in at around twenty grand – much, *much* more than we were expecting or could reasonably afford, but when you've been accused of loving your four-legged friends more than your partner of fifteen years …

'Let's just do it,' I said towards the end of the year. 'They really need some extra space.'

Of course, had we known what a dire summer was headed our way as far as accommodation bookings went, it would have been more sensible to have invested that money into something that *might* have attracted customers in the heat. You know, like a swimming pool, for example. As I continued with the bus tours throughout the summer I saw a lot of passengers were staying at venues with a pool, and we knew if we had one it would likely lead to more bookings for us too. But sometimes you just need to put passion before the purse. Much as I love my life in the country, what I love best is spending time with my dear animals and giving them lives their four-legged relatives could never dream of. I knew if we didn't invest in their new home then and there, we would never get around to doing it. We found the money and the idea was pretty straightforward … but then Mother Nature stepped in to play with us a little.

Every morning I go to the animals and give them their breakfast, and every week or so, I changed Helga's water – upending the trough to pour out the old, inevitably muddy water, then bringing her fresh buckets to top it up. In their wisdom, the designer of Helga's water trough thought it was a good idea to leave a space between the bottom of the bowl and the ground. The trough could be quite heavy and I'd hurt my back lifting it before, so I found the best solution was to get down on my hands and knees and prise it up from ground level. I'd done it countless times but on this particular day, I lifted it up and right there, a couple of inches from my face was a curled-up black snake. I shat my pants. And I swore, really badly.

In one seamless move I put the trough back down again lightly and was very pleased the snake hadn't flinched. It had been extremely hot of late so the snake had found the perfect place to nest, cool against the underbelly of the water. I raced inside to change my undies then went to get Jeff, because if anyone was going to die from snakebite, it certainly wasn't going to be me.

'What do you want me to do about it?' he asked, midway through some building/sawing/measuring task that he could usually be interrupted from (with only a slight grudge).

'Um, kill it?'

'Oh, for god's sake …' On went the boots and out came the rake and axe.

We moved the animals to a cordoned-off area of the pen, locked them in, and then made the plan. Jeff was to lift the trough and pin the snake with the back of the rake, I was to chop its head off. Even though my three animals were at risk, I really hated killing that snake. Its beauty was astonishing, its shock at the first blow palpable. I vowed that I would never ever kill another one, no matter what.

After my adrenaline had settled, Jeff came to tell me he'd accepted the quote to build the new fence.

'The guy asked if I wanted option A or B,' Jeff explained, 'and then I realised the quote wasn't for twenty grand. There are two options on the same quote and we have to choose between them, and the real price is only nine.'

We did a little dance that *for once* the gods of take, take, take had done us a small favour. We'd already mentally prepared ourselves for the twenty grand, so to get eleven back was like winning the lottery. Matt, the fence builder, promised to start work on Boxing Day.

Two days before, he called Jeff. 'Mate, I've got some wooden stump posts left over from my last job and wanted to know if you wanted them instead of the cheaper metal ones I quoted you on. Same price.'

Again, we couldn't believe our luck. Sure enough, at 6am on Boxing Day, Matt was there to begin work on what would eventually be called, after much deliberation, 'The Farm'.

I had considered 'Animal Farm', which in my view evoked an Orwellian utopia where animals and humans could be equal ... but which in Jeff's view evoked a film not at all meant for the kiddies.

Before the area was sealed off, we took the opportunity to go in and make the animals' new sleeping quarters. Unlike the basic metal shed we'd originally built for our old pigs, Rodney and Billy (and which now housed Winston, Wesley and Helga), this was to be quite the monument. Jeff's vision was for a quintessential workers' cottage – a throwback to Ned Kelly. Its walls would be clad in rustic wooden planks (though not fence palings) and, for its roof, he would use some rusty old metal. And so it came about. The new accommodation had three bedrooms, for use in different seasons. One had two windows for airflow in summer, one had one window for limited airflow in spring and autumn, and the last had no windows (for warmth in winter). In front was a covered veranda to provide the animals a shady spot to sit and admire their water view. If Helga didn't have a history of eating all things fabric, I know Jeff would have thrown in some giant designer cushions too. When I posted photos of it on Instagram, people naturally assumed it was a new villa for guests to stay in, or possibly a new house for Jeff and me … not just something 'for the animals'.

It took Matt five days to build a fence that is as wild dog- and fox-proof as any fence can get. It has a skirt around its base to stop them digging in, is two metres high, and is topped with barbed wire to stop those ferals climbing over. And those beautiful tree stumps are firmly in place to keep it solid.

We took a few weeks to get the animals used to their new farm, visiting it daily before walking them back to the pen in the bush behind the shed. Winston was always in the lead, Helga just in front of us.

Narrowing his eyes one day, Jeff said, 'Is that a tick on Helga's bum?'

'Nah, it's just a bit of mud,' I said.

'I don't think it is …' Jeff pushed.

I walked closer towards Helga and there unmistakably, right near her vagina, was a tick – the first one I had ever seen. I knew I had to be careful removing it, so I grabbed it close to her skin using my fingernails then pulled upward at a slight angle. It came away immediately; had barely begun attaching to her. It felt hard and menacing in my fingers and I threw it to the ground. I still regularly thank Jeff for spotting it and pushing me to investigate. We did our research: ticks can only attach to the soft parts of a pig – usually their ears, eyes and, as with this case, vulva. Later that night we told our neighbours about it, keeping them alert for ticks on their dogs. 'My pig had a tick on her vulva today' is a sentence I never, *ever* thought I would utter.

We kept taking the animals for walks to The Farm so they would be used to it by the time they moved in. Everything was going according to plan …

How very silly of me to think it all would run smoothly.

I've made no secret of the fact that I often walk around the property wearing Crocs and socks. You really can't beat them for comfort, though they're not the most practical or best protective wear for a farmer.

I trotted in to the old pen one morning to give the animals their breakfast, wearing my usual footwear because we'd killed that black snake and now anything slightly more than bare feet would do fine. As I stepped through into the third pen to feed Helga, a sudden movement caught my attention.

A brown snake slithered from beneath the pile of hay I'd just stepped on. Jeff says I'm prone to exaggeration. He's not the only one to say that. In my father's brief review of my memoir, he apparently told my brother Grant that it was 'good, but about ten per cent fiction'. Anyway, I *swear* that snake was four metres long if it was an inch. (Okay, so that would probably make it the longest brown snake ever known, but I *swear*!) It made its way under the little covered area where Winston usually took his afternoon naps.

I called Jeff. 'There's a huge brown snake in the animal pen,' I said, shaking with fear. I can handle spiders but snakes are *fast*, unpredictable and deadly. Our neighbour's son, Matthew, was bitten by one a few years back while he was nonchalantly watering the garden, and it took the ambulance over thirty minutes to collect him, then another forty minutes to drive him to the hospital with the best treatment! From that story we'd learnt that not every bite contains venom (he'd been very lucky), but I wasn't about to take any chances.

I'm not the only one in my family with a fear of snakes. There's my sister-in-law, Bec, who lives with her family in suburban Sydney. One day, she was on the phone to the local snake catcher, hysterically screaming at him to please come immediately and capture the snake on her driveway. The frazzled guy was taking down her address when my thirteen-year-old niece Sarah picked up the deadly creature with her bare hands and brought the snake inside. It was a piece of dried silicone.

Not the case here. Jeff came right away but not fast enough, if you ask me. Helga was eating some spilled food on the ground and it was *right* near where the snake had gone. I kept calling her sternly but didn't want to go near the snake myself, or approach her for fear she'd get all stubborn on me (as she is wont to do these days) and head right towards the snake.

'Helga! Helga! Here!' I kept saying, but she ignored me.

Just then, the snake reared up and struck out towards my pig. My heart skipped several beats. I felt like vomiting. My legs turned to jelly. I imagined the whole disaster playing out: Helga bit, Helga falling, Helga frothing at the mouth, shuddering violently, blood seeping from her eyes, my frantic call to the vet, the vet saying it was hopeless, me lying with my pig, stroking her, kissing her, telling her I love her and thanking her for coming into my life, having to go on a book tour to talk about her and fighting back tears every single time, of talking about her in the past tense, recalling the tender way David Attenborough spoke of her at her state funeral and ...

In a move that highlighted the utter skill of nature, the snake struck towards Helga, but plucked a mouse from the hay just inches from her trotters and swallowed it whole. Helga was none the wiser. Thankfully, the snake didn't seem to show much interest in her either.

Just as Jeff arrived, the snake reared up again and I knew this was definitely it – Helga's turn – but again its precision was breathtaking as it swiped another mouse from the hay. The rattling of the gate sent the snake into hiding beneath the pallet that served as the covered area's floor and also sent Helga running to see who her new visitor was. The rattling of the gate always sent her running towards it, bleach-blonde tail wagging excitedly (yes, it is natural) and snout at the ready for kisses.

'Where is it?' Jeff asked.

I was standing in the far corner of the pen. 'Under there,' I pointed to the pallet. 'Please, *please* be careful, Jeffy.' I was a housewife sending my husband off to war – again.

Jeff poked and prodded under the pallet with the handle of the rake in an attempt to get the snake to find its way out of the pen but, after several minutes, it was clear the snake wasn't budging for anyone.

'Leave it,' I said. 'He's probably lived here for months, there's no point making him angry.'

The animals are very good at spilling food and, no matter how frequently I clean up, there is always some on the ground. That means we have mice in the pen. Quite a lot of mice. And if you have mice, you also have snakes.

I knew the animals would be moving into The Farm in a matter of weeks, as soon as Jeff put the finishing touches on their house and then built the front gate to lock them in. But it couldn't come fast enough for me.

Three days later, I was in the pen giving the animals their dinner. It was later than usual – at dusk – and a bit difficult to see. Thankfully since seeing that brown snake I'd always worn boots into the pen because, as I was handfeeding Wesley some celery, the bloody thing went slithering right between my legs. (You can insert your own joke here.) I froze. Bless him, so did Wes. I suspect our animals have seen snakes on numerous occasions and know what to do. I shudder to think of the handful of times I've crawled into their pen after a few too many wines and lain down in their sleeping hut in the pitch darkness. Yes ... I confess that some nights I just can't help myself and, if ever I go missing, Jeff knows where he can find me. Just how close I have come to being bitten is anyone's guess.

As soon as the snake found the hole it was headed for, I stepped up onto the platform Jeff had built for the goats to climb on and shook the heebie-jeebies out of my body.

At night I had snake-filled nightmares. I had dreams that Helga had died a gruesome, bloody death and her cries of anguish actually woke me from sleep. During the day as I walked, twigs moved and turned into snakes. I had mini-heart attacks several times. We went away for a night and I knew – I was absolutely certain – that I would come back and all of our animals would be dead, having died alone and in pain. And day after day I considered it a miracle that old snake chose to keep to himself, preferring a bellyful of mice than to waste venom on an animal he would never be able to eat.

Finally, I just couldn't stand it any longer, and there was no time to pretend one of the animals was making this request.

'Jeff, we need to move the animals into The Farm ... today.'

I was not only playing Russian roulette with our animals' lives, but also with Jeff's temper. But he got it.

We made our way down to The Farm with the materials required to make it completely secure. But as we got there, the dam looked weird. Over the previous days I'd noticed a bloom on its surface – very small, nothing much to think twice about – but overnight, the algae had spread and it now covered about one-third of the water's surface. We immediately jumped online and googled the algae, identifying it as a dangerous type, one that could easily kill Helga. It was another hurdle to keep me from getting them away from snake bite.

Jeff raced off to the place he buys his mysterious farming chemicals from and came back with the solution required to kill the algae, but it would take up to five days for the dam to be safe enough for Helga to wallow in it. Though she rarely drank from the dam, we could not take that additional risk. Jeff went down there in his hazmat suit (really, no need to put me in this harm's way), sprayed the chemical on the surface of the water and waited for the blooms to die and disappear.

After four anxious days of waiting, just as we were ready to move them, we noticed a red-necked wallaby inside the fenced-off area. It seemed nature was determined to keep our animals in harm's way. Every day for an hour or so we would try to coax the wallaby out of the enclosure, but she just kept pounding into the wire of the fence headfirst, desperate to find her way out but unable see the opening in the fence where Jeff was to build the new entranceway.

I called Erin, a member of the local wildlife rescue team, who had helped us previously with capturing rogue macropods on our property. Since then, she and her partner, Jarrod, had become friends. Erin was working nightshift at the mines, so we called another guy to come and capture the stressed wallaby and release her back onto the property.

'Jeez, have you ever tried to catch one of them?' he said to Jeff while I was off driving the bus.

'No …'

'Well there's no way I can do it,' he said. 'You'll need a few more people and some massive sheets or something to trap her into a corner.'

She'll be incredibly stressed, Erin wrote to me later. *I can get there in a couple of days but maybe leave her alone until then.*

Every time we went into The Farm to do work, we again tried to coax her towards the opening, but each time she bounded straight past it in a blind panic to get away from us – the dangerous men who she must have thought were coming to skin her alive. I'd begun to have sleepless nights worrying about that damn wallaby (fearing she would be lonely and shock herself into a horrible death) – alternating between that nightmare and the one about snakes.

We were down there with our animals one day, enjoying a beer as the sun set. The poor wallaby still hopped around frantically, looking for a gap in the fence. Tired and bruised, with scratches from the fence marking her face and paws, she made her way to the opening but jumped straight past it again.

'I'm just going to go and open the gate,' Jeff said, referring to the new one he'd just installed. 'Just in case.'

'Oh, she's never gonna see that,' I said, ever the optimist when it came to one of Jeff's ideas. 'If she couldn't see a four-metre opening, how the hell is she going to see a one-metre gap? Just wait for Erin, she will know what to do.'

But Jeff went and opened it anyway. We opened our beers and focused on Helga and the goats instead.

'She's out!' Jeff said a few minutes later and, sure enough, there she was, bounding up the hill towards the olives where the rest of her mob were probably wondering where the hell she'd gotten to.

'Well I never ...' I said in half-concession to Jeff's persistence. 'Thank Christ for that.'

I texted Erin, *After eight days she finally found the entrance!*

Excellent because I had no idea how we were going to catch her! she wrote back.

* * *

Helga, Winston and Wesley had only ever known their little pen behind the shed. It's the place all of them have slept, eaten in and walked back to, day after day at Block Eight. Any walk to The Farm and the dam there ended with them following me back to their 'home'. So the day they moved was a hard one for helicopter-parent me – another situation to force me to acknowledge they're farm animals, not my children (even though the three of them never talk back and the same can't be said of teenaged humans). *If I wanted a response, I would have asked for one*, I say to Lucy about thirty times a day. The animals were out of sorts, scared and wondering why the hell they weren't returning to the one place they considered safe (apparently lethal snakes and tree limbs as large as men weren't dangerous). As Jeff and I walked away that evening they all cried out to me not to leave them and it broke my heart. I knew they would get used to it in time, but tonight, tomorrow night, maybe a full week's worth of nights, they would be scared and confused.

The entranceway Jeff built over the main gate is about five metres square and has a covered area that's divided into two: one where their food is kept and I can prepare it without hungry mouths and eager horns getting in my way, and another that was originally designed to be where they ate, but they chose it to sleep in instead – bugger the fancy three-bedroom terrace, they just wanted to be closest to the place they'd seen me last. That was okay, I didn't really mind – it was summer after all so they didn't need the bedrooms for warmth or protection against the weather.

But then one day it rained overnight, and water found its way under the entrance and onto the area where they liked to sleep. As I let myself into the gate, no one appeared to be home and then one by one, at hearing my noise, they emerged from the hut on the other side of the dam, sleepy and tussle-haired, yawning at the morning. As they excitedly made their way to me, I saw each of them was dry. It appeared they'd found their sleeping area and all agreed it wasn't too shabby.

Almost immediately, Jeff and his mother, Millie, set about demolishing the old animal pen. When we viewed it objectively (and without our animals in it), it had undoubtedly become a bit of an eyesore – one of the first (and ugliest) things our guests saw when they came onto the property. It took Jeff and Millie the best part of two days to take it apart, Jeff working to take down each piece, Millie making neat piles of materials so Jeff could reuse whatever he wanted.

When she isn't helping Jeff with jobs that most seventy-year-olds wouldn't have the stamina for, Millie is offering to make us cups of tea as we toil away. There's nothing quite as comforting as one of Millie's cups of tea, brought to you while you're sweaty and dirty, then sitting with her to talk about the beauty of the day, the crazy antics of the animals, or how much she is missing her cats back home.

Near the end of the demolition job, Jeff very carefully lifted a piece of aluminium and there was my old friend the brown snake, coiled up and happy. The animals were now safe but we didn't want to leave him there in the bush behind the shed so I called Erin, who'd recently told us she'd completed snake capture training.

'They basically stand you around in a circle, put a black snake in the middle and say, "Who's going to pick it up first?" and then after a few goes at that they do the same with a brown snake!'

You can have that, thanks all the same, I thought.

Erin was keen to grow her snake-capturing experience (*who does that?*) and was happy to come and get the snake, and to transfer him to a creek down the road. It was fascinating watching Erin and Jarrod get him in the bag, amazing at how fast the snake moved, and how adept it was at getting into tight, almost-impossible spaces. But Erin sure did know her shit and, after a few false starts, managed to get it into the snake-proof bag.

'I think he's a mulga,' she explained. 'Though he's brown in colour he's actually a black snake, but known as a king brown. They're less aggressive than actual browns and less poisonous, but can still be deadly.'

'Are you shaking?' I asked, thinking the adrenaline must be coursing through her veins as much as it was mine … and I'd been at least five metres away from the snake at all times. (Actual measurement may have been closer to twenty metres.)

'Nope,' she said, then she and Jarrod drove off to drop the snake far away from my trio of furballs.

It took Wesley, Winston and Helga about five days to settle in to The Farm. Every day I took them for a walk around the perimeter to show them it was fenced, to help them see they were safe in there – safer than they'd ever been in the pen behind the shed. They had an abundance of grass to graze on and Helga had a dam as big as an Olympic-sized swimming pool. There was plenty of shade, lots of gum trees to munch on and a big hill to climb. Jeff built the goats a three-level climbing platform, allowing them to get high up into the trees and away from Helga whenever she got into one of her moods, or took her mad half hour to chase them around and nip at their heels. *Maybe our human kids should have one in the yard too*, I thought.

We decided it would be a good idea to let the grass in The Farm grow long so the animals had lots and lots of it to eat. We were so sure they were going to eat all the grass that we'd debated over how wide to make the entrance.

'No need for the ride-on mower?' Jeff had asked.

'No, they will take care of all the mowing,' I'd said confidently.

By the time they moved in, most of the grass was at about ankle height. Of course they decided they weren't really into eating grass, having grown accustomed to the oats, pellets and bird seed they were usually fed (along with afternoon treats left behind by guests). So without nature's lawn mowers, the grass grew longer with each passing week.

By the time it was over knee height, the animals generally found walking through it unpleasant, especially Wesley, whose thick white fur is a natural magnet for grass seeds, bindies and other nasties.

It also didn't take long for Helga to start attracting more ticks – though thankfully on her eyelids and ears, not her vulva. Unlike the one on her rear though, these were smaller, softer bush ticks. I went into panic mode and made Jeff ask about treatment for Lyme disease at Farmers Warehouse and at the vet (so that he would be the one who looked stupid asking about a disease that doesn't really exist in our area). Bush ticks have their little meal on Helga's soft skin then fall off once they're full. I still pick them off whenever I see them because I don't want her to feel any discomfort, just like I can be found on all fours every morning wiping the sleep crust from her eyes. Anything for my pig.

I spent a day in the enclosure whipper-snipping the long grass. The animals generally hate mechanical sounds so I wasn't sure how they'd respond to one inside their pen. I started and, weirdly, none of them came to investigate. *That's it, they're all dead,* my stupid mind told me. *They've all succumbed to ticks and they're all lying dead in the sleep house.*

Don't be stupid, another part of my mind replied. *They're all fine, just napping. Do not go and disturb them – just keep cutting until they come to you because you might have to stop if Helga tries to attack the machine.*

I ploughed through the grass for a good ten minutes and still saw no sign of a single creature. This was very strange indeed. Finally, they emerged on the hill behind the dam – they'd been down there munching away on some of the long grass after all. The hairs on Helga's back rose up, just like they did whenever she got a whiff of a wild dog, and she ran towards the noise I was making. A few metres away, she turned and ran off again. Winston was the only one who wasn't scared – he came to inspect my handiwork and seemed to give me his approval, coming down to the newly cut grass and sniffing it for freshness. He's always been the most curious of our animals, and I like to think that he was checking up on me to make sure everything was okay.

Seven

Wilma V Cuddlington

I'm not quite sure why I've developed such a passion for animals so relatively late in my life. I kept a few until I was about fifteen, and once I moved out of home, I didn't even bother keeping goldfish. They just weren't on my radar.

But one day during my third year of uni, my friend Kirsti said out of nowhere, 'I'm going to Africa at the end of the year. Do you want to come?'

I practically bit her hand off. If I wasn't obsessed with Meryl Streep enough ('I had a farm in Africa'), then me insisting we tack on a trip to Egypt so I could see firsthand the sites I'd spent two years studying in high school sure sealed the deal. But as we started planning our itinerary, it became obvious to me that this trip was really about the animals, and seeing as many as we could. When the company running our safari advised that it was possible to take a side-trek for three days to visit the mountain gorillas of Zaire, neither Kirsti nor I hesitated.

To this day, seeing those magnificent animals in the wild is one of the highlights of my entire life. We trekked for a full day to base camp through a country on the verge of a horrific civil war, spent a stormy and Lariam-fuelled, crazy-dream-filled night in tents up a mountain, then the following morning followed the trackers to try to find the family of gorillas, headed by Marcel the silverback.

It took around four hours of trudging through thick mountain bush (no walking trails here, people!), avoiding stinging nettles, biting ants and slippery terrain along the way, but every single millisecond was worth it when I was the first to spot some of that black fur. The allocated hour we spent with that family of gorillas is etched into my memory in vivid detail – the size of Marcel's feet, connecting eyes with one of the females, watching babies frolic and play ...

Anyone who travels to Africa and does not take the opportunity to see the gorillas before they're gone is just plain crazy (plus, the hefty price you pay helps keep them safe from poachers). Sure, we saw just about every animal you'd hope to see on safari – leopard, cheetah, lion, giraffe, rhinoceros, hippopotamus, baboon, snake, elephant, chimpanzee, hyena, zebra, wildebeest ... the list goes on – but being *that* close to our closest relatives, well, words (for once) just fail me. I suppose those four weeks camping around Africa with Kirsti made me realise that animals and our relationship to them can be so rewarding, educational and uplifting. They really made me question the meaning of life. It's little wonder I've turned into one of those people who'd happily see only animals in their day, if it were at all feasible. Plus a little time with Jeff.

Do you have any human friends left? my friend Matt once texted after I'd posted a string of animal images on Instagram.

Nah, they only lead to disappointment, I joked.

But I do wonder what the world would be like if more people spent more time with animals. Quality time, I mean. Placing your head against theirs, hearing their heartbeats and their breaths, noticing how each and every animal has a starkly different personality – unmistakably unique in character and appearance. I can easily tell each of my goats' voices apart with my eyes closed. Call me crazy, but on some days I'm able to slip behind their eyes and see the world from their perspective. Is this why they have 'bring your pet to work' days? Well I guess part of me wants to take it one step further with a 'stop work and get more pets' life.

After we'd got Winston, Wesley and Helga, Jeff and I made the decision to only adopt rescue animals; to never again purchase one from a pet store, Gumtree (or other websites) or a farm. I've since developed a pretty militant attitude to puppy breeders. It is undeniable there are too many unwanted animals in the world and if you don't believe me, take a stroll through your local RSPCA next Saturday and see just how many desperate cats and dogs are waiting for someone to love them. With so many animals in need, it doesn't make sense for people to pay $5000 for a 'pedigree' puppy. I know of a local woman who has multiple bitches in heat at any one time and, based on my calculations, is making a cool million bucks a year breeding the canine *du jour.*

I also see it firsthand. Lucy and Charlie's mum Vicky raises unwanted puppies that are too young to be adopted, then desperately searches for homes for them when they've been desexed and are mature enough to move in with a family. The nights I've spent at her house with a puppy – who may not be a pedigree – that is the most loving, gentle, perfect pet for any family, only to listen to Vicky cry on the phone with frustration and disappointment when local families dismiss certain breeds and refuse to rescue an animal who should never have been born but for irresponsible pet owners who allow their pets to reproduce. No domestic or farm animal should be born in the hope you can make a quick buck from it, or the belief *someone* will eventually take the offspring off your hands.

This change in philosophy, after buying more than our share of pets from a shop (including Helga, I'm now a little ashamed to admit) began our regular search of the RSPCA's website Adopt-a-Pet. We do not have the time to commit to a dog or another cat, but aside from that, no animal on that site is out of the question.

One day there was a photo of who we felt to be the ideal addition to our little farm family: Alfie the sheep. Alfie was three months old, already desexed and vaccinated, and cute as a woolly button. I called the shelter and made my enquiries, but in order to house farm animals these days you need a PIC (property identification code), a piece of bureaucratic red tape that allows the government to track people who own them. Fair enough when the threat of mass disease is imminent, though to bring home a lamb who desperately needs a home, maybe not so critical. But then a rule is a rule.

It being the weekend, we were unable to visit the Local Land Services office to apply for our PIC. While I was sure we already had one, I had no record of it anywhere and I searched the nether regions of my laptop (finding a deleted poem about spider webs in the vineyard as a metaphor for racial intolerance that was going to win me the Nobel Prize for poetry), but came up empty on the PIC.

You'd think conducting a search on a government website to find your PIC would be straightforward – 'please enter your address' would be all they'd need to ask – but I've found that most government websites were either written by robots with English as their twenty-sixth language, or by civil servants who have never conversed with an actual human being since graduating from high school in 1943.

Okay, okay, I am the guy who made part of his living writing guides showing people how to use the internet effectively, but still. Getting a PIC (new or not) on the weekend proved impossible, and on Monday we were so busy cleaning villas that I didn't get away from the property at all. It was fair enough that the RSPCA wouldn't let you put an animal 'on hold' over the phone (even if you offered to pay in advance) because nothing could happen until they sighted your PIC. (A simpler solution only occurred to me much later when my friend Jenny said, 'You should have just given them mine and then when you got yours, transferred the lamb to it later.')

On Tuesdays the RSPCA is closed, so come Wednesday morning, I excitedly grabbed Jeff, picked up Mum and then drove to the Local Land Services office to get my PIC. A 'lovely young lass' (as Dad would say) behind the counter promised to expedite the application and, sure enough, within fifteen minutes the number had come through on email. We were driving towards the RSPCA when we passed the local Farmers Warehouse.

'Hey, look over there,' I said to Mum and Jeff, and pointed to a beat-up old farm ute with a lamb in a cage on its tray. 'I just know that's Alfie. We missed him.'

We got to the RSPCA and were told that we had indeed missed him by mere minutes. With only a few weeks to Christmas, it was pretty clear to me where a desexed three-month-old lamb was ending up on 25 December. You could adopt the poor thing for fifty-odd bucks, while one from a butcher or on a spit would cost multiple times that. Still, I wasn't going to become a crazy old cat lady, and knew I couldn't save every orphaned animal on the planet, even though we now had our one-acre farm enclosure just begging to be filled with more furry and feathered friends ... so I had to let go of the disappointment of not saving Alfie. I hope his end was swift and terror-free.

When a little goat popped up on Adopt-a-Pet, we dropped our mop (me) and drop saw (Jeff ... though that clarification wouldn't exactly come as a surprise to most) and raced to the RSPCA as fast as we could, PIC in hand.

One of the attendants took us out to the stables and opened the door, and little Wilma bolted straight to the massive pile of hay she knew was stored at the end of the row and happily began chomping away. Most people believe in love at first sight. I also happen to believe you can feel an animal's personality within seconds. Joel, the guy who looked after her, eventually picked her up and put her into my arms, and there she stayed for the next twenty minutes while we filled out the paperwork, barely moving at all, not struggling to be set down, just content to be cuddled.

It's not often that one of the animals' whole names will come to me right away. I usually start with a first name and wait for their personalities to appear before deciding what should come next – with Wilma all that cuddle time made my decision pretty easy.

So many of the staff came out to kiss her goodbye, I knew we were in for an animal that would work perfectly with Winston, Wesley and Helga. Wilma sat on the back seat of the ute with me all the way home, only bleating occasionally and quite content to just sit by my side.

She'd been found wandering on a road at about two days old, they estimate. No sign of her mother or any other goats – perhaps she'd been dumped. The thought of a kid so little and defenceless, desperately searching for the warmth and security of her mother just fills me with so much pain I can barely tolerate it. Some lovely soul picked her up and drove her to the RSPCA and over the following months the staff members took it in turns to take her home, bottle-feed her and get her to an age that she was strong enough to fend for herself, and then they put her up for adoption. We hadn't seen her in time when they'd originally listed her – her adorable photo must have caused quite a stir. The family who adopted her before us had a dog and, on day one, it took a massive bite out of her ear. They brought her back in to be treated and then rehoused. If her life hadn't been challenging enough, now she had faced the jaws of a dog, and half her right ear was missing.

Wilma is mostly white, but along the ridge of her spine, where the fur is longer and flowing, she has specks of grey. Her horns are shaped differently to the boys', almost with a kink at their end and when you look at her from behind, her long legs look like they're covered in woollen leg warmers with fringes. Oh, and the lashes! Each and every one is over an inch long so she's quite the classic Hollywood beauty – my very own Hedy Lamarr in glorious grey and white. Can you tell I was instantly smitten?

We dropped Mum home and took Wilma inside to meet Dad. I know my dad generally likes animals though not as much as me, and I suspect he's the reason Mum never got a dog after her cancer treatment was finished, which had originally been the plan. But on seeing Wilma, my dad turned all boy-like and he just couldn't take his eyes off her or stop saying 'the little darlin'', a phrase that takes me straight back to my beloved nan at Guildford, who also used to refer to my brothers and me as 'little monkeys'.

One school holidays when I was about ten, she'd given us fifty cents each to spend at the local shopping centre. Glen and Grant headed straight for the record store where (probably) Glen bought the Western Suburbs Magpies theme song on 45, and Grant bought Kelly Marie's 'Feels Like I'm In Love'. I headed straight for the pet shop, where I bought a budgerigar that they put inside a shoebox for me. It didn't matter to me that we didn't have a birdcage at home, that could all sort itself out later – I just had to have that bird. I guess some things never change.

As a kid I'd kept a range of pets, though none of them particularly successfully, aside from dogs. Sadie was our first, a big fat blonde Labrador whom I'd known since birth, and then her ginger son, Sam, joined the family. We eventually gave Sam to a neighbour and when we moved house, my cousin's wife, Barb, brought over her new puppy for us to meet. Suzy was about as big as a tennis ball, a ball of Silky Terrier fluff. Needless to say, my brothers and I were instantly head over heels and, in what was probably her intention all along, Barb asked us if we would like to keep her. What chance did Mum and Dad have? After a quick negotiation with Glen, Grant paid two dollars and the Kelly Marie single to change the dog's name to Lindy (after a girl he was besotted with; not a precursor to my Meryl Streep obsession and her role playing Mrs Chamberlain).

Aside from dogs, I often asked for goldfish (many died) and birds (ditto – prompting Grant to put me on trial for 'birder') and then finally I got my biggest wish, an adorable little guinea pig, Odie. A few weeks after I got him, Odie escaped his cage and was mauled to death by Lindy, as was her nature. Later, after a very old and failing Lindy was put down (always Dad's job, never mine or Mum's) I got the real love of my life, Bronte – a mongrel who I adored more than any animal (or human), a girl who got me through countless hours of lost love and loneliness.

* * *

Back at my mum and dad's, Wilma the goat made herself right at home, climbing up on Mum's furniture and nibbling away daintily at her pot plants. When baby Helga had visited them, she'd seemed out of place, running around sniffing crazily as if trying to find the part of the garden where she belonged. Not Wilma. For her it was as if she had a right to be there. *So this is my new caretaker is it? Alright then, I'd better make myself comfortable, because who knows how long I'll be staying here.*

We got to Block Eight and wondered how our other animals were going to react to the new addition to the family. Winston and Wesley were curious, then dismissive, giving her a little nudge in the rump with their horns just to show her they were bigger and meaner, and not to be messed with. Helga wasn't quite as gentle, and after a brief sniff of Wilma's bits, began chasing her with an open mouth, intent on taking a chunk out of her flesh. By this time Helga was an adolescent sow – a teenager, if you like – with all the attitude and mood swings you'd expect. Still, at least Helga's adolescence was nothing compared to what Rodney's and Billy's had been.

When I wrote the *Helga* book, Jeff begged me not to include a certain scene involving the male pigs, but sometimes artistic integrity calls for the whole truth, and nothing but.

My publicist had secured me a prime spot for an interview on ABC Radio National. I went into it with a very clear mantra: *Promote the book for Mother's Day. Promote the book for Mother's Day.*

Midway through the interview, the journalist said, 'Now, I believe adolescent male pigs present particular challenges.'

With the lovely benefit of hindsight, I suppose she was expecting me to talk about how non-desexed male pigs can get aggressive and territorial and that is why we were forced to make the heartbreaking decision to find them jobs as studs around the Valley. But unfortunately I've memorised many of our stories, so sometimes I find them flowing out of my mouth on autopilot, and without censorship.

'Yes, they learn how to masturbate,' I said. 'So they will trail their penises along the ground until they reach that point ... and whatever they are producing can hit you in the face. That happened to Jeff once.'

It was a remote interview so I was unable to gauge the reaction of the journalist and couldn't hear any response in her voice.

Oh my god, I thought. *You've blown it.*

After I left the studio, I called Jeff. 'Well that was the worst interview ... ever.'

'I am a little surprised you went there ... I mean *all* the way there. You even said "the money shot".'

I had images of my publisher's Managing Director calling me direct to tell me I had disappointed him.

'Well that's the end of hoping for a boost in sales for Mother's Day,' I said, so bitterly disappointed in my big mouth and my brain's inability to control it.

But then, sometimes, the world turns in mysterious ways. An ABC print journalist heard the interview and thought it made for a good online story. A few days later, Jeff and I were on the front page of the ABC News website. A lot of people read it, countless people wrote to me to say they'd seen it, and Benjamin Law even tweeted about it, creating the perfect social media mini-tornado.

A few weeks later, I was giving a wine tasting down at the Wine Room and, as often happens, the guests started asking questions about how Jeff and I had ended up at Block Eight. I mentioned Helga and then the story developed further.

'Oh!' one of the women interrupted excitedly. '*You're* the masturbating pig guy! My colleagues and I had quite the chuckle over that in the tea room one morning.'

That's not how I'd prefer to be known, but there are worse nicknames if my school days are anything to go by.

* * *

Back at The Farm, Wilma had speed and street smarts on her side, and bolted from Helga, whose little legs can't carry her potbelly very fast for very long. But there'd been such determination in Helga's movements that I knew it wouldn't be long until she succeeded in taking a bite. We needed a new solution.

It was time to pick up our tools again – this time to build Wilma an enclosure within The Farm. We hurriedly erected a reo and star picket fence with materials from Winston's old one, brought down the old hen house to keep her dry, and set her up with hay, straw, water and food. She liked her little home immediately, but really came to life whenever we went in there to keep her company.

More than any animal we've ever homed, Wilma is people-oriented. Unlike her 'brothers', who like scratches and being brushed but that is the extent to which you can touch them, Wilma lets us smother her in cuddles and kisses and it is an almost-daily occurrence that she falls asleep in my lap, breathing deeply and contentedly against my thigh, not a care in the world. If we stop scratching her, she uses her hoof to take a hold of our hand and pull it towards her belly, urging us to continue. For their part, the other animals rarely pay Wilma any attention unless I am in there with her; suddenly jealous of the affection she receives.

From the outset, Wilma loved to dance. She quickly learnt how to climb on the roof of her house and there she would tap away like Shirley Temple, copying our moves from one side to the other, that little mouth of hers permanently fixed in what seemed to be a smile.

At night as I left them all, I couldn't help but worry that she was lonely in that little house all on her own. I knew she'd be able to find her place in the goat hierarchy easily enough, but winning Helga over was never going to be easy, as Helga hadn't ever had to deal with any animals smaller than herself – and worse yet, with someone who stole away some of my focus and affection.

After Wilma's third night with us, early the next morning I made my way down to The Farm to give her some love. But about fifty metres away from their enclosure I could see that Wilma's space was empty. Then I heard her high-pitched little bleat, that excited *I can see you coming* sort of cry and there she was, next to Winston and Wesley, sitting almost between them, munching on some grass. As I let myself in the gate, the noise woke Helga from her slumber in the three-bedroom terrace on the other side of the dam and she bolted towards me in anticipation of her breakfast. Partway through her trot she saw that fluffy white-and-grey little thing and altered her course, again making an open-jawed bolt towards Wilma's rump. Obviously Wilma had experienced this onslaught more than once and she was like lightning as soon as she sensed Helga was on the chase, the pig giving up after only ten metres or so – out of breath and only now seeing me, being reminded that breakfast was on offer. I couldn't chance Wilma with Helga out here in the open, could I? What if she ever got her cornered?

I gave everyone breakfast and went to inspect Wilma's enclosure. The reo sheets had been pushed inward – someone had either broken her out because she wanted to be part of the family, or someone had tried to break in with a view to having a nice feast. I mended the fence as best I could then placed a set of ladders against the reo to provide a barrier, so the naughty culprit would be kept from head-butting or full-body rolling their way in.

The next morning, Wilma was there again, sidled up next to Winston outside of her enclosure. Helga was fifteen metres away and seemed she couldn't care less. It appeared that a truce of sorts had been called and in time I learnt that the only things any of them ever fought over were food … and me. It was nice to feel wanted.

* * *

We thought it would be a fun idea to introduce Wilma at a wine tasting, just to give her a small break for an hour or two from that marauding pig. (I wish I could say Helga is perfect in every way, but I can't. She's not me, after all.)

At this tasting we had a group of twelve twenty-somethings, so the presence of Wilma was embraced with open and enthusiastic arms. No one was really interested in hearing about our wines, just our goat. Wilma made her way around the table as though she was greeting them all personally. At the head of the table sat a girl wearing a strap dress and while Jeff and I were pouring wine Wilma thought it would be a good idea to nibble on the ties of the straps and, in one swift move, had them completely undone. Wilma was so stealthy, the girl had no idea it'd happened until her top started falling down.

'I bet you've trained her to do that!' one of the boys joked.

'Trust me, that's not really our style,' I said and everyone laughed.

As the tasting progressed, Wilma danced for the guests (appreciated), shat everywhere (not so appreciated) then nibbled away at what looked like very expensive straw handbags (met with horror). *Maybe goats and wine don't really mix after all*, we thought. Though I couldn't deny it, Wilma was as close to a dog as I'd gotten since having Bronte and dammit if I didn't want her by my side every minute of every day.

We often took Wilma for walks outside The Farm, just to give her a little break from the bullying she sometimes received.

On one of those days, two of our guests had organised to go on a helicopter wine tour. Jeff and I were very excited – we'd seen hot air balloons land on our property but never a helicopter. Watching it hover then come in to land right near the villas was one of those surreal moments as the two of us sat on the ground, with our goat between us.

'Don't you think it's kind of bizarre we have a property big enough for a helicopter to land on?' I said to Jeff.

'It's so cool,' he said, his face in his phone, taking photos and videos.

Once the pilot had switched off the ignition, we walked over to say hi.

'Gorgeous day for it,' he said.

'Welcome to Block Eight,' I said, and shook his hand.

'And who do we have here?' he asked.

'This is Wilma,' Jeff said and we all laughed as she ran about, excitedly inspecting the chopper.

Later as he took off, the three of us sat on the grass, waving goodbye to our departing guests, the wind from the helicopter's blades blowing upright the hairs along the ridge of Wilma's back. But safe between the two of us, the noise and gusts from the machine didn't bother her at all, she barely moved a muscle.

'Well that was a first,' the pilot said to us when he returned later that day. 'I can safely say I've never had a goat sit to watch me take off.'

Every time I go down to The Farm, thanks to a little doorway Jeff has left from the animals' space into the entryway, Wilma meets me at the gate, her tail wagging excitedly (earning her the nickname Willy Wagtail), her little face peering into mine with love and anticipation. She bleats her happy sound and bounds around in circles. It's very similar to how Jeff greets me every morning.

'Oh, she's just like your dog,' friends often say (about Wilma, not Jeff).

Wilma makes eye contact with me, while the male goats generally don't. I suspect because she was raised by humans and has no recollection of being raised by goats, she sees more of an equal in our faces. I swear she is clever enough to manipulate any situation involving a human to get precisely what she wants. I watch her bound around The Farm, teasing her brothers and her nemesis, Helga, and I have no doubt that as she gets bigger she will be the ruler of that roost … and perhaps be a little too much for us to handle the heavier she gets. Her mischievousness is so endearing but I wonder what it bodes for the future.

* * *

Not long after we got Wilma, the *Weekend Australian* sent a photographer to take some shots of us to promote an excerpt they were running of the *Helga* book. I've been known to be quite happy to pose for photographs, but it's not exactly Jeff's favourite thing in the world. I think he'd prefer to be banned from buying cushions for life than to have to endure a photoshoot. Nick, the photographer (whose work is stunning) clearly takes his job very seriously, and was keen to get in among the animals. What ended up being two photos for the publication was a four-hour shoot for us. Jeff was so *thrilled* by the end of it and even I, I have to admit, was a little worse for wear. Who'd have thought that I'd *ever* grow tired of posing? But with us all the way were Winston, Wesley, Helga and Wilma. At one point we were posing with Wilma on my lap and Helga (a bit like Jeff) was getting tired of having a camera poked in her face. Her attitude had begun changing; that teen rebellion was kicking in. She gave Nick a good hard bash with her neck (pig talk for 'Will you just piss off now?'), but if he was at all concerned he showed no sign. Eventually bored with him, Helga came towards me and sniffed baby Wilma in my arms then, in one fell swoop, snapped at her stomach. Poor Wilma's high-pitched scream was bloodcurdling.

'That's it, Nick. I think we'd better stop now,' I said, my voice wavering with stress.

We left The Farm but Nick still hadn't gotten 'his shot' so we moved over towards the house, letting Wilma come as a post-traumatic treat. While Jeff and I may have been exhausted and beyond forcing fake smiles, I swear that goat lapped up every single second of the attention and, though she's not even featured in the *Helga* book, there she was, full-paged in the *Weekend Australian*, this little goat with a story to tell.

* * *

In time, the highest platform of the goat-climbing frame became one of my favourite spots on the property. It is the spot where I begin and end every day – sometimes for just ten minutes, other days for upwards of an hour. There, while the animals eat their meals, I lie on my back and watch the leaves and branches of the gum trees swaying in the wind. It is quiet and peaceful and the sun always warms the spot. After eating, the goats will come and join me – Wesley for scratches and brushes of his thick, fluffy white coat; Winston to lick the salt from my skin or to have his underbelly or brown cheeks gently tickled.

Helga fashioned herself a sleeping hole beneath the platforms. It's the perfect size for her body and a suntrap for early morning where she can usually be found snoring softly away. Wilma falls asleep in the crook of my arm, and it becomes my nirvana. I crave for nothing more, wish to be no other place. I could spend all day, every day down there and never grow bored. Compared to that, the realities of running the business and completing my chores are a sobering hangover, an unwelcome intruder from the high of being with the animals in an altogether simpler and untethered life. While I am up there, I can't help but ask myself, *How could I ever leave this place and take our animals away from it?*

Most afternoons, Jeff will join me. We are fathers to a motley crew and without fail we find ourselves laughing at their antics. In those moments, under the dappled light of the gum trees, we often just sit to take in deep breaths and appreciate how fortunate we are that we made the decision to end up in the country.

'God I love it down here,' I say almost every time.

'We're so lucky,' Jeff agrees. 'I hate to think what we'd be doing in that tiny courtyard in Annandale ...'

'I'd be reading cookbooks and you'd be shopping online for cushions, probably.'

'You really have blown this whole cushion thing out of perspective.'

'Rubbish!'

'You know you have, just admit it.'

'Here's your intervention, Jibbuz. *You* need to admit that nothing in the world quite tickles your design fancy like buying a neat little cushion.'

'But really ... you can't say I'm obsessed.'

'Can't I? Can't I, Jibbuz? Can't I?'

'Did I see you counting your cookbooks the other day?' he said, making his lethal chess move.

'No!' I lied.

'How many have you got?' he asked with a laugh.

'Twenty-three.'

'Toddy … how many?'

'I lost count after four hundred and couldn't be bothered starting all over again.'

'Four hundred! No way! You're the one with the problem, not me! There's no way we have four hundred cushions on the property. Not a chance! I win, you lose.'

I thought to myself, *Holy shit, even at thirty dollars each, that's twelve grand I've spent on cookbooks.*

'Toddy, you spent over two hundred on *Fat Duck* alone!'

'Shut up! Go and play with Winnie; he's looking at you, wondering why you're ignoring him.'

'Twelve grand …' he muttered under his breath as he walked up to Winnie to take a gentle hold of his horns.

I must remember not to include this bit in the next book, I made a mental note before walking up to Helga to give her belly rubs and allow her to nuzzle into my hand.

It is Wilma who has done this to us. I mean, I wrote a book about my pig for Chrissakes, so there's little doubt how much affection I have for *her* … but this little goat really is something else. Part of it is knowing what a horrific and lonely start to life she's had. Part of it is wondering what would have become of her had we not rescued her from the RSPCA. But I'm not the only one who feels this way.

Visitors to The Farm absolutely love Wilma too. They love the cuddles she gives and some fully grown adults crouch down on all fours to let my little goat climb all over them.

Well, not every visitor. One day I let Wilma out to play with Mel and Jesus's daughters, and poor Amelie ended up in the dirt, the victim of what this overly defensive goat father would summarise as a 'gentle little nudge' ... though Amelie's tears might have suggested otherwise.

* * *

Sentence I Never Thought I'd Utter Number 478: My goat has pus coming out of her vagina. (Let's face it, I can't imagine too many other scenarios where I'd be required to say the word 'vagina'.)

Wilma had recently had her first heat (Is that how you say it? Maybe it should be *Wilma had recently been hot* ...) and a few days later I noticed white liquid coming from her behind. I consulted Google and saw that it wasn't uncommon to happen after their first cycle, but called the vet and explained the situation, just to be on the safe side.

'I'm quite close with my goat,' I heard myself saying, shuddering at the implication, but the words were already out. 'I mean, I haven't noticed any before today.'

'Is it a lot of liquid?'

'No, a few mils ...'

'Oh, that's okay. Is she behaving normally?'

'She just danced for ten minutes on a raised platform ...'

'I'd say she's perfectly fine then. Keep your eye on her and make sure she doesn't go off her food, or the amount of pus doesn't increase significantly.'

It was just another day down at The Farm.

Eight

The Birds

Although I tried to keep birds growing up, they were never really my favourite kind of animal. I suppose after you've been attacked by magpies countless times at cricket ovals in forty degree heat while watching your brother play the world's most boring sport, and swooped by angry sandpipers near another oval in Toowoomba, birds just proved beyond a reasonable doubt they couldn't be trusted. Of course as a kid, watching Tippi Hedren being completely terrorised by the feathery flappy things in Hitchcock's *The Birds* did nothing much to improve my perception of them. Aside from all that, they also had a habit of dying on me.

But when we moved to Block Eight, I knew keeping chickens was non-negotiable. I mean, who moves to the country and doesn't have at least one chook? Chooks came and went, as did the ducks and quail – most lost to fox attack or some mysterious illness that meant they just wound up stiff one morning. Each of those birds was to serve a purpose, to provide us with a supply of eggs for our guests and ourselves, so when we decided to keep peafowl, we were definitely straying from the only-birds-with-purpose mantra.

Peacocks sure do root a lot. They're very efficient – both at choosing when to mate with the fowl, and in the act itself, which is harsh (they pin her head down with their beak) but thankfully also very fast. As is often nature's curse, it's the female who has to do all of the work: the thankless task of sitting on up to eight eggs for around six or seven weeks, making both the offspring and herself vulnerable to attack. When a chick is hatched, we still think it's a miracle, so much to the point that we hate to part with them, or put the females through the anguish of having their babies taken away. But we have sold some of the chicks in the past. It's not like we keep every single bird ever hatched on our property; just one or two *too many*. They make great alarm animals and will always alert us to a truck or larger vehicle coming onto the property; they eat mice, which is also helpful; they look pretty and act funny – but aside from that all they do is eat … and shit. Peafowl shit is big, they're not exactly fussy about where they drop one, and it has a god-awful stench if you happen to step in it.

The owner of the transport company who used to deliver our wine to wholesale buyers had been asking Jeff for months if he could buy one of our peahens to take home to his peacock, Andrew. We were resistant because they're a pain in the arse to catch and it's stressful on the bird. But when Jeff insisted we keep another three hatchlings from the 2017 season, it felt like letting go of one bird was sensible, and we agreed to do it for no cost. The day Susan (as she was later christened) was to be taken away still felt somewhat soulless, sending one of our own into the great unknown, but Jeff had asked all the right questions about where she would be living, and had given instructions on how best to settle her in.

'How many peafowl do we have now?' Jeff asked.

'Stop being stupid,' I snapped, probably cross over having to unpack the dishwasher. 'Spencer, Kate, Tom, Shelly, Freddie, Freddie Junior and Susan. We had seven, now we have six.'

'Hmm ...' he hmmed and walked off, though probably because I'd been short with him.

The next day I went to feed the fowl, knowing Kate was sitting on another set of her eggs and rarely came to feeding time. I counted our six fowl, just as I'd insisted to Jeff we had. This being a rare occasion when she was off her eggs, I thought it wise to go and check how many she was sitting on. I walked around the front of the shed to the spot under the house where she'd chosen to camouflage herself and her clutch, and there she was.

'Jeez, Kate, that was lightning fast,' I said. But I somehow knew she would not have snuck back so quickly or quietly, as any time a hen is coming from or going to her eggs, she races about gaggling frantically in an attempt to ward off predators. I ran as fast as I could back to the feeding area. Six fowl. I did one of those old school double takes, scratched my head and said 'ha'. I ran back to the place where Kate had sat – she was still there. Again, 'ha'.

Welcome to the Taj Mahal of chook pens, built by Jeff. He's got baby Wilma on his knees. I'm holding Stevie, and Nicks is supervising from up on high. *Photo © Nick Cubbin*

A drone view over our vineyard and the main dam, towards our house, with the Brokenback Range in the distance. *Photo © Jurds*

Wesley Chesney is the most calm and angelic of our goats … until it comes to tucker time or flies!

Photo © Work of Heart Photographic Studios

The goat who followed me kilometres home, Winston Buttworth-Jones, remains our most inquisitive.

Photo © Work of Heart Photographic Studios

Wanda posing. I can tell the goats' voices apart from a long distance, and each one has a uniquely charming personality.

Photo © Work of Heart Photographic Studios

Shirley is our shyest animal but leaps for joy with her twin, Warren, when there's some interesting food on offer.

Photo © Work of Heart Photographic Studios

A close-up of Wanda showing off those lovely Beyoncé curls.

Photo © Work of Heart Photographic Studios

Like most pigs, Helga loves to rub snouts with her 'mum' – she's still my baby girl despite being twice as big as me! *Photo © Work of Heart Photographic Studios*

Wilma likes to think she's higher than Jeff in the mammal hierarchy. She's probably right. *Photo © Work of Heart Photographic Studios*

I've given up trying to stay clean when I'm with the kids (here with Wesley).
Photo © Nick Cubbin

When we collected Wilma from the RSPCA, she stayed cuddled up in my arms for nearly an hour. *Photo © Jeff Ross*

Fresh from an afternoon nap, Winston emerges from the sleeping-cottage that Jeff lovingly built for the animals. *Photo © Work of Heart Photographic Studios*

The goats' favourite food is olive leaves, which is helpful in keeping the trees well pruned. *Photo © Work of Heart Photographic Studios*

I called Jeff. 'Are you sure they actually left with Susan?'

'Yeah, he just sent me a photo of her on her new perch,' he said. 'Why?'

'Um, I think I owe you an apology. Yesterday when you asked how many peafowl we have, I thought you were just being dumb, but ...'

'I knew it! We have seven, don't we?'

'Yep!'

'I knew I wasn't going crazy!'

'Well not about this, at least. Where the hell did she come from?' I wondered aloud.

Spencer had been crowing to announce to the world he was mating, so his cry must have drawn her in from ... somewhere. None of our neighbours kept peafowl so she must have been living wild in the bush. Maybe she was one of Kate's babies we'd previously sold and whoever had bought her got sick of her and had dumped her in the National Park at the back of our property. Needless to say, she had a home with us, and just when we thought we were thinning out our flock too!

* * *

A few months later, our neighbour called to say Spencer was on her property. It was one of the few times Jeff and I had taken a night off from Block Eight together, and we were at a resort celebrating my birthday.

'That's unusual,' I said to her, 'because he's never roamed before.'

'Should I feed him?'

'No! Whatever you do, don't feed him! You'll never get rid of him then. Just leave him and we'll come and try to get him when we get home.'

The following day when we got home, I saw Spencer (whose previous owners had placed a red identity band around his leg) outside our villa. I texted Jeff, *Spencer's back*.

So is someone else, he replied with a photo of another peacock on the border of our two properties. He was smaller than Spencer and had a shorter tail, and no red band.

Spencer's crows had alerted another family of fowl in the area. The male, Intruder (later shorted to Trudy), brought not two, but three females in his harem. For days on end we tried to chase him off the property. He made Spencer very uneasy, on-edge. Then they started cock fighting. For hours, they'd flap and kick and peck at each other, but no matter how hard we tried to chase off or capture Trudy, nothing worked. After about a fortnight of fighting, the boys called a truce and our family of seven, then six, then seven, peafowl, instantly turned into eleven. When people tell us of the feral peafowl problem in Canberra, we can all-too-well relate.

* * *

The same day Trudy moved in, Kate was missing from her place under the house. Her eggs were shattered. I looked everywhere for her but couldn't find her and began to assume the worst: that she'd been attacked and a goanna had come to eat her babies.

I remembered that in the past she'd shown a fondness for the garden bed at our Barrington View Villa and when I made my way down there I saw her, hiding in a corner with her five babies, two of them her signature white. After some kerfuffle we managed to capture them and put them in the special cage we'd built for the chick-raising purpose. We now had sixteen fowl! Thankfully I'd already convinced a local to take all of Kate's babies, no matter how many she had, but that still left us with eleven …

We found a home for two males and two females and called a professional bird catcher to come and get them.

'Nope, not peafowl,' he said to Jeff over the phone. 'They're impossible.'

'Don't you know of any way …?'

'Just dope their water. That's the *only* way, believe me.'

But we just couldn't stand the thought of drugging them to catch them, so for the time being, they were all ours. When it came time to separate the five chicks from Kate, our beloved first peahen, it was just horrible to think of all that stress we would be putting her through, so I called the buyer and asked if he'd consider taking her with them. To my surprise, he said yes.

Luckily for him, the two white ones are male and will put on a stunning display when their tails are fully grown. *Unluckily* for him, the other three were also male … as were the two chicks Kate hatched the following season.

'The neighbours hate me,' he joked.

'It must get very noisy at mating time.' I empathised.

'No … because they go roaming, I mean. Mine aren't noisy at all.'

'Oh mate,' I said with a chuckle. 'Just you wait until they've grown their tails and fight each other for domination. It's going to be chaos.'

'Do you think so?' he asked nonchalantly. 'I love them.'

'Seven males and one female! It's going to be like an all-night sing-along!'

For the record: ours are strictly non-refundable. (That's now in print.)

Now, a full year later when I count the peafowl, I think we are at nine instead of ten, but I've given up counting. It is what it is. I thought I'd won the lottery the day a woman who lives about four kilometres from us left me a note in our mailbox. Judith had read my book and wrote, *I noticed you have peafowl and I wondered if I could buy a peacock from you? You see, almost two years ago my male and three females just disappeared ...*

I called her up immediately. 'Judith,' I said. 'Today's your lucky day.'

* * *

It isn't just peafowl that have taken up residence at Block Eight.

One afternoon, when we were at our neighbour's having drinks (food was always a secondary consideration at one of our get-togethers), I got a call from two of our guests who reported seeing a fox nibbling away at a lame kangaroo. I couldn't stand the thought of leaving nature to take its course on this one, so we decided to call a member of the local wildlife rescue team, who turned out to be Erin, and she brought her partner, Jarrod.

They arrived late in the afternoon and we took them to where our guests had reported last seeing the kangaroo. Armed with our bottles of beer, we began the hunt for the injured roo, intent on scaring away the ravaging pack of foxes munching away on its flesh. The sun was setting and the light was fading, so we each got out our mobile phones to light the way down the rows of grapes. We searched and searched, and I was ready to call it a night, when Erin and Jarrod appeared, carrying what looked to be a dead weight in a body bag. It was actually a wallaby wrapped inside a blanket. Macropods are incredibly skittish and nervous animals and the only way to calm them, if at all, is to 'turn their lights out' by covering their faces in darkness and restricting their bodies. In one deft move, Erin and Jarrod carefully placed the wallaby in the boot of their hatchback and told us they would do their best to help him and get him home to the rescue area at her house so she could examine him and assess his chances of survival.

'This is a wonderful property,' Erin said after they closed the hatchback.

'Thanks,' I said. 'And thanks for coming out tonight. I hated the thought of him being out here alone to fend for himself.'

'You did the right thing,' she said with a smile. 'Have you ever considered releasing kangaroos on the property?'

'I'm happy for you to release them whenever you like,' I said as I finished off my beer, 'I love animals, so they're welcome any time.'

'It's a little more involved than that,' Erin said. 'I'll be in touch and let you know more about it.'

We exchanged phone numbers and waved them off.

For us, the evening continued as per usual – more drinks, more arguments over who was getting control of the music for the night, more pondering whether we should open another vineyard's wine or just stick to the tried and true – our own. But as we got home close to midnight, my mind kept thinking of that poor wallaby and I knew I wouldn't be able to ignore its fate.

The following morning I texted Erin to see how it was faring.

He had a paralysis tick inside his ear, she wrote back, *which I managed to remove and now he is in recovery, so hopefully that will be all we need to worry about.* Thankfully, we must have gotten to him before the fox had done any real damage.

All day as I went about my chores, I kept thinking about him and whether he would make a complete recovery, and whether Erin would bring him back to his home so he could return to his mob. I left it as it was, not wanting to harass Erin too much, but the following morning I couldn't help myself and texted to ask her for an update.

I went out to the enclosure this morning and he was gone, she wrote. *So he's probably fine, though we may never know.*

Over the following weeks Erin and I talked some more about releasing kangaroos on the property. It involved me hand-rearing orphaned or recovering joeys, then releasing them into the wild, knowing they would always be semi-tame and would generally keep coming back to me, even as fully grown adults. Naturally I signed on the proverbial dotted line faster than an incumbent Republican President undoes all the progress made by an outgoing Democrat

President. I registered as a member with the group and paid my twenty bucks, assuming it would fast track me to my dream of kangaroo rerelease. I envisaged my very own TV series with a roo who could understand me and save little kids who'd fallen down wells ...

Erin came to inspect our animal enclosure then reported back to Wildlife Rescue that we had a suitable place to release macropods. And then I waited for them to bring me an orphanage's worth of needy animals. And I waited some more.

Finally, twelve months in, patiently waiting to become a saint of the macropod kingdom, it was just after dusk when I got a call.

'Todd, this is Cortnie from Wildlife Rescue. Look, we have a situation I was hoping you could help with.'

'Okay ...'

'A bloke has rescued a kangaroo from his dam. It looked like he was drowning – he's a very large male. The bloke went in and managed to get the roo out and he nearly drowned doing it. But they're both out now. The roo is by the edge of the dam and he's not moving.'

'And what would you like me to do?'

'Can you go and catch it?'

We only had Barry the Barina at the time – not exactly the ideal animal ambulance, particularly for a bull larger than a human. 'And then do what?'

'Probably take it to the vet. They'll just put him down.'

'Um ...'

'We're kind of desperate and I had no one else to call.'

'I've never rescued a kangaroo before ...' I ventured.

'Could you try? For me?'

I seriously considered it for a few moments. Jeff and me in the dark at some bloke's dam, capturing a full-sized male kangaroo and shoving him into the back of our Barina. Would he even fit? While I can't deny we've done some downright stupid things since moving to the country, even to me this one spelled disaster, if not death.

'Hmm ... I don't really think I'm the right person for this job,' I said. 'I've never caught a kangaroo before and I'd hate to stuff it up and cause him any more injuries, or stress. Sorry, Cortnie.' *We're probably better at handling dead things* I thought of adding.

'Bugger,' she said and hung up the phone.

Months later, I received another call from Cortnie, in distress.

'Todd, I'm sorry, I've tried everyone else and no one is answering and I just wasn't sure who else I could turn to ...'

'What is it, Cortnie?'

'I need some ducklings rescued up in Branxton. Seems the mum has abandoned her chicks and they've got a few of them that need saving.' *Yes!* I thought. *Ducks we can manage, full-sized male kangaroos, maybe not.*

'Okay,' I said, 'I'll do it. What's the address?'

Perhaps it was my inner child trying to make amends for my multiple counts of birder, but I didn't hesitate to grab Jeff and drive the ten minutes to collect those little ducks in distress. We'd hand-raised eight ducklings before (all but two taken by foxes), and had some hands-on experience with the peachicks, so we knew two little ducklings would be a walk in the park. But by the time we got to the house, they'd only managed to catch one, and didn't know where any of the others were. We took a look but couldn't see any at all so took the little one home with us.

Being wild, he was very determined to peck at our hands any time we went to handle him, but we could tell just by looking into his eyes that he was a fighter, a survivor. How many days had he been without his mother? We set him up in the peachick's bird-raising cage and gave him some food and water. He was curious but timid.

'I'm just worried,' Jeff said sounding gravely serious.

'He'll be fine ...'

'Worried that he'll die of loneliness ...'

'Oh! Come on, then!'

We drove the ten minutes up the road to see our mate Trevor at the local pet shop. Though we'd sworn against buying animals from shops and farms, the local hatchery had no ducklings for sale and the local RSPCA had none for rescue. We were damned if we did, and our little rescue duck would probably die if we didn't. I chose a large white one from a small crate in the pet shop to be his mentor and we immediately named them George and Martha, after characters in my favourite play, *Who's Afraid of Virginia Woolf?*

On the whole, they got along famously. George (the wild duck) really enjoyed cuddling up next to his domesticated counterpart and together they huddled under the red light we'd also bought for the mission – along with bags of starter food, and straw for a bed. We set them up on the daybed in our unfinished villa so they got lots of human interaction and once comfortable, at night we'd let them out of their cage to settle in between us and watch television (with a towel to keep me protected against their inevitable pooping, though sometimes they missed and I'd run into the bathroom to wash shit off my neck, arm or ankle). Martha loved cuddles and to be stroked, George was way more pragmatic and tended to use us for warmth, or come to us if he knew there was food on offer.

For his part, Leroy the cat was curious but never much bothered and from our past experience we knew any bird we brought into our home would be safe from a cat who generally loved nothing more than to pin down a feathery nuisance if he came across a bird in the wild. Both the ducks would eventually fall asleep – usually with Martha cradling into my neck and George keeping his distance on my hip or thigh. They were lovely nights, and we brimmed with pride and gratitude that we'd been afforded an opportunity to rescue George and employ Martha to help bring him safely back to the wild.

Once every two days we'd run them a nice bath and they'd clean themselves, drink and have a whale of a time – the bathroom floor covered in more water than anyone would ever think it possible for two baby ducks to splash about. On warmer days we took their cage out into the sun and let them feel its warmth and eat fresh grass shoots and then, as time so resolutely passes faster than you ever want it to, Martha grew too tall for her cage and both of them had developed their lovely waterproof feathers.

It's always a bittersweet moment when you release one of your hand-raised animals back out into nature. I hated seeing Helga move outside after raising her by hand but aside from the odd cuddle and bit of affection, I'm sure she rarely thought twice about living back with us, with our hard floors, small litter tray and lack of sunshine and fresh air. I knew Martha would be fine – we still had two white ducks on our medium-sized dam and she'd fit right in with them – but I worried about little George and whether the other native kids would embrace him or forever see him as an outsider.

They swam off together – Martha confident and excited to explore her new surrounds, George uncertain and struggling to keep up with the much larger bird and her determined kicks. For the first few mornings they came to feeding time at the dam together, Martha gobbling up as much as she could, George staying a little distant, the striking green feather beneath his left wing making him easier to spot among the many wild ducks that lived with us. One day I was late feeding them, and Martha had walked about one hundred metres towards where we lived until I called her all the way back to the dam.

Then George disappeared. He wasn't at feeding time two mornings in a row. I hoped he was one of those further back on the water, or else had moved over to the other dam where some of our other ducks chose to live. Then, on the third morning I went outside our villa and there he was, sitting on the grass where his cage often sat in the sun, waiting for me to feed him. Over the coming weeks he came and went, sometimes bringing a new friend with him, as if he'd said to her, *We don't have to wait here every morning to be fed like all the other stupid ducks. If we go up to the shed first thing in the morning, the chooks and peafowl get fed there way before us at the dam.*

It became increasingly hard to spot George but, even a year later, I will look into a duck's eyes or see that green feather of his, and know it is him. There is a knowing look of mutual recognition, and on my dreamier days, a thankful nod coming from him.

* * *

As Martha grew, it became hard to ignore that her colours had changed, and the dark grey feathers and markings she'd developed were those more traditionally seen on male Muscovy ducks. One day I saw 'her' humping one of our white ducks, and I knew a quick name change was required. So Martha dropped her M and became Arthur. Our two white ducks, Merv and Drake, who had lived the longest of all the birds we'd ever brought onto Block Eight, soon went off to sit on their eggs and I wondered how many of those babies would survive. I often went looking to see if I could find where they were nesting, but I never found them and soon weeks turned into months and I knew they were never coming back. I was once more charged with birder.

It's the unfairness of this one that gets me: had we not rescued George and got him Martha/Arthur for company, and had we not released Arthur onto the dam, Merv and Drake wouldn't have wanted to nest ... making them vulnerable to fox attack.

Still, every day I trek down to the edge of the dam to feed Arthur, maybe George, and the scores of other birds who permanently live there – mostly Purple Swamphens and Eurasian Coots. One of the coots has a white tail feather and I named him Frank (for no particular reason), and another has one foot missing – he hops out of the water, eagerly pecking up as many pellets as he can – and I named him Dennis.

* * *

We were driving around Rutherford gathering together bits and pieces for Jeff's latest project (it might have been a project he was building, interior designing, or something else – I really couldn't say for sure). He was on his phone while I was driving – a job I usually choose to take to keep my mind focused on something other than cushions, MDF and structural pine.

'The RSPCA have some ducks for adoption,' he said, and by now these kinds of statements between us couldn't be interpreted in any other way.

'What time are they open 'til?'

'Four.'

'Great, we'll go on the way home.'

They had seven Muscovy ducks for adoption. Seven! If I thought we had a problem being overrun with peafowl, just wait until these suckers began mating. The Farm was complete, so they'd be nice and safe from predators, but first we needed to hand-raise them until they grew their waterproof feathers.

'Jeff, we can't possibly keep seven of them inside. They stink so much, and that cage just isn't big enough ...'

'We'll work something out,' he said and once again we were bringing home animals we simply hadn't prepared for. But they were animals who desperately needed a home and some love, and we had enough of that to go around.

We got to the RSPCA and signed up to take all seven of the ducks (I quickly named them Liesl, Louisa, Friedrich, Kurt, Brigitta, Marta and Gretl) and just as we were about to leave, a staff member came out from one of the back rooms.

'These guys are here to take all of the ducks today,' the lady serving us said.

'What? All ten?'

'No. What? Seven, you mean?'

'And what about my three? The little ones?'

I just looked at Jeff.

'Okay, we'll take those too.' (Maria, Captain and Uncle Max.)

We hastily built them a cage outside our villa, complete with a little swimming pool, a medium-sized doghouse for shelter and a red warming lamp. Every two days we captured them all, took them inside for a bath, then moved their cage to another spot to allow them to eat more grass and stay clean.

I went out one morning to feed them and three of them were dead – one had tried to escape, as he was stuck between the edge of the pool and the far back corner of the cage. When we lifted their water bowl, we saw the tell-tale entry point, a hole where a small-sized snake had burrowed up into their cage. Muscovy are known for their curiosity and ability to attack small snakes and reptiles, so the snake had probably just been defending itself. Now the seven von Trapp children were orphaned.

After a few weeks, most of the birds had developed their waterproof feathers so we were literally days away from releasing them onto the dam down at The Farm when I happened to walk past their cage and noticed all of them were huddled desperately against the far corner of the cage, far away from the safety of their house. *That's weird*, I thought and almost kept walking. *No, you'd better go investigate*, I thought again, and went back to do exactly that.

'Jeff! Jeff!' I screamed as though I was the one getting attacked. 'Get out here. Quick!'

Jeff came running out expecting me to be mid-battle with a pack of hungry wild dogs.

'It's in there!' I pointed to the duck cage. 'Quick, Jeff, get it out. It's horrible and it's got one in its mouth!'

Jeff peered into the cage and saw the large goanna, now partway through eating one of the ducklings alive. Bones cracked as it casually chomped away. All the other ducks were so petrified they were clamouring to get as far away from that enormous lizard as they could – just as I was. Jeff ran to the shed and came back with his lethal weapon of choice: a broom handle.

Jeff heroically ripped the top of the cage from their pen and started poking towards the goanna, who didn't take too kindly to having his lunchtime feast interrupted. The goanna hissed at Jeff, its powerful jaws snapping around the carcass of the duck to try to take a chunk out of Jeff's wooden pole. He poked some more, really shoving his arms and face inside the cage to try to get at a better angle to scare off the goanna.

'Jeff, please, be careful!' this distressed damsel cried out from a *very* safe distance.

I wasn't exactly afraid of lizards, but goannas sure did have sharp claws and I knew a bite could cause major infections. Besides, it just made no sense putting both of us in danger when Jeff was so adept at those kinds of situations. I'd happily tend to his oozing sores, if it ever came to that.

After a few more pokes and snaps, the lizard eventually sensed Jeff's determination and finally took its leave, bolting off into the bush at an incredible speed, the sound of crunching bones still audible. It climbed high up the trunk of the nearest tree and seemed to look back to the living ducks, giving them a menacing wink to tell them it'd be back.

We patched the hole in the cage and refilled the ducks' pool and within seconds they were all frolicking in it – if they'd been traumatised by seeing their brother or sister eaten alive, it looked as though their diagnosed-by-me PTSD wasn't going to last very long.

The week after, we released the ducks onto the dam. Watching them flap their wings, shake their heads with pleasure and dive beneath the water was a beautiful, magical moment. It didn't take long for them to realise the mammals were fed about five metres away from the edge of the dam, so every feeding time, I not only had three very excitable goats and an impatient pig to contend with, I also had six raspy, snorting ducks at everyone's feet.

Unlike the previous animal pen, where the ground was a constant source of mouse food, The Farm now has six lovely ducks, who are so incredibly efficient at scavenging for every morsel of spare food that you barely ever see a single grain or seed left behind. As a result, months after they'd moved in I had seen only one mouse – hardly a feast for hungry snakes. Now my little family was safe from wild dogs, foxes, falling tree limbs, *and* snakes.

* * *

Erin called me about a month after we had settled the six remaining von Trapp ducklings into their new home. 'Hi Todd, I've got a little duck with a damaged leg and I was hoping you'd let me release him onto the dam inside The Farm so he'll be safe from any predators.'

'Of course, bring him over!'

Erin brought him over in a small box and released him onto the dam and he swam about like a boat with his outboard engine slightly above the water line, his bung foot splashing up water in his wake, working with great effort to avoid going around in circles. It was the first time he'd felt the freeing buoyancy of water since someone had caught him to be rehabilitated by Erin. We showed her around The Farm and petted the goats and Helga, and by the time we looked again for the duck, he'd completely disappeared. For about thirty minutes we fished around in the reeds but could find no trace of him.

'He's very good at hiding,' Erin said, but I couldn't help but fear that his leg had given out on him and he'd sunk to the bottom of the dam.

The following day, there again was no sign of him but then on the third day I saw Helga sniffing around one of the reedy patches near the side of the dam. When I pushed her away (met with unappreciative grunts), there was our little duck, almost invisible to the world. He eventually grew in confidence and later, when Erin dropped off another four ducks (these ones brown with blackish specks), once he saw his relatives out on the dam he painstakingly paddled out to greet them. From then on, the five of them were a regular family, just hanging out, though rarely with our Muscovy ducks.

* * *

Another time, when I went out to feed the animals, one of the white von Trapp ducks was missing. They're very good flyers and can easily get over the fence. (One day I spotted one on the outside and worked for over fifteen minutes chasing it before I literally threw myself on him and carried him back inside, ignoring his pecks at my hand.) But never before had I been to The Farm in the morning and not had all six come waddling up to me to be fed, the braver ones happily by hand. I could only assume he'd flown the coop overnight and been attacked by a hungry fox, or one of the wild dogs that Helga and I sometimes chased off together.

I sat on the goat-climbing frame watching everyone eating. It's always sad when we lose a bird, though in truth it's a fairly regular occurrence. The only ones we ever keep in a cage are the chickens, Stevie and Nicks, and that's only at night – aside from that they are all open range.

Then, I saw Helga sniffing around an upturned feeding crate, which is not unusual if she thinks there's a tasty treat hidden inside. In one deft move she flicked up the yellow plastic and there he was, our missing duck. I hate to think how long he'd been stuck under it, perhaps even overnight. He was dirty and disoriented, and clearly starving by the way he marched straight towards the oats scattered on the ground.

I ran right up to Helga. 'Good girl, Helgy. Good girrrrrrl,' I said, giving her lots of loving scratches and kisses on the top of her head. But that's my Wonder Woman Helga, saving the world one hidden duck at a time. I like to think it wasn't a coincidence, that she heard him stuck inside there and deliberately lifted it to set him free, knowing he was now a vital part of our little ecosystem, and that a world with all those lovely ducks significantly decreases the chances of her getting bitten by a snake.

To return the balanced eco-system favour, Helga has developed quite a taste for raw duck eggs, so she's single-handedly keeping our bird population under control. *Good girrrrrrl.*

Nine

Waz n Shirl

I was giving a talk at Cessnock library to promote the *Helga* book. It was lovely and comforting to speak to a local audience, where many people (they later told me) shared similar experiences to Jeff and me. It also felt nice to laugh in the face of our joint struggles against the land, running a small business and various industries.

At the end of the talk I opened the floor up to questions. A six-year-old hand shot straight into the air.

'I want to know what animals you're going to get next,' the little girl said.

'Hmm … I don't know,' I said honestly. 'We are only going to get rescue animals from now on, so I guess it depends what animals need our help the most.'

She seemed totally dissatisfied with my response, but another hand shot up in the air before I had the chance to elaborate.

'What about sheep?' a lady asked. She was about seventy and in the audience with her daughter and granddaughter, all of whom had read and loved the book, she told me.

'Funny you should ask that,' I said and went on to tell the story of Alfie and how incredibly close we'd come to saving him.

'Well I have two sheep you can have,' she said.

'No, no … we are only *rescuing* animals from now on. Those who need a good home,' I explained.

'Well these need rescuing; I can sell them to you,' she persisted.

'Oh okay … so they need rescuing *and* you make money off them. Sounds like a win-win for you,' I said a little dismissively.

After the talk, the lady gave me her card and said I should call if ever I wanted the sheep. 'They're twins,' she explained, 'and very, very small. They're too small for us to use for meat and nobody wants to buy them unless we separate them, and I just can't do that to them.'

'Okay, I'll think about it,' I lied. This certainly wasn't part of the plan. But then why had fate made us miss out on Alfie?

Mum, Dad and Millie (who were also at the talk) came to dinner with us and I started making jokes about the sheep and how this woman wanted money for two perfectly good animals who probably had a nice little home with her.

'Sounds to me like they're going to end up on someone's Sunday dinner table,' Dad said.

'Oh, don't say that,' I pleaded as my vegan meal arrived.

'To me, she sounded pretty desperate to find them a home,' Jeff added unhelpfully.

'Should we?' I asked him.

'What do you think? You know you can't help yourself!'

So I texted the woman, *We will take the sheep. How much do you want for them?*

Whether she knew it or not, the price she quoted was actually less than what we would have paid to save Alfie from the RSPCA.

If the ram isn't desexed can you please ask your husband to band him for me? I said in a later text, after we'd established how this was all going to work.

* * *

A few days later we drove to the town of Kurri Kurri to collect the new additions to our little farm. We may not have had the Barina any more, but that didn't mean we'd gone to the effort of putting an animal cage on the back of our ute. The idea was to put the two sheep on the back seat with me. We hadn't even bothered to bring a sheet or plastic tarpaulin to keep the upholstery clean.

The sheep were farmed by an elderly couple who raised their own animals for meat. In short, these two sheep just didn't have enough flesh on them to warrant slaughtering them. The man had been raised on a pig farm across the road and grew up watching animals being slaughtered for meat … and yet it was obvious he'd grown particularly fond of these two as we watched him feed them by hand. They were the height of medium-sized dogs, self-shearing (another skill I wouldn't be forcing Jeff to learn – like the farrier he'd had to become to keep poor Wes's and Winnie's toenails under control), with very sensitive eyes. On the whole though, they were rather skittish and I realised I'd never had anything to do with sheep … ever.

We paid our cash, I signed a copy of my book, then we said goodbye to the people, promising to take good care of their little sheep, who were now about six months old.

'What shall we call them?' I asked as we drove towards home.

We ran through a string of names that didn't quite fit the bill, but like all expecting parents we would never share the possibilities with anyone else. We eventually settled on Warren and Shirley … yes Beatty and MacLaine. Brother and sister, cute to look at, and rather fabulous.

'Waz n Shirl' (as their names were quickly shortened to) were scared to be away from their home for the first time in their lives, and Waz went to ground, burying himself as far into the car seat as he could, meaning Shirl more or less had to lay on top of him. I got shat on, the delightful aroma filling the back of the car like a thick green gas cloud and sitting heavy in the back of my throat as I wound down my window and felt tears sting my eyes. I stuck my head out like a dog addicted to the rush of the wind in his hair.

Jeff decided to take a different route home, and by 'different' I mean the long, long, long way home via one of those roadworks where you have to wait at an automated red light for about half your life. Before setting out on the entire forty-minute journey to the place, he hadn't thought to look at the petrol gauge, and now we were sitting on empty and had to pull in to get some fuel. All the while the sheep kept shitting on me, then standing in it, smearing it all over themselves, the car seat and my arm.

I don't think there has been a single animal we've brought onto the property with an actual enclosure ready and waiting for it. The amount of times we've winged it, strung together a bit of wood with a bit of metal, cable ties to hold it all together … We'd originally decided to put the sheep in the makeshift reo and star picket area of The Farm that we'd cordoned off for Wilma when she arrived.

'I'm not sure Wilma's reo enclosure is going to keep the other animals out,' I said, as we got closer to home.

'Well where the hell are we going to put them?' Jeff asked.

'What about the chicken pen? Just for a day or two until this rain clears up. We can make the reo stronger in the meantime.'

As we got home, the stench of the shit pellets in the back of the car finally got too much and I nearly heaved. It was a meaty, grassy, sulphur-and-sludge kind of stink. I managed to grab a hold of Shirl and placed her safely inside the chicken pen but just as Jeff reached for Waz, he released a bladder full of urine. The back seat of the ute looked like the bottom of a zoo exhibit.

'You settle them in while I go clean this up,' Jeff said and I was pretty chuffed with my end of the bargain.

Sheep are very shy, very timid animals. There was no Wilma cuddle, no falling asleep and snoring in my lap like she or Helga had done. If I had food to give them, they would come to me. But aside from that, I was of no interest to them whatsoever. If anything, I was something to be petrified of.

The next day, Jeff came home and surprised me with a stock fence to place inside The Farm. The reo one we'd constructed for Wilma had proved useless, but a professionally manufactured steel structure would keep the smaller animals safe from the larger ones – just until everyone got used to the new state of play. Besides, this way the sheep could graze on grass all day and, when they'd mowed down their little patch, we could simply move the fence to a fresh new area.

Once they saw the lovely long green grass after our recent rains, Waz n Shirl settled immediately into their protective custody section of The Farm. Helga was curious – she would approach and sniff deeply and, on one or two occasions, tried to get herself a mouthful of soft fluffy wool. Winston and Wesley couldn't have cared less, but Wilma was very intrigued. The sheep were exactly the same size and height as her and if ever anyone was going to be her friend, surely animals of her own stature could be trusted.

We decided to keep the sheep separate for about three weeks, just to make sure there'd be no lamb on Helga's breakfast menu. Over time, I've learnt that Helga is not vicious or malicious, she's just stubborn and will tell you when she is unhappy with you – like when the others go near her food, or when I tell her she can't rip apart my shoelaces or sniff my crotch. Her open-mouthed head bash that meets any of these refusals could be misconstrued by others as a bite, but in truth she's only ever actually nipped my mate Scott, and poor Wilma. Though sometimes Jeff is convinced he's a goner ... and also Charlie got a wee little nip once.

Waz n Shirl eventually became curious of Jeff and me. They loved eating bread out of our hands (even better if I was courteous enough to toast it for them) and would sometimes sniff our faces in an attempt to recognise us, but never responded well to our insistence on giving them pats or cuddles. It took a while for them to settle in health-wise too. An unexpected delight of keeping sheep was having to regularly wash down their hind legs with hot soapy water, inevitably getting more shit all over our arms. Now when I think of all the times my mum called me a dag growing up, it has particular poignancy and pungency.

* * *

'There's a dead animal under the water tank in The Farm,' I said to Jeff one day. It wouldn't have been the first time we'd found a dead thing on the property – that stench was unmistakable.

We'd hand-rolled the ten-thousand-litre water tank from one of our villas the five hundred metres or so down to The Farm. We'd removed it from the villa because the cicadas in the trees above it shat so much that it tainted the water a tea-coloured brown. This was something no one ever tells you about building a villa in the bush, and having a professional tank company install a tank next to it. Even though we'd triple-filtered the water so it was safe to use, nothing quite got out all that colouring, so we decided to connect two villas to one tank and move the spare one down to The

Farm. How funny we must have looked barrel-rolling this enormous metal structure across our main paddock. Turns out we'd burst the tank, and after paying two hundred dollars to have it filled with lovely fresh water, we watched it all run slowly out the bottom, the leak not noticeable until it was filled to the top.

'How do you know it's under the tank?' Jeff asked of the dead animal.

'I can smell some flesh rotting. It's rank. I looked around everywhere for it but couldn't see anything.'

'That's weird, man,' Jeff said, 'because I thought I smelt something the other day too, but I couldn't see anything.'

'Will we just leave whatever it is under the tank?' I asked, always eager to avoid another corpse-handling episode.

'I guess.'

The next day I went back and the smell was even stronger. As I bent down to feed Warren his toast, the stench smacked me square in the face. I patted him and he turned around to run away, and a waft of his rotting ball bag went up my nose and down the back of my throat. I gagged.

The thought that his testicles – those once huge appendages that were now blue and shrivelling – were rotting on the outside of his body sent shudders along my spine. We'd banded Wes but had never smelt anything like this. Warren's balls had been so large (a nod to his so-vain namesake, perhaps?) they'd become like a gangrenous limb.

I jumped onto Google. It wasn't uncommon to smell a sheep's banded balls, or tail in the case of docking.

'But he just seems out of sorts,' Jeff said after agreeing his poor dried-up dangleberries were the source of the stench.

161

'I really don't think he's well. Shouldn't we call the vet, just in case?'

At Block Eight, I say 'we' for Jeff to handle building, repairs, spraying crops, moving dead things and anything mechanical. Jeff says 'we' for me to order water, contact guests, call the vet or organise our winemaking.

I explained the situation to the veterinary nurse who answered the phone. 'I'm just worried he may be too old to have been banded,' I said. 'Google says they shouldn't really be banded after about three months old.' (The word 'Google' probably causes more eye rolls in surgeries and hospitals than any single word in the English language.)

'Well, my dad had lambs and he always banded them,' she said reassuringly. 'And basically if the band is big enough to go on then they're not too old for it.'

'I think maybe we should have the band removed. Is that possible?'

'It is ...' She hesitated. 'But it's a very complicated procedure, because some of the nerves and tendons may have died already. Believe me, it's better to leave the band on. But keep your eye on him and if he goes off his food or seems really off-colour, call us and we will come and see him.'

I joke to my mother that Dad has two hobbies: calling bingo (they call it 'Housie') and visiting medical professionals. If doctors and the like didn't exist, I just don't know what Dad would do with his time. I'm not one to throw stones though, I'm sure my name has a different ringtone at the local vet. *It's Todd again. He's helicopter-hovering over a pig with one stray white hair ...*

Waz's balls eventually did fall off, though unfortunately I couldn't find them to serve them to Jeff for breakfast.

* * *

It finally came time to let Waz n Shirl into the general population. I'd been delaying the decision for more than a week – they just seemed so timid and small compared to the big goats and Helga but at the same time they'd been cooped up long enough and needed more space to run around and eat grass. On their day of release, the sheep positively bounded out of their small pen and ran off to explore all that their eyes had drooled over for the previous weeks – hills to climb, food buckets to forage in and more grass than they'd ever seen in their lives.

For Wilma, I'd developed an alarm: a loud call of 'Run, Wilma!' whenever Helga was trying to sneak up on her, or else making a rampaging beeline for her. It just seemed to make sense to use the same cry for the sheep, so that everyone at The Farm knew when to be alert. I used it often enough to keep everyone safe from my inquisitive pig (*I wonder what wool feels like in your mouth?*) and poor Wilma still ran even if I sounded the alarm for the sheep who were near Helga on the other side of the dam. In time, those little sheep learnt their place in the pecking order – in essence, the very, very bottom.

Though Wilma was the boss of them, she also quickly learnt they were the closest things she was ever going to get to having pint-sized allies in The Farm. Most days when I approach, the three of them are hanging out together, grazing, keeping each other alert for butting horns or wrestling sows.

Whenever I take the animals for a walk around the perimeter of their enclosure, the parade order is always the same: Helga in front, Winston next, Wesley a few metres behind, and straggling up the rear are the youngsters, who run about and frolic like the naughty kids at the back of the school line. Wilma darts in and out of the adults to tease them, and then races up to the sheep to nudge them into action.

The three of them bolt around the perimeter of the dam, chasing each other in some unknown game, the sheep getting so beyond excited they bound in joyous leaps, skipping through the air like their lives are the happiest they've ever been. The sight of them doing this always gives me the giggles. The trio remind me of a group of kids from one of the movies I watched when I was a kid, like *E.T.* or *The Goonies* – a bond of innocence, carefree, with a feeling of invincibility keeping them together (and definitely separate from the older, slower, more serious residents at The Farm). Sometimes Warren even lets me scratch him under the chin, and he still loves to sniff our faces, just to see what's going on there. Shirl, much like *her* namesake, loves to sing at the top of her lungs. If her friends could see her now.

Ten

Helpless

Helga became quite the star after 'her' book came out, though she only displayed diva behaviour occasionally. I lost count of the number of people who wrote to tell me how in love they were with my little pig, and some even shared stories of their own pigs too.

I can't quite put my finger on why Helga attracts so much attention and fondness. At Block Eight, our guests love to visit The Farm, and Helga is always keen for love and affection – poking her (usually muddy) snout through the fence and grunting excitedly to receive scratches on the top of her head. Though I think I'm probably the only one who kisses that soft, wet snout. We often have strangers show up to the property, and I'll run out with my book-signing pen and pre-posed 'Blue Steel' selfie look ... only to find that no one is all that interested in me. They just wonder where to find Helga.

Australians have a long love affair with pigs. When I was growing up, Porky Pig was one of my favourites – and then a little later, Miss Piggy. Doris the alcoholic pig was one of the country's favourite characters in *A Country Practice*. *Babe* is still Australia's third-highest-grossing film of all time and now our children have gone mad for Peppa. So what is it about pigs in our pop culture?

It's all about the eyes if you ask me. Helga connects with people through eye contact and at times it's intense. There's wisdom there; a silent knowing. I'm still waiting for her to grow out of her nuzzling – as so many articles suggest they do at the age of one – but by her second birthday in July 2019, Helga still loved to suckle into the meaty part of my hand. Some days, when her mood is right, she comes barrelling towards me, throws herself on the ground and expects tickles on the belly, scratches on the chin and deep, soothing strokes on the top of her head. Being over one hundred kilograms or so, getting down on the ground isn't as easy as it used to be for the old girl. Then if one of the goats gets too close, she growls and leaps up to tell them off for interrupting her day-spa time.

I still marvel at this creature, at the way she brings her back leg forward if you scratch her thigh, at the kinks in the 'hair' on her left rump, at how delicately she closes her eyes, and how those long lashes remind me of that silly Muppet.

And then there's that adolescence I've spoken of. Helga kindly requests not to be told what to do and this includes any number of things she shouldn't do like, on one occasion, chewing a metal bottle top. If she's scolded during a moment she's knowingly being naughty, we are likely to be met with a heavy bash of the head, sometimes with mouth agape and if her teeth connect with your skin they can inadvertently cut. She did this once to my elbow and it flared up with fluid, a hideous elephantiasis deformity I eventually had to get drained by the doctor.

'It's from my pig,' I said to him and was met with a *you're a bloody weirdo* kind of look. There's nothing more reassuring than getting that look from your GP.

Jeff and I are pretty well in tune with Helga's moods these days, however. We know when to get out of her way, when not to coax her down for a belly rub, or when to stand still and let her chew on our shoelaces until she moves on to the next, more interesting thing. On the days she lets me, I place my head against hers and give her soft kisses. There is an enormous amount of mutual trust in these moments and I wonder how different a pig she would have been had we allowed her to keep living inside with us. Undoubtedly she'd be more responsive to discipline and not be so insistent on having things her way but frankly I'd prefer to endure the odd crazy moment than see her cooped up inside for most of her life.

* * *

In winter, something wholly unexpected happened. Wesley the goat morphed into a marshmallow! It was like someone had washed him and stuck him in an industrial dryer. Almost overnight, his short fluffy coat grew several inches and he suddenly resembled a huge white cloud. It looked like someone had spent a little too long using their Barbie crimper around his neck and head, and the rest of his coat was so thick I was forever brushing out leaves, hay, dirt, sticks, poo pellets and then one day, an oat. My goat had an oat in his coat.

Sometimes it's the smallest things in life that amuse, and I spent that whole morning giggling to myself, making up a series of rhyming picture books starring my critters. *My Pig Does a Jig in a Wig, My Duck Found a Buck in a Truck* and *My Lamb Ate Jam by a Dam* … all coming soon to a store near you. Or maybe not. But Wesley's *pouf bouffant* always brought a smile to my face, reminding me of Kath Day-Knight's shocker of a perm. Most days he sidles up to me wanting a brush and a stroke, and I love the lanolin scent his coat produces.

* * *

Helga isn't the only animal in The Farm who likes to play rough. One summer we had our friends Linda and Jason over for a beer, and they brought their daughter, Annabelle. Linda Lunnon is a local artist of breathtaking skill, so we'd made the decision to fill our final villa with her art. I also commissioned her to complete a portrait of Helga. (Yes, I'm one of *those* people.) But this is no simple pencil sketch, let me tell you. Linda does most of her art using scratchboards – a kind of high-resolution lino carving. After the success of the *Helga* book, I wanted to immortalise my pig (even further) and there was only one person for the job.

Jason brought his camera to take photos of Helga and wasn't afraid to get down and dirty, lying on the ground to get the best angle and not even flinching when she came right up close to him.

'Jeez, you're being brave … or stupid,' I said and he laughed. But I just envisioned the news headlines the next day: 'Book Pig Not So Lovable After All'.

All the animals were behaving, however, and it was decided to let little three-year-old Annabelle into The Farm so she could be near her dad. I was in the process of feeding the animals and very conscious of Helga's mood and, between the two, had forgotten to give Wilma her dinner. When I looked at her, she had metre-long globs of drool streaming from both sides of her mouth, so I went to feed her.

'Todd! Todd!' I heard.

Winston hadn't been able to help himself from one of his favourite pastimes, and he had butted Annabelle as she stood on the dry edge of the dam. She kind of somersaulted head first into the dirt and was a little dazed and confused so picked herself back up. And this, of course, was another opportunity for more fun for Winston, who again butted her, and she fell back down onto her bottom. Jeff, Linda and I all bolted to save her. Jason had only just noticed what was going on and ran from his prone position in front of Helga. Poor Annabelle was in tears, though thankfully not hurt, and Winston was sent to solitary confinement inside the stock fence to contemplate what he'd just done.

To their credit, Linda and Jason kept calm the whole time, and after a brief cry and a minute or two to pull herself together, Annabelle was back to being her inquisitive self.

I heard from Linda later that night that Annabelle had spent the entire evening raving about her afternoon … especially Winston the goat. Neither of us could believe the tiny little girl hadn't been severely traumatised by the whole event!

There are bigger people who've suffered less harsh Winston clashes but who genuinely fear for their lives. Lucy was once butted in the shins and now turns to a helpless mess any time Winston so much as looks her way. My brother Glen insists on walking inside The Farm with a giant stick, though he'd never use it, I'm sure.

* * *

Winston is the reason behind so much of how my life on Block Eight has turned out. Though my pigs Rodney and Billy came first, it was the day Winston followed me home that really first prompted the idea that I would keep more animals than just two pigs, a few chooks and some ducks. He was the reason I got Wesley and then, having fallen in love with the personality of both of the goats, I knew I had to get Helga when after Rodney and Billy I thought I'd sworn off pigs. I'd rescued Winston from an uncertain future; we'd bonded so beautifully and I had almost lost him when his original owners had come to reclaim him. (Thankfully they later changed their mind ... in exchange for cash. More fool them, I would have paid a million for him.)

The morning after Annabelle-gate, I noticed Winston had a stream of fresh diarrhoea running down his hind legs.

If there's one thing in the world Winston hates more than rain, it's having someone touch his hind legs – it brings about instant head-butting – so my attempts to wipe him clean were futile to say the least. But then in an altogether un-Winston-like way, he didn't eat his breakfast. I could tell just by looking at him that he wasn't his normal cheeky self. He looked sad. He didn't want to approach me, and walked off whenever I walked towards him. I've seen many of our animals have off days and this, coupled with his runny bottom, made me think it was just one of those.

That evening when I went to feed them, Winston was in his bedroom. He is usually the first to run to me for food and once he realised I was there he ever so slowly emerged from their terrace house and came towards me, but stopped about five metres away. The others were happily munching their dinners and I got close enough to feed Winston some cauliflower greens but after about six or seven he'd had enough and walked back towards his bedroom.

Ever fearful of being labelled 'paranoid' by vets, I decided to leave things be and see how he was the following morning. He was still in bed when I arrived but slowly walked towards me, again stopping metres from where I stood. He showed no interest in the oats he usually got for breakfast so I took a handful to him and watched him take a few bites. On the positive side, there was no more diarrhoea.

He walked away from me and went to stand in front of a tree, his head bowed, and just stood staring at the trunk. There was no spark at all to his personality, no inkling to join (or head butt) the smaller animals. I told myself he'd get better and not to worry.

Jeff joined me later that day for dinner feeding. If there is one thing to test how Winston is feeling, it's plain rice crackers. He devours them so desperately his mouth becomes a robotic destroyer. He won't stop until the packet is empty, which he needs to see clearly for himself. But on this day he ate one, then two, and then spat out the third before walking gingerly back to the terrace. Jeff followed him to hand-feed him some greens from the vegie patch, but Winston only nibbled at them half-heartedly before heading inside to his bedroom.

I went back to our villa determined to call the vet when they opened the following morning. I don't know why I didn't think to call their emergency line. I suppose I didn't want to be accused of Goat Munchausen syndrome. Maybe I also just assumed he was a bit sick and everything would be fine.

The following morning Winnie was still in bed when I arrived. He was weak. One minute after the vet opened I called and asked for a house visit.

I stroked my goat tenderly. 'Help is on its way, Winnie. Don't worry, you'll be feeling better in no time.'

I left him to relax and went to prune the grapevines. I was already weeks behind, and took any opportunity I could to head up and do some pruning. About a third of a row in, I saw the vet's number on my phone and I answered immediately.

'Hi Todd, it's Beth from Singleton Vet. I just thought I'd call and mention that you might want to bring Winston in.'

'Really?'

'It sounds like it might be a worm infestation and for that the prognosis is never good. We will need to put him on a drip and doing that in the field is never easy. So I just thought I'd float the idea.'

The thought of getting a one hundred kilogram floppy goat into the back of the ute wasn't an easy one to entertain.

'I'd really like you to come out and see him first,' I said, also worrying how stressful Winnie would find the drive. 'If you then think he's better off at the surgery, we'll somehow find a way to bring him in.'

Beth agreed on the plan and hung up the phone. I chipped away at some vines but her words sliced away at my concentration, deep welts in my conscience. *The prognosis is never good.* All along I'd assumed Winston had a bug, a cold or a small bout of food poisoning and now a medical professional had told me he was as good as dead.

I put the shears in their holster and walked back towards our villa. The more I thought about that cheeky brown-faced head-butting goat – and the way he danced, and greeted me with that familiar bleat every single morning – there was nothing I could do to stop myself turning into a blubbering mess. Here I was, a forty-five-year-old man crying once again over his pet goat.

'Toddy? What is it? What's wrong?' Jeff practically fell on me when I walked inside.

'I … I …' I couldn't get the words out. I took a deep breath. 'The vet says Winston might be dying and I can't stand it. I just can't bear the thought of losing him.'

I was so racked with guilt for not acting sooner. Me and my stupid determination not to be seen as an overreactor, a hypochondriac projecting onto our animals.

I pulled myself together so that I could at least speak. 'I can't just stand up there pruning. I need to be with him.'

'Come on,' Jeff said. 'I'll drive you down. Don't worry about cleaning the villa, I'll do that. You just go be with your Winnie.'

Winston was again in his bedroom, his back to all the activity of the other animals, and my arrival. I approached him slowly and he stood up, his head hung low, his eyes so incredibly sad.

'Hold on Winnie, not long now. Just hold on for me,' I kept whispering but whenever I touched him he shied away, telling me he just wanted to be left alone.

I went to the driveway to meet Beth. I like her; she's a no-nonsense vet, the same one who told us Leroy was obese (the first ever to use that word) and that if we didn't put him on a diet he was in for a world of pain. To his credit, Leroy embraced the new diet and lost twenty-five per cent of his body weight over a year or so. He's a much happier, chirpier cat as a result. Beth followed me down to the farm and, at the sound of two cars, Winston came to inspect.

I hate to corral any of our goats by the horns but Winston hasn't worn a harness for over a year and I knew if I didn't grab a hold of him and drag, there was no way we'd be able to treat him. I pulled him into the separated feeding area and Beth set about examining him.

'With goats if it's not worms, it's usually worms,' she said. As Winston is always very adept at spitting out the drenching we give him, it's quite possible he'd not had a proper treatment, she explained. I fought back silly tears of guilt. 'I'm going to take a blood sample, give him some antibiotics and anti-inflammatories and try to give him this drip too,' Beth went on. 'Do you think you can hold him?'

Have I mentioned that Winston doesn't like to be held? I cornered him up one end of the area and used my bum to squish him gently, taking a tight hold of his horns. He struggled for a few seconds but then surrendered. Beth worked quickly to administer the treatments but it wasn't until she inserted the needle for the drip that he really protested.

'This is subcutaneous so he's really going to feel this,' she said. He had a fever and the cool fluid would also help him feel more himself.

I kept shushing Winston and stroking the top of his head the way he likes, but he was whimpering. His soft little cries of discomfort, pain and annoyance just about blew my heart into tiny smithereens. To see this big, bulky unit of an animal reduced to a quivering, frightened mess was soul destroying. To think it was me, his (former) best friend, holding him down so this strange woman in her green overalls could jab him with her needles over and over again.

'Do you like working in the field the most?' I attempted small talk to take my attention away from Winston's pain and the dark cloud of tears building just behind my eyes.

Beth had to keep moving the needle to fill different parts of his body with the fluid and every time she stuck it in him, those whimpers came to tell me just how disappointed in me he was – how betrayed he felt and would never trust me again. *I chose you! I followed you home dammit. And for what? Look how you go and treat someone you apparently love. Please let me out. Please Toddy, please. I'll never head butt another kid again just please take this pain away ...*

Finally, after a proper drenching, it was time to let Winston go. I'd held him in place for over fifteen minutes, his eyes wide with fear and confusion the entire time. He was so shell shocked by the whole thing that, when I opened the gate, instead of bolting off he just staggered out dazed and confused. I wanted to go to him, to extend my arm in peace and let him lick it, but I had another job to do. Jeff came to help me catch each of the other animals to get their own drenching.

Used to any number of handlers and vets, Wilma waltzed right in like the VIP at an invite-only event. Wes had to be dragged in by the horns but took his treatment well enough. Then we ran about like great galoots trying to catch the sheep for their turn.

'Your goats are very large. They're both overweight,' Beth said. 'Obese actually.' And there again was that word, the finger of blame that I was slowly murdering our animals anyway, so why feel so shocked when they fell ill? I silently promised myself that things were about to change. I wish Beth had been a doctor when I was younger, and my parents had taken Fat Toddy to her for treatment.

I resisted the urge to stay at The Farm for the rest of the day but Jeff and I returned at dusk to feed the others and check up on Winston. He ate a little, took a sip of water, but could barely look at me. *You!* his eyes stared accusingly.

That night I went to bed early. My dreams were jolting, infuriating, repetitive mites come to gnaw away at my flesh. In them, I was packing for an upcoming author tour but after I'd left, I realised I'd forgotten very important things. I barely slept a wink.

I knew I had to take drastic action to protect my cheeky, clumsy, lovely goat. I ordered in a five-thousand-dollar goat bed and organised with the vet to send us a round-the-clock nurse to sit with Winston. I sat Jeff at one end of the bed alternately feeding Winston peeled grapes and polishing his horns while I sat at the other end of the bed and gave his hooves a pedi. Mum brought over one of her hand-knitted blankets for him and we took it in turns to wipe his brow with a warm, damp cloth.

At least ... that's what I would have done had Jeff not been around to keep me grounded.

Instead, at daybreak I forced myself to go for a run when all I wanted to do was go and check on Winston. As I ran, his whimpers played over and over in my mind. I'm sure I was quite the sight for any neighbours who passed while I was on the road when what I really needed was one of Mum's notes she used to write me for school sport's carnivals. *Please excuse Todd from today's run. He has a sick goat and needs to stay with him.*

Finally I got back to The Farm and did a quick headcount. No Winnie. I counted again. And then I knew, in my heart, that it was over. He'd died overnight – alone and frightened and the last thing he'd known of me was pure torture. I quickly said hello to everyone then ran over the slippery ground to their terrace. As I got closer I saw the white of his coat, he was lying on the ground. *Please no, please no, please no*, I chanted internally.

Just then, he lifted up his head. When he saw me he slowly got to his feet. I reached out to pat him but he flinched, and I couldn't blame him for that after all I'd put him through. I'd left some wombok overnight and brought it from the feeding area to give to him and he nibbled away at it feebly. Gone was the ravenous goat I'd always known.

'Oh Winnie, please get better. Please stay strong for me,' I said to him, finally managing to get close enough to stroke his neck, avoiding the places the needles had been and the newly shaved patch where the blood sample had been taken.

My other animals were annoyed they hadn't been fed their breakfast yet, so I set about the task, trying to keep everyone happy.

Beth called and said that Winston's samples showed only minimal worm activity so we could rule that out.

'Oh my god, that's such a relief,' I said like someone had just saved me from the firing squad. 'But what do you think it is?'

'I'm still worried about his fever and the look of his blood so I'm sending that off for further analysis, we'll know more tomorrow. How does he seem today?'

'About the same …'

'Okay, keep your eye on him. I'll call as soon as I know but if he gets any worse call our emergency number.'

We were still far from in the clear. Winston made his way over to be near the other animals, but not close enough to join in, and nowhere near me. Not by a mile. After a few minutes of standing on the perimeter of the activity, he took his leave and walked back to his bedroom. *At least it's not worms*, I thought. *There's still hope.* I dragged myself away from The Farm and went to clean villas, completely forgetting to do certain jobs and having to go back over my own work, glad Jeff wasn't around to notice. By dinnertime, Winston wasn't back to himself, but his head wasn't hanging low and he wasn't refusing to leave the bedroom. He socialised with everyone else, and over the next few minutes he ate more and seemed to have a little more energy. He even leant in to lick my arm – a peace offering I accepted so gratefully my heart skipped a few beats – and, when Warren approached to join the love-in, Winston made to head butt him.

'I never thought I'd say this Winnie, but I've never been happier to see you head butt and I'd like to see more of that, please,' I said. Every fibre of my being clung to these signs of hope.

I reported back to Jeff, who was busy toiling away on the last villa. Beth had called him to report that nothing abnormal was in Winston's blood.

'If I had to bet I'd say it was food poisoning,' Jeff said to her. 'He's always fishing around Helga's bucket and maybe there was something in there he shouldn't have eaten.'

'Yes, a strong possibility,' Beth agreed. 'There may also be something stuck in his gut which would prevent him from chewing his cud so watch for that. If there is, we will need to bring him in for x-rays.'

When I visited The Farm at dinnertime, Winston met me at the fence, licked my hand through it and greedily chomped down his (and others') dinners.

He butted Wilma out of the way and she reared up to challenge him, hoping he'd still be weak and too ill to defend himself. But he solidly stood his ground and she ran away, quickly realising she'd bit off way more than she could chew. Best of all, after he finished eating, he stood licking my leg for a good ten minutes. That cheeky look was back in his eye and when Jeff brought down a beer for us to toast his recovery, Winston even challenged him to a little wrestle.

As his personality came back to the fore, we watched him wait eagerly at The Farm gate when we brought fresh bins full of water to pour into their troughs. (Winston demands to sup his water straight from the bin before it is tainted with his siblings' scents.) Goats have the most remarkable way of drinking, using the ends of their pursed lips as though sucking up through an invisible straw, slurping as they do and licking their lips satisfyingly at the end. I wish we had a glass-bottomed trough so I could film it from beneath. An instant YouTube sensation.

We never found out what took Winston out for nearly five days. I replay his whimpers over and over in my mind and I can't erase them. They creep up on me during odd moments and I have to push them back down deep into the recesses of my mind. How anyone could intentionally hurt an animal, or support an industry that refuses to acknowledge they suffer pain or fear, is utterly beyond me.

'Do you miss eating meat?' I still get asked about twenty times a week.

'Not in the slightest.'

For every sheep, goat or pig whose name I do not know, I have Winston, Wesley, Wilma, Helga, Waz n Shirl to remind me. Even if their vet and food bills are one of our more considerable expense line items ... But I couldn't care less about that.

* * *

After Winston was better, I felt it was the right time to expand our menagerie. I was still checking the RSPCA website every couple of weeks and, when I saw Wanda, I knew she was the one for us. Wanda is a brown goat with thick spirally woollen curls and a cute-as-a-button brown face. I thought most people would think she'd be high maintenance with all that wool, but I also knew that whatever new skill needed to be mastered … I'd force Jeff to do it.

We got to the local RSPCA shelter and were taken through to their stables. Wanda had been the victim of an animal hoarder – poorly treated, malnourished and very skittish. She'd learnt that humans couldn't be trusted, so wouldn't let us near. But I also knew that, like Warren, in time Wanda would grow to trust us. Once she saw how animals *should* be treated she'd lap up her new life of luxury at The Farm.

The only problem was, Wanda was sharing her stable at the RSPCA with two other goats. They looked like twins – more deer than goat – and it soon became obvious that Wanda used them for protection. Whenever she was separated from them she would panic and begin to fret. How could I take her away and make her face that upheaval all alone?

Whitney and Wanita had been found wandering the streets of Cessnock. Nobody knew where they had come from. Whitney was all white with tiny horns protruding from the top of her skull. Wanita (named after Vicky's mum, Juanita) had flecks of black running through her coat. Both goats were thin and sleek with tall hind legs, which meant they were able to leap about the stable with great skill.

'You want all three, don't you?' Jeff asked. Sometimes I wonder why he even bothers asking such rhetorical questions. It's not that I *wanted* all three … it's just that I worried how lonely Wanda would be without her new pals. And if we didn't take Whitney and Wanita, who knew where they would end up and what horrors they might have to face?

'Okay, we'll take all three,' I said to the stablehand. He was the same guy who a few months before had placed Wilma into my open arms.

Poor Dawyl the ute had only just got the stale stench of sheep pee out of his back seat, when we crammed three goats into it. They lay one on top of the other and just resigned themselves to a new move. Every once in a while, Wanda stood and lifted up her head to allow the breeze from the open window to ruffle her dreadlocks.

Wanda Bey Cleckheaton was born, and before long Whitney Britney and Wanita Juanita had their full names chosen for them too.

We settled the three of them inside the stock fence within The Farm, but within a couple of minutes, Whitney and Wanita had clear jumped the fence so they could roam with the other animals. A quick shake of the food container always brought them back inside. They ended up being true escape artists, capable of leaping just about any fence, often balancing on a narrow piece of wood after leaping from a bolting start. All three of them were so wary of us, even more than the sheep had ever been. They'd clearly had no exposure to human affection and avoided Jeff and me at all costs, running away from us whenever we tried to approach for a quick scratch, or even when we had food in our hands.

But then, little by little, their hard façades began to melt and, after a couple of months, Whitney Britney was the first to break. Like Wilma before her, she often sought me out, came to lick my legs and demand to be scratched under the arms. Then slowly Wanda would let me hand-feed her and stay for a second or two of scratching before scuttling off. But Wanita, after many months, stayed painfully shy and cautious.

Of course, introducing new animals into the mix always has a flow-on effect to the established hierarchy. Wilma had already started bossing Waz n Shirl around but now that there were three new inmates – and of her kind – she quickly took the opportunity to show them she was boss of the younger kids. It was poor Wanda with her stand-out-from-the-pack woolly coat that quickly drew the shortest straw and instead of trying to compete with the goat herd, she sought the mateship of her cousins and was regularly seen hanging out with Waz n Shirl, as though they took the time to compare their coats and how best to keep them free from knots and debris.

And every morning, I still begin exactly the same way – by taking that walk around the perimeter of The Farm, my crew following me with great excitement in anticipation of their breakfast. Except now Wilma generally puffs out her chest to prove she is no longer at the bottom of the goat ladder.

Eleven

All Creatures Great and Small

Home to scores of native fauna, coming across dead things isn't exactly a rarity at Block Eight.

A few weeks after Erin, Jarrod and I had saved a wallaby, I was walking by the dam in front of the villas when I saw a small kangaroo up to its neck in the water. It was motionless. My heart sank. The only thing I could think was that it was stuck in the mud on the bottom of the dam and had been struggling to set itself free but now it was exhausted and at any moment was going to sink beneath the water and drown. I called Jeff but he was out at Bunnings and that could mean he'd take anywhere from one hour to twenty-three days to return. I swear, the number of hours I've lost pushing trolleys behind Jeff at Bunnings …

But here, with this roo, this was *my moment*. At last, my chance to prove to the world that the marmalade-boiling half of the Block Eight duo actually did more than look pretty and tell a few jokes. I raced up to the shed, grabbed Jeff's waders and ran towards this rescue with vigour. This magnificent feat of human strength and compassion was going to go down in the history books as the turning point, the moment that Todd was officially declared a real, *bona fide* farmer, a mover among those who refuse to shake.

Cue the music. It's the opening notes of *Chariots of Fire*. There are tears in my eyes but I wipe them away – masculinely – with the back of my hand. I rip my shirt off and my muscles are already gleaming with perspiration. I look out to the water and mentally calculate the distance to the roo. I reef my shorts off to reveal a dazzling (both in vibrancy and tightness) pair of red Speedos. The wind picks up and suddenly there are enormous waves at the edge of the dam. Cut to the roo: its head starts disappearing beneath the waves. I lunge into the water – slow motion as I'm horizontal above it – then I'm powering through the water (such a beautiful stroke, it must be noted) towards the little creature. The music swells to a crescendo but ...

It was all a three-second fantasy and instead, there I was by the side of the dam squeezing myself into a pair of khaki waders. I hastily climbed into the rubber pantsuit, taking just a second to marvel that if any article of clothing on the planet was ever invented to be *the least flattering* then surely this was it.

I felt like a fattened chook whose cavity had been stuffed with one too many lemons. Parts of me bulged in grotesque ways and my package was contorted into such a painful squidgy pancake that I feared it would never work again. *But this is no time for vanity. A drowning roo needs me!*

I raced back to the dam (picture a hippo running in high heels – waders weren't meant for running in either). My heart was pumping with adrenaline, and my mind started working out a strategy for how to grab a hold of the roo without its claws ripping me to shreds. I had a vision of the roo and me, locked in a firm embrace, its arms around my neck, its head resting delicately on my shoulder. I would carry it to shore like a hero and there we'd collapse to the sand and both struggle to get our breaths back. There would be a quick Instagram selfie during the rescue, too. There needed to be photographic evidence, after all, if I was to receive my medal for bravery.

But as I got to the edge of the dam the roo was no longer there. My heart sank – it was underwater! *It's drowned! Hurry, it's drowned!*

I would have to wade in and find it in the murkiness, drag it to the edge as fast as I could and perform CPR and/ or mouth-to-mouth. No roo was going to drown on my watch.

I stepped into the dam when, out of the corner of my eye, I saw a totally drenched roo in the reeds by the dam's edge.

The cheeky thing had been in there taking a morning bath. I shrugged, sighed, peeled off my waders and went back to our villa for a cup of tea. I needn't have worried; my days of finding roos in dams were far from over.

In all the time we've been at Block Eight, among the most horrific moments was 'rescuing' a dead roo from the main dam in a rubber blow-up boat six weeks after we'd moved in. As I went around Australia promoting the *Helga* book, it was rare that anyone let me pass without repeating that story.

Now, seven years later, as I was going to feed the ducks one day, it happened again! There in full and plain view of all the villas was a bloated grey roo, smack-bang in the middle of that previously unblemished vista. While I no longer worried what impact a rotting roo would have on the quality of the dam's water, it just wasn't good enough to have our paying guests wake up and sip their morning coffee while staring at a carcass, or have their al fresco breakfast on the deck ruined by the wafting smell of rotting roo.

I've often made jokes that Jeff does all the dead animal handling and, much as I'd love that to be true, over the years he has, on occasion, insisted that I get my hands dirty too. I loathe the feeling of a dead chook's feet in my hands, its heavy weight dangling as I carry it to the boundary of the property to hoick it over the fence, where animals can at least make use of its meat. I've swept up dead rabbits whose entire insides are a writhing mass of maggots and I do this not because I want to, but because the joke of me calling on Jeff to do it every single time has worn very, very thin (for him, at least).

'Why can't they do it themselves?' I asked Jeff one day, when guests spotted a small corpse under the deck of the house and called on us to remove it.

'Toddy, come on, be reasonable,' Jeff said.

'Can you do it?' I pleaded.

'No way, you're coming too!'

'I'll do all of the cleaning for next week.'

'No you won't. And even if you did you'd be so shitty doing it. It isn't worth it.'

'I'll give you a ten-minute massage every day for a week …'

'Go and get some gloves. You're coming with me.'

There are only so many times a boy like me can charm his way out of facing maggots.

So here, with another dead roo on the dam and Jeff out to lunch with Millie, was my chance to prove to Jeff (and indeed the whole world) that I wasn't afraid to do some of the corpse-handling myself.

Hello world, this is Todd. I'd like to announce that today you can no longer laugh when I call myself a farmer.

I headed down to get the enormous six-person rubber boat my uncle had given us just weeks before. It was meant to give us hours of entertainment during Lucy and Charlie's stay next school holidays. But now it was on hand for a grimmer task.

I would remember to take rope and gloves this time, so no roo flesh could go melting through my fingers as it had through Jeff's. But even inflating the boat on my own was going to take hours, so I channelled Jesus's ideas-man philosophy and decided there had to be a more efficient way.

Surely, we didn't need all that brouhaha when I could simply get in the dam and push the roo to shore. This was what fearless farmers did – just strolled into the water and dragged the dead thing out. So I went to fetch those trusty waders and even decided against gloves – I was definitely up for pulling it with bare hands. No sweat. No big drama. Just get it done.

I'd gained weight in the weeks since I'd last put the waders on to rescue what I thought was a drowning kangaroo, so now instead of a stuffed chook, I looked more like the marshmallow man from *Ghostbusters*. It was so tight around the crotch that my voice rose two octaves.

I started wading in from the villa side of the dam but quickly saw the roo was a *long* way in and went instead to the other side of the dam where there was natural bush ... lots of lovely long grass for deadly snakes to hide in. But surely snake fangs couldn't pierce what felt like six inches of rubber against my skin ... could they?

I wanted to hurry before our guests checked in, and little things like drowning or lethal venom would have to be put to the back of my mind. Jeff would come back from his lunch (and an obligatory browse of the nearby homewares store) and I'd have simply vanished.

And Todd was neither seen nor heard from again ... until the year 2035 when the dam was drained for a housing development and there lay his skeleton inside a rather fetching pair of khaki waders, the body of a roo clutched in his oh-so-masculine right hand. He left us while wrestling a massive roo, literally, to the death, bless his dear ambitious soul.

I took slow steps into the dam, one deliberate foot at a time. I had a long stick to poke in front of me to check for potholes or fallen trees. The water in the dam is murky and has a visibility of practically zero. I took another cautious step and now the water was up to my knees, another and it was at my thigh, another two and it was at my waist. The waders really only come up to chest height and the thought of that murky water seeping in wasn't all that appealing. But still the roo was a good twelve metres away. It was time for Plan B.

I waddled over to the other dam, walking the full hundred metres in my waders, to where our kayak lay abandoned at its edge. We'd bought the kayak from our mate Chris on a whim years ago and it'd probably been used a grand total of four times. I dragged it back across the grass to the other dam, frequently swapping hands because the small rope loop at its bow dug deeply into my fingers. Once back at the dead roo dam, I eased the kayak about two-thirds of the way into the water then trudged all the way back to the other side of the main dam to fetch the oar that'd been sitting there well away from the boat, for whatever reason. It would have been more efficient to take my waders off before the walk but by now I was hot inside them and they were stuck to my skin. As I stepped into the dead roo dam again it was difficult to tell if there was a leak in the rubber or if it was just filling up with my own sweat.

I was fully clothed beneath the waders so the plan to ease myself elegantly into the little seat of the kayak didn't quite work – my hips were too wide, I couldn't manoeuvre my feet into the boat and it began to rock erratically from side to side. I took a deep breath and steadied it, then eased my clumsy feet into it like an evil stepsister does into a glass slipper. Then it came time to wedge my hips into the seat, grazing both bones as I did so. *Yes Prince Charming, it fits!*

The boat moved forward and, suppressing the thought that I'd never get out of the kayak again, I surprised myself with how gracefully I could row out towards the roo. I mean, the kayak was positively gliding over the water and I'm sure I looked like I belonged there. I took a moment to silently congratulate myself. Then rowed on.

It's not often I spend any time on the dams, and yet every time I do, it strikes me just how peaceful and lovely they are – this one especially so, with its wall of whispering casuarinas on one edge and beautiful ghost gums on another. Ducks moved out of my way and I swear I heard them snigger as they did, deflating my confidence ever so slightly.

'Hey Don, check out this geezer! Did you see him trying to squeeze himself into that boat thing?'

'It's the getting out I want to see. Now that's really gonna tickle my fancy.'

After ten or twenty strokes I made it closer to the roo.

But I overshot my mark and I was the Titanic headed straight for the iceberg. Bang! I hit it with a dull thud. That's when it all came back to me, the stench of that rescued carcass seven years previously, and here I was thinking I could simply stroll up to the bloody thing and nonchalantly drag it to shore with my bare hands. How time so effectively erases memory. *Herk!* I howled, swallowing down bile. *Herk!* It echoed back to me from the bush.

I put myself into reverse and thought of my next plan of attack. I would row towards the corpse, poke it towards shore with the oar, rinse the oar, and repeat. I edged the kayak closer and reached out to push the roo but, as I did so, the boat dipped to the right and for a split second I saw myself falling in, my face planting against the roo's rump. I could practically taste its stink inside my mouth and my stomach whirled in horror. But somehow I managed to steady the kayak, swung it around for another go, then reached out again with my oar.

The blade of the oar touched the fur of the roo's rump and immediately lifted some off like a well-boiled spud. Grey flesh was revealed beneath … along with another waft of rotten stench. *Herk!* I yelled out again, and again caught it back in echo. I pushed the oar to the roo again and another flap of skin fell off. After a few more gentle nudges the rump looked like a leg of lamb slit in readiness for cloves of garlic.

The roo may have been dead but I still wanted to save some of its dignity (having lost all of my own thanks to the waders). I just couldn't stand to see any more flaps of skin wisping in the water, so I made the decision to nudge the body with the tip of the kayak instead.

I put myself in reverse again then drove the boat full steam into the rump of the roo and it worked! It floated about a metre towards the edge of the dam. *My plan was really working!* But as the roo floated, it turned on its side and in that moment I saw that its face had completely melted away. In its place was a skull with streamers of flesh and tendons. *Herk!* I really gagged that time, the threat of vomit rising from deep in my gut. I swallowed hard against it.

Jeff will be so proud of you, Toddy. Keep going, you'll get it, I said to myself. *Just a few more pushes!*

I shoved the roo two more times but with each determined push I was slowly overhitting the mark, so by the third strike the kayak swung swiftly to the right and the side of the boat connected with the roo … about fifteen centimetres beneath my elbow. I panicked that I was going to fall in, and there's nothing like thinking you are going to fall that will make you end up in the drink. The boat teetered on a knife's edge above the body. I closed my eyes and whispered silently, *Please no, please no, please no. Not that. Anything but that,* and somehow the gods of dead roos smiled down upon me and they righted the kayak again so I was once more saved from copping a mouthful of ribbon-like skin.

I corralled my strength and intellect (whatever was left of it) and worked determinedly to guide that roo to the edge of the dam – *bash row row, bash row row,* and finally I got it there, the dead roo's face turning towards me with complete nothingness – not even a thank you for getting it away from whatever critters had munched away on it. I heaved again as the stench intensified, the animal now three-quarters exposed, and as the puke crept deep into my nostrils my cheeks blew up to swallow back everything that wanted to see the light of day.

I couldn't bear the thought of heaving the roo fully to shore, remembering how it'd turned Jeff all funny years before, so I left it there slightly hidden in the reeds where no one else could see it. I turned the kayak around and rowed back to where I had entered on the other side of the dam.

Now shoving your rubber-clad arse into a kayak is a darn sight easier than squeezing it back out again, let me tell you. Though the water was shallow, I really didn't want to eat mud. Somehow, I needed to put all of my weight onto my hands which were placed either side of the seat, steady that weight until the boat no longer wobbled, then crawl out of the seat backwards until my feet were clear of the fibreglass. The kayak shook from side to side like an amusement park ride, water splashed into the boat's cavity and my dangleberries were forced even further inside my body, but eventually I hauled myself free of the tiny prison. Clear of the water I ripped off the waders and found myself to be a delightfully moist mess, sweat running down me in rivulets. What a sight.

But Jeff was still at lunch, and having mastered dead roo removal, I definitely had a swagger to my step, and I had another job to do before he returned. The neighbours had a tree on our boundary and its limbs had grown longer and longer so that it was now obstructing our driveway. *Now I'll show him I'm not afraid of anything, I'm gonna chop down that frigging tree on my own*, I thought. He'd wonder how the boy who wanted to be Maggie Beer suddenly transformed into a lumberjack.

The problem was, I never taught myself how to use the chainsaw. I suppose I am a little afraid of that machine – of all machines on our property, actually. I just don't see the sense in lopping off your own limb and shrugging afterward as if to say, *I guess I never really learnt how to use the thing.*

Jeff had almost done that for me one day when he couldn't get it started, and so asked me to help him. The plan was for me to hold down a particular lever while he pulled bloody hard on the starter cord. I was standing to the left of the machine, Jeff behind it.

'I can't really push it in at this angle,' I complained.

'What do you mean?'

'Well … let me get behind you. That way I can reach in properly and press it down more firmly while you pull the cord.'

I was crouched behind Jeff, as if he was getting ready to take a seat on the top of my head. But now my hand was pushing very firmly on that lever and I could see the action clearly. It all made perfect sense and would work seamlessly, thanks to my brilliant idea to change positions. Jeff pulled the cord in a sort of half-arsed manner.

'Jeez, Jibbuz, you'll need to tug harder than that. Pull it! Pull it frigging hard!'

I saw Jeff's muscles tense, he wrapped his fingers around the end of the cord and then with all the strength he could possibly muster, his sharp elbow came smacking into my forehead. I fell back and my eyes immediately began to water. If I were a cartoon I definitely would have been seeing stars.

'Oh my god, I'm so sorry! Sorry Toddy. I am so, so sorry!'

It was refreshing to hear him sound genuinely remorseful. Whenever I bash my head on an open cupboard door or, as I so very frequently do, into the stupidly placed glass rangehood in the house, I silently turn around to see if he's seen me do it. Inevitably, and it doesn't matter where he is, he will have watched the whole thing unfold and before I even have a chance to rub the sore spot, Jeff will be doubled-over in uncontrollable fits of giggles. It especially tickles his funny bone when it's someone he (apparently) loves, when he knows he shouldn't be laughing at their pain. That sting often hurts more than the original injury, and it royally, absolutely gives me the shits.

I do try to get him back though, such as the night after one of these giggling fits, when I turned on the bathroom light and closed the door so Jeff would think I was in there. Then I squeezed myself beneath the tiny space under the bed. As Jeff wearily pulled down the covers in readiness for sleep, I shot my hand out, grabbed hold of his ankle and yelled as loudly as I could. It is one of the greatest scares I've ever pulled off and his reaction made me laugh out loud for weeks afterward. If he thinks it's okay to laugh at me when I hurt myself then I think it's okay to never, ever stop jumping out from behind closed doors and hidden corners to give him a fright. All is fair in love and war.

On this occasion with the chainsaw however, Jeff managed to hold in his laughter, possibly because he'd just come within inches of murdering me – sending my nasal bone shattering into my brain and causing me to keel over instantly. At least we would have been nominated for the Darwin Awards.

Even had this never happened, I wouldn't trust my uncoordinated-to-say-the-least self to use a chainsaw. So, naturally, when it came to removing the tree before Jeff and Millie returned, I went into the shed and grabbed his tiny handsaw, the one with a blade as big as a banana.

I marched up to the tree overhanging the driveway. From a distance, trees look so easy to conquer, yet it's funny how once you get up close you quickly realise their limbs are the best part of a foot wide.

I sawed and sawed and sawed, lifting my arm high for the limbs above my head. As I hadn't thought to bring eye protection, I did so with my eyes closed to keep all the sawdust out.

A fallen tree limb is heavy, particularly when you have to drag it over one hundred metres to the pile in the bush behind the shed. But I managed to remove four heavy branches and was onto my fifth one, the highest and heaviest, when it broke free and landed with a thud on my arm, which then landed hard on the barbed wire on top of our boundary fence. The blood flowed thick and gel-like but I was part-way through the job and it was a five-minute walk to our villa and I knew if I didn't just get it done I'd never finish, so I dragged that almighty bough all the way back into the bush as blood pooled into my hand and left a nice trail behind me as I walked.

Finally back inside the villa I took a photo to send to Jeff.

What happened? he texted.

Wild dog, I texted back.

He responded with a photo of his finger covered in what was clearly tomato sauce.

What happened?

Wild chip, he texted in response.

I waited anxiously for Jeff and Millie to return, not telling them of my life-changing, awe-inspiring dual feats for the afternoon. They'd be driving up the driveway so that would be a dead giveaway, and then when Jeff went to inflate that huge boat to retrieve the roo I'd suggest we go down to scope it out first so he could see I too can handle dead things ... when the occasion demanded.

'So what've you done while we've been gone?' he asked when they got back.

My heart sank. I was a farm dog wanting praise. My Farmer Hall of Fame nomination instantly vanished.

'You didn't see?' I asked, even though it was clear he hadn't.

He looked around the villa and shrugged.

'I cleared that tree on the driveway,' I said. 'I thought you'd notice?'

'Funny that,' he said, though I failed to see the humour. 'I said to Mum on the way out, "Look at that tree; I really need to clear that." But then I didn't think about it on the way back.'

'I also got that roo out of the dam,' I said, cutting to the chase.

'You should have waited for me, silly.'

'Oh, don't worry. I got it to shore but I thought I'd leave it for you to drag out into the bush.'

These stories always prompt people to ask just *what* is in our dams to result in so many dead kangaroos. Actually, it's more likely that kangaroos like to be near water when they feel death is imminent. Besides, we've let Lucy and Charlie swim in the dam many times and hey, they're still alive. Maybe it's time we got their weeping sores checked?

* * *

We hadn't hosted a wine tasting in the Wine Room for some time and, as per usual, left setting it up to the last minute.

The table was cleaned, glasses were staged, wine was chilled, everything was *just so* … Except there was an unmistakable whiff of dead roo in the air. We ran out of time and it was way down in the ditch behind the Wine Room, and that meant only one thing would work: hand-to-carcass combat.

Naturally, I suggested that Jeff should complete the task while I polished glassware, but he declined and we went ahead with the wine tasting, hoping no one would see our new black-and-decaying friend over the ditch. It was a morning wine tasting, starting at 10am, but as it progressed and the sun heated up, there was no ignoring the stench that enveloped our wine-sipping guests.

'You think I should say something?' I whispered to Jeff.

'Won't that just draw more attention to it?'

'Jeff, I'm chewing on the stink, it's so bad. He's your friend and no one wants to talk about him.'

'My friend?'

'Well, I did ask you to take care of him …'

Then I went back into the room and made a joke about the joys of living in the country and, before long, twelve curious wine tasters were outside catching a glimpse of Jeff's mate, with teary eyes and fighting back vomit. We didn't sell much wine that day.

A few days later, we were driving on our way to the supermarket when we came across some roadkill at the end of our road. It always incenses me that idiotic drivers can't be arsed to slow down for kangaroos, who naturally have zero road sense. And why should the kangaroos? They're wild animals, not rally drivers. The roadkill was fresh, blood smeared across its face. There was no sign of life.

'Still, we should move it out of the middle of the road,' I prompted Jeff.

'And once again, "we" means me?'

'Well ...'

Jeff faffed about in the back of the ute looking for something.

'I don't have any,' he eventually said.

'Any what?' I said testily. We were stopped in the middle of the road and, while not exactly a ten-lane highway, I didn't want to stall any longer than we needed to.

'Gloves,' he said. 'I thought I had some.'

'Oh for Chrissakes, Jeff! Can't you just grab it by the tail and drag it into the bush over there?' I snapped. (I had no reason to be snappy, but I figured my 'rage' might make him act without questioning why I wasn't dragging the roo myself.)

'Me? Why is it always me? I'm not putting my hands –'

It didn't matter what he was saying, I had a point to prove. I could push a faceless kangaroo to the edge of the dam without Jeff, so I could certainly move a dead thing to the side of the road. I noted that it was a male, so there was no need to check a pouch for joeys, then I grabbed hold of its thick tail and dragged the heavy weight to where one of the neighbours' bushy areas met the boundary fence. Blood had left a trail out of its nose, along the bitumen and there were drag marks in the dirt.

'Now that wasn't so hard, was it?' I said facetiously.

'Sounds to me like you've got a new job title,' Jeff said with glee.

'Piss off!'

'*Ohhh, I can't touch dead things, you'll have to do it,*' he said, impersonating one of my whines.

Which prompted the thought, if I was capable of dragging a dead roo, was I also capable of murder?

* * *

Since an altercation with an angry kangaroo a couple of years ago, I'd maintained a healthy respect for the animals, particularly the larger males. If they were in my path on the property, I generally altered my course to avoid them, just in case they were having a bad day. To this day I keep a wary distance from those animals, with their very powerful back legs, muscly chests and long sharp claws.

One day I went to set up for a wine tasting for our guests at the Wine Room and noticed a huge male grazing nearby. As I approached, he saw me and growled like a rabid dog. He had tiny ears, so I named him Nero.

'Whoa, okay,' I said aloud to him. 'This is your turf, I'll back off.' Then I waited patiently for him to hop on his angry way. Block Eight was these creatures' land after all, and we are merely passing through.

Another day, I was walking from pruning the vineyard to feed our animals and needed to pass through a mob of roos near the main dam. There is only so much cleared land between the water and dense bush so I kept as close as I could to that snake-infested scrub. Most of the kangaroos scattered as I got near, but the two huge males stayed behind. I recognised Nero and he started making a threatening noise that sounded like *berk berk berk*, calling me out on my cowardice. He hopped past me, continuing to make that menacing heckle and I could have peed myself with relief when he didn't stop to fight.

And that left just one. I turned around to face him. We made eye contact and dammit, he started jumping straight for me.

'Why me? Why are you bastards always after me?' I asked him loudly.

I raised my hands in the air then took the sharp electric shears from the holster on my belt.

'Please don't.' He hopped another metre closer. 'Oh please don't, mister,' I said.

At the last minute he diverted from his course and hopped ahead of me. That's when I heard Nero's familiar chant: *berk berk berk.* He does it to me every couple of weeks or so, just to make me shit my pants.

Twelve

Well and Truly Over
a Barrel

Lots of people have asked if Jeff and I regret our tree change – and the answer to that is a resounding, firm and fundamental *absolutely not*. But some people also ask if we would do things differently. While rescuing animals and caring for them is challenging and costly, one of our biggest joys on the property is watching them thrive. Tasting our own wine and olive oil was more rewarding than all of my years in the corporate world, and hearing how much our guests love Block Eight never fails to bring a smile to our faces. But while all this happiness helped make our days enjoyable, there was a new set of challenges lurking just beneath the surface; more threats that could derail our years of hard work and give us many sleepless nights, wondering how we would pay the next bill. If it wasn't Mother Nature coming to menace us, it was the industries we relied on to sustain us that would be our undoing.

When I was in Canberra promoting the *Helga* book, a local contacted me and asked if she could pick my brain. Charlotte was interested in buying a winery and wanted to know my opinion.

Until speaking with Charlotte, I hadn't really put my own thoughts in order. Would I encourage someone to buy a winery? I must have told the story a thousand times – that when we decided to make our big tree change we'd never had *any* intention of becoming farmers. That lasted until the evening we first moved in, when we first tasted a bottle of Brokenwood wine made out of our grapes. It was only then, realising that Block Eight had grapes capable of making great wine, that we decided to make that death-defying leap.

'How hard can it be?' has sort of become our motto now.

I remember another property we looked at during our search for the perfect tree change – it was on a quiet, bush-lined lane. The main house was stunning and had been hand-built by the owner, a builder by trade. The property had a lovely in-ground pool, a large shed that had been partially converted into living quarters, a one-bedroom villa to rent out for accommodation, and council approval (with plumbing in place) for a further two villas. The entire plot of land was just over five acres – a mere blip by Block Eight's standards, but more than enough space for us, after the relative confines of our tiny inner-city Annandale property. They had wanted roughly the price we ended up paying for Block Eight, but we'd made a low ball offer and they'd refused. Jeff knew how much I loved it and encouraged me to make another offer, but I could tell his heart wasn't set on it and what was the point of moving if we weren't equally in love with our new home?

How very different our lives could have been. How much more manageable, affordable and altogether *achievable*. Would I go back, if I could, and buy that property? No. But I still can't help but wonder.

So the piece of advice I gave Charlotte was to ease herself into winemaking slowly and ever so cautiously.

If we were to do the same over again, first up, we'd get our accommodation in order: do a quick renovation on the house, jazz it up by removing any net curtains and filling it with statement-piece cushions, and start letting it immediately so we'd know we had some regular income coming in.

Next, we'd get our vines back to good health, but wouldn't feel as though we had to pick every bunch of fruit ourselves and turn all of it into wine. We'd start small, building our brand slowly, buying existing stock, with one (maybe two) wines of our own for a year or two and selling the rest of the fruit to someone else. Maybe we would even do a deal with a winemaker who could buy our fruit and pay us in our own-branded wine.

In taking on fifteen acres of grapes as one of our first tasks at Block Eight, we poured hundreds and thousands of dollars into wine production. Yes, we eventually sold out of most of our wines, but the cost in producing them meant the opening of each of our villas was pushed back again and again, further and further, and in any strategy for the future of our business, accommodation was always going to account for at least seventy per cent of our income, if not up to ninety per cent. Why then, were we investing so much in making wine?

Even though we were selling it above cost price, sales came in dribs and drabs, and that disappeared into the business without making a dent. We genuinely enjoyed the process and loved the final product, but it wasn't exactly sensible when the carefully considered plan for our tree change that I had painstakingly pointed out to anyone who'd listen had been one solitary idea: open accommodation.

Up front winemaking costs included seventy-five grand for a tractor, ten grand on barrels and other winemaking technology, and five grand we were obligated to pay for water under the local irrigation scheme. *Then* for every bottle of wine we produced, we were up for around $6.50 ($1 in harvesting costs, $1.50 in winemaking costs, $1 in chemicals, $1 in bottling, $1 in bottles, caps and cartons, and $1 in labels). And none of that includes paying ourselves for countless hours of labour. Add ten per cent in GST and twenty-nine per cent in government wine tax (which some of us get back, thankfully) and you begin to see why smaller wineries like us charge over $20 a bottle. If our fruit can produce up to 30,000 bottles of wine, then we need to find the $200,000 every year just to make the stuff without paying back the cost of expensive equipment.

If you can sell each bottle at wholesale for $15, it's more or less worth your while. In the beginning, we had several wholesale customers who would pay between $10 to $15 a bottle. These customers would buy anything between half a pallet to six pallets of wine (300 to 3600 bottles), and we'd get a nice injection of funds to invest into our following year's production. One of the catches to selling at wholesale is that you're responsible for freight, which can add up to $2 a bottle, but so be it.

Another of my frustrations about the wine industry is that the buyer dictates payment terms. For the majority of them, that's three months from the date of delivery, and some of them like to order well in advance. So it's not uncommon to get an order for a delivery due in six months' time, which means you're waiting nine months for payment. That's *if* they pay on time. We had one buyer take over twelve months to pay us ten grand – a paltry amount to a big company like them but crippling for us.

From harvest day to bottling day, depending on the varietal, you can be waiting from three to eighteen months for the wine to be ready, so that your next harvest sometimes comes around before you've been paid. In the case of red wine, sometimes two harvests. With careful planning, selective fruit-selling and lots of determination, you can somehow find a way to make wholesale work at $15 a bottle, and anything you sell at retail is the non-dairy icing on the vegan cake.

In the six years since we started selling our wine to wholesale buyers, the market has changed considerably. Online buying clubs have become enormous, and customers love that they can buy quality wine cheaply. It's driven price expectations down very low. Nearly every winery I know has an excess of stock and is desperate for funds, and wholesale buyers aren't stupid – it's their job to know the state of the industry. So when our biggest customer started dropping their price to us, despite the cost of winemaking *increasing* each year, we began to see things weren't as rosy as when we'd begun.

We'll offer you $4.50 per bottle, came the email from our biggest customer.

Is that plus plus? I replied (industry talk meaning the GST and wine tax are added on top of the stated price).

No. That's net.

But that's below cost … I said.

Yes, I know, he replied. *And that's all I am prepared to offer. Take it or leave it.*

This was no shit wine we were talking about! It was award-winning, highly reviewed wine that could cellar for up to twenty years. And the crazy thing was, because they were offering that price for 4000 bottles, I seriously considered it – we could have done with $18,000. We would have made a loss, but at least we would have some cash. I knew they would sell the wine for a 300 per cent mark-up (around $13), which was still 65 per cent less than its retail price (thus showing their customers what an incredible bargain they were getting). But by doing so they would completely decimate our brand and any hopes we had of selling wine at full retail ever again. We would make a significant loss, and they would make $9 a bottle. Sounds fair, right?

Of course once *they* started offering less than $5 a bottle, and desperate winemakers started taking it, word got around and before long *all* of our wholesale buyers started offering the same. One of our most loyal buyers offered us

$5.50 for the same wine two years later, to then sell it to his customers at around $30 per bottle. But the offer came during March, when our accommodation bookings were so slow we felt we had no choice and I stupidly, short-sightedly accepted the offer in a desperate grab for cash. It was a full seven months before the order was placed and the bill was paid. Naturally I asked for more money but was given a list of reasons for why that wasn't possible.

'But that's just on this order,' the buyer insisted. 'I'll look for other ways to use your wine and I promise, mate, I will pay more for those.'

Two weeks later, another order came in for a different promotion of the same wine, and not a cent higher than we'd been previously paid. I rejected the order.

'You told me you have lots of that wine and now you're telling me it's not available? Seems odd,' he said.

Maybe to you, 'mate'. But not to us.

When the brutal reality of the industry began to rear its ugly head, Jeff and I spent hours and hours deliberating our best course of action. The television would be switched off and we'd just sit across from each other on the couch, talking through ideas and discounting those that didn't feel like the right thing for our business.

Though we were talking predominantly about the challenges of our business, those moments with Jeff strike me as the ones we need the most. So many couples just fall into the inane TV and device habit after work or after the kids have gone to bed, with so little interaction with the person we've chosen to spend the rest of our lives with. But in turning the distractions off for an hour or two with nothing but each other and lively conversation to pass the time, it reminds me how special a person Jeff is, and how our relationship is founded on mutual respect and admiration. In our fifteen years together I don't think either of us have ever left a single thing unsaid, both complimentary and more challenging topics. I suppose that's why we work so well together and seem to be growing stronger as a couple with each passing year.

Besides, how can you not love a guy who, mid-conversation about Christmas plans, turns to you very seriously to ask, 'Do you think fish saliva tastes fishy?'

And about three days later follows up with, 'But do fish even have saliva?'

* * *

So we run a vineyard and don't get paid for it, and we make all that wine and get paid less than what it costs to make, and the wholesalers clear anything from $12 to $25 a bottle! Where do we sign on the dotted line? *Hello? I'd like to pay* you *to take some of this silly wine off our hands please. Hello, anyone? It's cheaper than free!*

The fallout from this part of the industry is that retail wine buyers (that is, the public) don't *want* to pay $39 – or even $29 – for a bottle of wine when they know they can get it online, via their club, or at the local liquor store for way, *way* less. And if they can't get that exact wine, then they can find a similar one from the same region.

We even had one of our friends contact us by email to say, *I wanted to buy some of your wine but saw it cheaper online. Rather than pay them, I thought I would pay you direct … if you can match the price.* The online price was from a customer who had bought six pallets, and our mate wanted six bottles.

Of course we can, I wrote back.

We have other friends who think they're saintly because the clubs they are members of promote a sense that they are single-handedly keeping young winemakers in business.

'Yes, but I'm a good wine Samaritan,' our friend said and it was true, you could see the halo beaming atop her head.

But if you really dig down into most wine clubs' business structures, you'll find out that most only care about their own profit margin – some buy the fruit, bottle in scale, pay a winemaker their base cost then a nominal 50c to $1 each bottle as 'profit' while the club makes a clear $15 a bottle. But at least that model gives winemakers work, and gives new or unknown winemakers a chance to get their name known.

We could no longer sell our wine in bulk to wholesale buyers because it wasn't worth it. Our individual customers generally buy no more than a few hundred bottles a month, so what the fuck were we going to do with the absolute shedload (eighteen thousand bottles) of wine we had in storage? Not to mention the potential for thirty thousand more each year moving forward? We certainly didn't have the money for marketing and PR to try to build a brand that could warrant charging $30 a bottle, nor did we have the forty-odd grand to pay council for the privilege of opening a cellar door (plus the building and staffing costs).

The reality of the wine industry is that anyone who cares about supporting the winemaker or grower should only buy direct – before we become the same as the milk industry. Only direct sales truly contribute to a winery's success. But it won't be $3 a bottle like it is in Aldi, and not even $11 like it is online. So what is a bottle of wine worth? If you owned a vineyard, I assure you you'd be answering that question very differently.

* * *

For Block Eight it seemed the writing was well and truly on the wall. There was only one thing we could do. We made the soul-destroying decision to reduce our vineyard. The previous owners had already removed five acres of merlot grapes and, after chatting with local real estate agent Cain, we knew having more vines didn't add value to your property – in fact, having *fewer* vines could increase the value. The only things we had to lose were costs … and time spent in the vineyard.

By now, the vines were nearly twenty years old. They were producing amazing fruit and made outstanding wine, but we couldn't justify the time and money spent on keeping them in production. Even selling the fruit didn't do much better than break even. Because our vineyard is old and falling down in places, we also can't send the cost- and time-efficient harvesting machines through to pick because our infrastructure can't stand the heavy shaking, so we are forced to hand-pick all of the fruit, which costs a bomb. So we reduced the vineyard by roughly half. It still hurts to say it, and to see those vines in disrepair.

The thing about reducing a vineyard is that it's easier said than done. We needed to kill the vines, remove the infrastructure (wires, poles, irrigation) then return the land to flat ground. We started the project with gusto – removing vine crowns with the chainsaw then chopping away at their bases – but as the enormity of the task started to overwhelm us, and summer turned into winter with its demand to prune the vines we were keeping, and all the while the accommodation business kept up its momentum, we soon felt swamped by the whole thing.

Two years later and the vineyard still didn't look as it should. Half the vines were more or less dead. We were no longer harvesting them for fruit and they were an eyesore of lifeless grey limbs and long overgrown grass, a messy mass of falling-down poles and wires that perhaps one day we would get around to removing. But in the meantime, we needed to upgrade the remaining vineyard, which was in desperate need of new infrastructure, and so the cycle went around and around and the grapes continued sucking up more and more of our funds to give us so little in return.

Not only would we be producing less wine, but in turning our backs on below-cost wholesale deals, we'd lost our three largest customers who could take seventy to ninety per cent of each year's production between them. As we came to rely solely on our existing customers and guests, our stock levels remained mountain high, never diminishing. We steadfastly refused to bow down to the wholesale buyers, however, and figured that, as we gave our guests complimentary wine on arrival, and have been known to tipple a little ourselves, any of our own wine we used for either purpose would save us money in the long run. If we never have to buy another bottle of wine to drink until the day we die, but just slowly make our way through our perfect-for-cellaring stock, then we are still in front.

But there's only so many of our eighteen thousand bottles of wine we can consume ourselves. So we made the decision not to make any wine from our grapes but to sell them instead – except Chardonnay, because we had run out of that. We secured a good price to sell our Shiraz, and had three different buyers for our Semillon. And good old Toddy, just unable to help himself, spent all that money before the season was anywhere near done.

I'd forgotten about that little lady called Mother Nature.

Earlier in the season we'd experienced a hailstorm and, though it appeared to have done little to no damage to the grapes, a lot of the young berries had been hit and these died out on the vine. Our yield for the year was almost half what it was the previous years, and our grape buyers were left short, and they weren't happy. What we made from selling the fruit barely covered our harvesting costs.

When it came time to harvest the Chardonnay, the birds were so hungry they took most of it, so we decided to buy grapes from another farm – the first time we'd ever had to resort to those measures. Still, we had our Shiraz to come and it was the one we were being paid the most for ... or would have been paid the most for had the frigging crows not come and decimated the entire crop overnight. We cancelled harvest and kissed goodbye to fifteen to twenty grand, the sum I'd already mentally spent on putting a floor down inside our villa, and paying back Mum and Dad for a loan we should never have taken.

We decided to take another year off, bowing down to Mother Nature and asking her to spare us some of her destruction, just this once. But even worse things were to come.

* * *

'So Charlotte,' I said, winding up the call to my information-seeker in Canberra, 'making your own wine is a joyous, amazing and incomparable thing in life. Many people make money out of the wine industry but we simply aren't among them. Invest in your brand – get it known, get in restaurants and bars and magazines and on social media, win awards, promote your cellar door – your future has to rely on you selling at a reasonable but not astronomical retail price, and riding out the storm of wholesale buyers who feed off seeing you in a position where you're desperate enough to lose money.'

* * *

As winemakers struggled to make ends meet, other business in the Valley thought up new ways to bring in some well-needed cash. Before long, one industry started to dominate.

My brother Glen used to work in restaurants, which often meant he would come home quite late (or early, depending on how you looked at it), and often after a few (or several) drinks with his workmates. In 2004, when his husband, James, was doing a bit of work for me during normal office hours, they were rarely on the same social wavelength. One night, Glen came home and got it into his head to play an ABBA CD, as you do at two in the morning, when your partner is asleep in the next room. The song he really wanted to play had a scratch across it, so the player wouldn't acknowledge it. This didn't deter my brother who, once he gets a notion to do something, will generally follow it through to the death.

As he sat cross-legged on the floor in front of the CD player, it went a little something like this: the song wouldn't play, so he would hit 'back' on the remote control. The previous song, 'I Do, I Do, I Do, I Do, I Do', would start playing the familiar horns and brass of its opening bars. *That's not the song I want,* Glen would think, and hit 'forward'. Again, his song wouldn't play. 'Back'. Horns and brass. *That's not the song I want.* Forward. Back. Horns. He must have done this about twenty or thirty times, the only noise coming from the living room those same few bars, when James finally exploded.

He stormed into the living room, screamed, 'It's broken!', snapped the CD in half and threw it into the bin. I would have given anything to be a witness to it, and it's among my favourite Glen stories.

Jeff offended just over half the world when he said anyone with net curtains deserves to die. Well, now I'm about to alienate myself from the other half. I do not believe in weddings. Like James with my brother's ABBA CD, I want to scream, 'It's broken!' too.

Thanks to Paula Yates, when I was younger I saw myself getting married to a bride wearing a red lace dress with a long train, but I suppose I always knew it wouldn't be someone in a dress across the altar from me. So the idea morphed into me being the one wearing red – a red tartan suit, perhaps. But then the older I got, the more I began to realise that, actually, a wedding ceremony just didn't sit right with me, red suit or not.

Marriage is fine, and ever since it was made legal for same-sex couples I'd be a wealthy man if I had a dollar for every time someone asked whether Jeff and I were going to.

For the record, we're not, ever. It's something we neither feel the need nor desire to do. But I do understand why marriage can be an important agreement for people to enter into. What I don't get is why people also feel the need to spend thousands of dollars on a ceremony in which they stand in front of hundreds of people to say they love each other, then have those hundreds of people congregate in an impersonal and public place to share bad food and shit wine, and to listen to speeches that only make sense to the person giving them. Then the bride and groom dance awkwardly to one person's taste in music on a dance floor that is three-by-three-metres square.

Maybe I'm over-simplifying the whole shebang ... but I still don't get it.

True, I'm happy enough to sing in front of fifty people at my thirtieth, and show a video of me dressed as multiple Meryl Streep characters at my fortieth, and I have been planning what to do at my fiftieth for nearly seven years (oh, just you wait and see!) ... But ask me to be a groom for the day? Not on your life!

It's the minor details that seem least unique: the thumbprint tree, the names in lights, the cheeseboard engagement memento, the wall of drinks, succulent wedding favours, releasing of balloons/doves/floating candles (or, I don't know, bloody wild monkeys) ... all the ways people try to make their day 'special' when they're just jumping on the bandwagon of whatever trend is popular at the time.

The flow-on impact from all these people choosing to get married in increasingly lavish and 'unique' ways is that the wedding industry is ridiculously huge, at around two billion dollars a year in Australia. Just think how far that money could go in doing something meaningful, like helping starving people eat, giving animals shelter, saving farmers from drought or, hell, even being selfish with it and buying a new car or a house to live in! But once a handful of brides or grooms starts a trend, everyone wants in on the action, including choosing the loveliest place to get married.

On their website, *Lonely Planet* mentions the 'Disneyland aspect' of the Hunter Valley wine region. Not only do we have international concerts, Christmas lights, snow in July, Ferris wheel, chocolate festival, camel rides, horse-drawn carriages, hot air balloons, smoky barbecue days, thrill flights, hand-made markets, farmers' markets, disco buses, llama walks through the vines, pop-up this and that, and the list goes on ... but now we have become the wedding capital of Australia.

It seems every person and their goat are opening a wedding venue in the Valley and there are lots of reasons local councils aren't putting a cap on how many are being granted permission to open. Every single one throws another chunk of cash into the council's coffers, thanks very much. We have barn venues, marquees, chapels, open-air, purpose-built, restaurants, cellar doors, accommodation venues … all vying for a slice of that rich wedding cake.

Some of them will do anything to make a quick buck, even converting their living rooms. As long as some couples have a grapevine to look at, they don't seem to care if it's in your living room, or that you don't have council approval or insurance. In one weekend, a venue can make anywhere from ten to forty grand gross on a wedding and, if they're smart enough to do fifty or sixty weddings a year … well, anyone can see how those figures add up. Which is all well and good if you're running a wedding venue, but if you're trying to sell expensive wine or accommodation in the same area, things might not be so lucrative. As we all-too quickly found out.

The more wedding venues councils allow to open, the fiercer the competition. And that means a price war to attract as many weddings as possible. When you throw in extras like late curfews, BYO booze (and, often, food), hire your own staff, then you end up with budget weddings for people who do not have the cash to spend on additional extras like good quality local Hunter wines, or staying at mid- or high-priced local accommodation. In general, wedding guests drive to the Hunter Valley late Friday afternoon, have a meal at a large sharehouse or local pub, go to an early Saturday afternoon ceremony followed by a long boozy reception (where non-Hunter wines are served), then wait for the hangover to subside before driving straight back home on Sunday. They do not have the desire, time or funds to spend on visiting a local cellar door; they prefer to stay one night rather than two; and, after paying for petrol, a new outfit and a present, they prefer to spend as little on the accommodation as possible.

Our neighbour called me one day to ask, 'Was there a wedding in our street last night?'

'Yeah, there was,' I said. 'How did you know?'

'Not a single person in the cellar door today. For the first time in fifteen years, not one visitor on a Sunday. Can only mean one thing – all the accommodation on our street was booked out by wedding guests and they aren't interested in tasting or buying wine.'

'That sucks. I guess we're lucky because we still get booked,' I said, trying not to focus on the negatives. 'But we've noticed very few wedding guests buy any of our wine or anything else we're selling, so we're losing out there …' I couldn't help myself. I didn't go into how it also often meant bowing to the pressure of providing discounts on the accommodation.

'Last week one of their guests came here for a quick wine tasting, then used our toilet to get changed for the wedding!'

'Cheeky buggers!'

'Yep. Didn't buy anything, of course. Just made me do a one-hour wine tasting so they could hit me up for a changing room.'

'Did you tell them to fuck off?' I asked.

'Ha!' He laughed. 'What can you do? Charge them twenty bucks to use the loo?'

After talking with other local businesses, we could clearly see the main reason driving people to visit the

Hunter was beginning to shift. I spoke to my mate Paul at one of the cellar doors.

'Sales are down twenty-five per cent on last year,' he said grimly. 'And last year was down on the previous year. All these hens' and bucks' and thirtieth birthday parties ... no one wants to buy.'

I hadn't really thought that with weddings also come hens' and bucks' parties. Increasingly, local cellar doors are visited by larger groups of millennials who pay for a wine tour (thankfully we offer this service), but their main aims of the day are to have fun, get drunk and do it as cheaply as possible. Buying expensive wines is not even a vague consideration.

I had to remind Jeff that we are fortunate we're offering an 'essential' service: a bed for the night.

Ever the financial realist, he was quick to point out, 'But even that isn't enough to capture the wedding market, and we're having to go even further, offering lengthy payment plans, discounts and added flexibility to bridal parties, all of which pounds hard against our bottom line'.

I'm sure without him I'd be Kylie Jennering our net profit figures and make it onto *Forbes*.

* * *

So what does all this mean for the future of the Hunter Valley wine region? Businesses will survive, sure. Some cellar doors (and the breweries and distilleries!) are a heaving noisy mass of young people on the weekends and, for some, business is absolutely booming. They tend to ask a tasting fee and recoup some of their costs that way but they generally sell their products at twenty to forty per cent less than boutique wineries, which they're able to afford through sheer scale. Or else they're evolving their offering and providing add-on experiences like chocolate, oysters, cheese, or other pairings – all moving further away from what the focus of the region once was: wine.

On the tours I run, I regularly get the feedback that people are seeking 'memorable experiences' and I've had some groups emerge from cellar doors saying they loved every single wine they tasted but because the winemaker or staff member hadn't made them laugh, or responded to some of their jokes, they didn't enjoy it and therefore hadn't purchased any wine. For our part, Jeff and I very quickly came to the realisation that the experience we offered our guests was much, much more than the alcohol we poured. Wine played a part, and sure, our ultimate aim was to sell some, but we know it is just one aspect of what we do.

I cast my mind back to that beautiful time we spent at Maggie Beer's farm in South Australia before our move to the country. In many ways it was the main impetus for Jeff and me to end up at Block Eight. Of course we were there for the food, but Maggie's produce is part of something bigger – her story, her farm, the history of her restaurant, her books, her brand, her beautiful personality ... all set against the backdrop of her stunning property. It had become a destination in its own right. How many Hunter businesses can truly say that of what they have to offer?

And if our region is becoming the wedding capital of Australia, then we could either join in or graciously bow out, because holding onto 'how things used to be' or insisting on sticking to our original master plan would necessarily end in failure. As we saw it, the solution wasn't to open yet another wedding venue – that was painfully obvious. It had to be about evolving our business, or creating a new one, that supported this ever-growing customer demographic.

While we love living in the Hunter Valley, Jeff and I also needed to remind ourselves that what brought us here originally was business – an opportunity to be self-sufficient instead of relying on corporations with their ever-increasing demands. We loved Block Eight, initially, for its privacy, solitude and quiet, but at its core, it always needed to pay us a living.

We just needed to figure out a way we could keep doing that.

Thirteen

The Dry

When Jeff and I decided to transition to a plant-based lifestyle (meat-eaters, cue obligatory grimace), Jeff went cold turkey immediately.

The day after making his decision, he went to a local café. After shopping for cushions he'd worked up a hunger and was ready to flex his newly found vegan muscle.

'Do you make the pumpkin soup with chicken stock?' he asked.

'Yes, we do.'

'Okay I'll just have the green salad and a large flat white, thanks.'

A few minutes later, the waitress came to Jeff at his table. 'Actually, the chef has just told me she uses vegetable stock, not chicken – would you like the soup instead?'

'Yes please, that'd be great,' he said, rather impressed there was a real vegan offering in such a small café in an industrial part of town. After the waitress left, he watched her deliver the pumpkin soup to two women eating at a table nearby. It was topped with sour cream. *Cream*, he thought. *I don't eat that any more. Shit! I forgot to ask for soymilk in my coffee.*

Just then, his coffee was delivered. By now he was a little embarrassed about all of his demands and, knowing there was another request coming, he decided not to mention the cow's milk in the coffee but instead said, 'Can I please have no cream on top of my soup?'

'Of course, no problem,' the waitress said politely.

A few minutes later she came back with Jeff's soup and put it next to his untouched coffee.

'Soup with no cream on top,' she announced. 'There's enough cream in the actual soup to make it delicious anyway.'

Jeff sat for what he thought was the appropriate amount of time and when he figured he could make his escape without drawing the attention of staff, he got up and left. He came home without having eaten any lunch and made himself his standard go-to: baked beans on toast. You can take the boy out of England ...

While he was grappling with these situations, I thought I would make my life easier and be vegan just at home and that I'd be okay with vegetarian options when eating out. But after three or four weeks, I knew that my conscience wouldn't allow it. After all, I was vegan for three reasons: health, animal welfare and the environment. Well, the dairy and egg industries are just as bad as the meat industry on all three counts, if not worse.

Since going vegan, we've seen a significant shift in the volume and variety of plant-based ingredients at supermarkets and meals at restaurants all over Australia. Being vegan is no longer awkward or difficult, and it just makes sense on so many fronts. I always say I'm not a vegan preacher – to each their own and all that – and if you want to eat meat then that's your prerogative and you won't hear a thing about that from me (unless you challenge me with some illogical arguments).

I spent most of my twenties as a pescatarian. My philosophy was pretty simple: I enjoyed fishing and didn't mind hacking off the head of a fish, yanking out its guts then eating it. My parents lived on the Central Coast and I quite enjoyed taking out their little dinghy to cast out a line in the hope of catching fish (usually leather jacket, though of course Grant, my ever-legendary brother, once caught a baby shark), mud crabs, or blue swimmer crabs. I'd do the gutting or the crab freezing and happily serve up a meal. But towards the end of my twenties, the lure of pepperoni grew too strong and I caved.

In about 2016, we had our friends Theo and Sarah out from the UK with their kids, Gabe and Hebe. Sarah is the cousin of my friend Meredith so her husband, Lachlan, and son, Jack, also joined us, along with baby Ivy. Gabe was about nine and because he'd never been before, he really wanted to go fishing. As we had silver perch in our main dam, I offered to take the older kids out in the dinghy Dad had lent us. Dad had also given us some hand lines, and before long Gabe caught a pretty big fish. As I hauled it onto the boat, it flapped about crazily, as caught fish are wont to do. Jack found the whole scene horrifying and wanted to be rowed to shore, but I insisted it would all be fine, I just had to remove the hook from the fish's mouth. We wouldn't be eating it, this was just for fun.

The hook was lodged so far into the fish's mouth that it took me several goes to get it at the right angle to remove. Every time I jiggled the hook, the fish writhed in such immense pain that its body practically folded in half and the blood flowed so freely it started dripping onto the floor of the boat. Jack started crying.

'Almost there, kids,' I said all chipper, but the bloody hook just wasn't coming out.

I pulled and wiggled and angled and yanked with all my might, each time sending the fish into a painful spasm. Finally after about eight goes, I got the hook free, and in the process I'd mangled a corner of the fish's mouth. Gabe got his requisite photo and was very proud of himself, but for the first time in my life I'd been in tune with a fish's pain and I swore that I would never catch another again, and I have not. I also banned people from fishing at our dam, but as fate would have it anyway, in 2019 a hungry pelican moved onto our property and took care of whatever stock we had left in the dam ... or so I thought.

I was cleaning one of the villas facing our second dam about a year later when I discovered the pelican hadn't been as thorough as I first thought. The second dam relies on natural rainfall to fill and by that point we hadn't had a decent downpour in about two years. It was sitting at around twenty per cent capacity. Where once the water was deep over my head, I could now walk on dry mud inside one of the channels leading into the dam. While cleaning, I noticed a white thing floating on the edge of the water and thought that perhaps a guest had left behind a ball or something. On closer inspection I saw a few of these mysterious floating things.

I walked towards the dam. Littered all along the edge of the water were twenty, maybe thirty dead silver perch, each about the size of a football. Their dam was so stagnant that they hadn't been able to survive.

I called my regular corpse handler.

'We have a gross job to do. You'd better bring some gloves and some garbage bags.'

Jeff trudged down a few minutes later. 'Oh my god,' he said like he was about to vomit. 'This is going to be so bad.'

And it was. There were so many dead fish in the dam that we needed to get the tractor bucket to hold them all. We counted over thirty, each about five kilograms. Twenty-year-old fish, succumbed to the drought.

'This is the most disgusting thing I have ever had to do,' Jeff said with a groan.

'What? Worse than hauling out that dead kangaroo?'

'Yes! Ten times worse than that!'

'Oh give me fish over mammals any day,' I said. Though later it did take about ten minutes of constant skin scrubbing to get the smell of dead fish from my hands.

It was as if all those dead fish were a sign of the apocalypse: the planet is sick and we demand more from it than it can provide – heed its warning or ignore the signs at your peril. Maybe it's time for Jeff to dig us a shelter underground and stock it with baked beans, food for the animals, tofu ... and wine.

* * *

I've heard most of the jokes about vegans but I take them on the chin. A waiter at a restaurant once told me, 'I know you find buying meat from a butcher disgusting, but buying vegetables from a shop is grocer.'

Another time, I prepared a table full of food for a Christmas celebration for my whole family, and we invited Pete, Ange, and their daughters, Tejay and Jorja, to join us. We even splashed out on fancy crackers and read the obligatory jokes and riddles aloud.

My riddle said, *What is served but never eaten?*

'Vegan food!' Pete said.

Most people don't agree that animal suffering is something to feel morally guilty about, and some insist it doesn't actually happen. Buzzwords like 'organic', 'free range', 'ethical' and 'RSPCA-approved' all mask the true conditions faced by animals raised for, and at, slaughter. So let's say we as humans are born to consume meat and that's the way we've always been. Why change now? For every research paper I've read about the adverse effects of a diet high in animal protein, I know every one of us has heard of a medical professional telling someone that the solution to being low in iron is to eat more red meat. So let's dismiss the potential health benefits of a vegan diet because we humans just *have* to eat meat.

But what about the environment?

It wasn't until I went on tour to Dubbo to promote the *Helga* book that the absurdity of our current situation in Australia really hit home for me. The Hunter Valley is in drought and has been for some time, but it is absolutely nothing compared to how dry it is out in Dubbo and the surrounding areas.

There I was, driving along roads bordered by farms where animals raised for human consumption – the same animals that have been introduced to this harsh landscape – were struggling to survive. Not only do they need water to live, but they also need to eat lush green crops to fatten up for slaughter. But of course we as a nation stripped the landscape of most native plants (which can mostly cope with periods of drought) to turn them pastoral. Since then, global warming – itself a side effect of the industry we're trying to salvage – has meant less rain in rural areas, which is where we choose to raise meat for the majority of the population. It isn't as visible to most of us, who live in coastal areas, where it naturally rains more often.

The farmers I spoke to in Dubbo were bordering on despair. They were paying tens of thousands of dollars to bring in hay and feed for their animals from another state, where fortunately there was enough rain to grow crops for meat-producing animals to eat. As I drove, I watched these bony animals forage for plants to eat – mostly the dead grass patches intermittently dotted throughout the vast dirt plains. Then I would come to the next farm and, for whatever reason, they had access to more water. Their fields – the ones right next door to dust – were a sea of lush green.

I despair when I see advertisements by water conservation bodies telling us to shorten our showers and turn the tap off while we brush our teeth. Cutting three minutes from your shower will save around twenty-seven litres of water if you've installed a water-efficient showerhead. If using less water in the bathroom is all it takes to conserve water resources, more people should be like me and Jeff – since moving to the country our weekly shower count has fallen dramatically.

'I don't see the sense in showering every day when I'm just going to get dirty the second I begin work,' I said to my friend Pet, and her face twisted in a horrific kind of disgust. Most days her nickname for me is 'Dirty' something or other. 'Dirty Vegan' for example. Or 'Dirty Homma'.

But consider this. Just imagine that as a country, we all agreed to make every Monday meat-free. Let's assume that on any Monday in Australia, around (a very conservative) half of the population eats around three hundred grams of meat (again conservative). The Institute of Mechanical Engineers estimated that to produce one kilogram of meat requires a minimum of five thousand litres of water. So by choosing not to eat meat for one day, you're saving 1500 litres of water (that's close to *three hours* of water in the shower ... at the very least). And if only ten million of the approximately twenty million Australians who eat meat went meat-free on Mondays, that would save fifteen *billion* litres of water every week. That's about thirty times the amount of water in Sydney Harbour. Showering less isn't going to fix the dire situation our planet is in, but eating less meat will.

If fewer animals needed to be farmed, then the fifty one per cent of all greenhouse gas emissions caused by livestock and their by-products would also decrease.

So if you hate those pesky vegans going on about animal welfare, and wish they'd shut up for your children's sake … think about what kind of planet your kids will inherit, as we try desperately to keep twenty-seven litres of water out of our shower drains but consume the equivalent of thirty Sydney Harbours' worth of water every Monday.

This does beg the question, 'What do vegans eat anyway?'

If you asked my ten-year-old second cousin Theo, he'd tell you 'crumbed tofu'. Every time he calls me, it coincides with Jeff's and my favourite meal: crumbed tofu with spring onion jam. I could eat it every night of the week, much like I used to say I could have eaten pepperoni pizza every day for the rest of my life.

'Again?' Theo groans.

'Yeah, and tonight your mum is making it for you too.'

'Get out!'

'No seriously. She told me she's making you go vegan so you're gonna have to kiss those steaks and your favourite chicken parmy goodbye.'

'Nahhhh …'

'I've already sent your mum the recipe for eggplant parmy, and tofu parmy – you'll love it.'

'Aww, you're just pulling my leg.'

'You'll see.'

'Those vegan cupcakes are pretty good, but.'

* * *

Sometimes I wonder if, as a wine producer, I'm just as culpable as the meat farmers. Some people might tell me

I may as well start eating meat, because growing grapes is *just as bad* for the environment. Not quite. *The Economist* estimates that it takes nine hundred and sixty litres of water to make one litre of wine. How many days per week are you drinking a litre of wine versus eating three hundred grams of meat? In going vegan, I'm no longer consuming around one hundred and ten kilograms of meat each year, which means I alone no longer require over half a million litres of water just to eat meat. That's the equivalent water required to make almost eight hundred bottles of wine. Much as I love a sip or two, I don't think even I could drink that much in a year. I suppose the real point here is that I'm trying to be more conscious of the things I consume (as well as grow) and, where possible, I make choices that are having better impacts on our planet and its inhabitants. Any step taken by any of us to adjust this chronic environmental imbalance is at least one step in the right direction.

Jeff has a saying: 'why let perfect get in the way of very good.' I take that to mean we *are* making a difference to the planet by not consuming meat and dairy, and though making wine isn't saintly, it's far less damaging to the environment than raising or eating meat. Besides, when I have a few glasses of wine in front of Netflix, the only animal it causes harm to is me. But I'll take my chances.

* * *

Closer to home, in the last few years the drought has started having disastrous consequences on our property. While we get water pumped in from the local river to water our crops (it's expensive and there's never a guarantee that we will get any despite the yearly fee), that water only goes into one dam, not all three of the ones we have. And it wasn't just our second dam – and its resident fish – that suffered.

Over the summer, we watched the depth of Helga's dam inside The Farm decrease by centimetres on a daily basis. You could literally see the previous days' levels drying up in the sun.

We didn't think all that much of it – Helga still had enough to wallow in, the ducks could still paddle about – then one day Wesley got ill. If there's one alarm you can't ignore at Block Eight, it's Wesley not being interested in his tucker. Nothing comes between my fluffiest goat and his food – not even a heavy-set determined lady named Helga.

I called our friendly vet Beth and asked her to come out, just as she had done for Winston's mysterious illness. And so I went through the trauma once again, of watching poor Wes get stabbed repeatedly with needles as we tried to restore some energy in him through a painful drip. Unlike his brother, however, Wesley just stood there silently taking the torture, until the very end when he let out a deafening, excruciating groan. As if to say, *Alright Toddy, I've done my best but that's about all I can bear.*

In a few days, his condition improved but, despite the tests, Beth couldn't put her finger on what was wrong with him.

Then it was Wanda's turn. And if Winston and Wesley had shown signs of illness, Wanda looked like she was on her deathbed. She could barely stand up. It was definitely time for me to order that fancy goat bed and round-the-clock nurse.

Since Wanda was smaller, we were able to rush her in the ute to the veterinary surgery. Beth walked into the treatment room.

'Oh god,' I said with a moan, 'I was so hoping it wasn't going to be you. "Oh here comes the paranoid goat boy again."'

'Well we discussed who should take on the case and, thanks to you, I now have more experience in goats.'

The perfectly behaved Wanda was poked and prodded, tested and probed, but nothing appeared to be wrong with her. She was given an ultrasound for the *very* unlikely scenario that she was pregnant, and the whole examination set us back a cool few hundred bucks.

And then it dawned on me. 'Jeff,' I said one night, 'what if the animals are drinking the stagnant dam water?'

By that time it was probably less than twenty centimetres deep and about as big as half a tennis court. It often served as Helga's and the ducks' toilet. It was brown and smelly, and had started showing signs of algae.

'If we don't do something soon they're all going to die!' I bellowed dramatically from stage right, the back of my hand pressed delicately to my forehead. Of course I could have pretended one of the animals was sending Jeff a message to fix the problem, but this time he could see the stress in my eyes so I could save that tactic for another, more personal request in the future.

We thought about all the potential solutions, but nothing was going to solve the problem as quickly as it needed. Jeff went off to his mysterious builder's/farmer's/handyman's outlet and came back with a massive hose, some connectors and a plan. If we temporarily disconnected the water in the olive groves, put the hose on the tap at the property's perimeter, then turned on the pump, it might be strong enough to get water from our main dam into Helga's. And it was. For two weeks we let the water run and almost instantly the mood inside The Farm improved. The filthy white ducks now had enough depth to dive beneath the surface and clean themselves, Helga had enough water to submerge herself in the hot summer sun and, if they happened to drink any of it, all the other animals now had access to water that was cleaner, fresher and wasn't about to cause them any harm.

But the drought also had another immediate impact on our livelihood. We didn't realise it at the time, but the earth was so dry, our vines (which like to draw moisture from deep underground) didn't have enough water to get through the season and produce abundant, plump grapes. As much as we dripped water onto the soil's surface, the vines, sun and weeds greedily lapped it up and nothing was able to penetrate further underground. As a result, when the vines came to full life late in the year, their canes were short and stunted, and the amount of fruit they were able to produce was reduced by almost half. Even then, the amount of juice was reduced significantly because there wasn't as much moisture in the fruit.

We'd already made agreements to sell all of our Semillon and Shiraz that year, and at full yield that could have grossed us around thirty thousand dollars, but at under fifty per cent yield, it barely made it worth tending the vines at all, as picking them alone costs the best part of ten grand not to mention all the costs in the lead-up to harvest. But we soldiered on.

If the vines were thirsty, the drought also made a lot of animals very hungry. Kangaroos had no fresh grass to graze on, so turned to our lush and sweet grape leaves and this lessened our grape yield even further. Local council had allowed the development of a major new town not far from us and, in so doing, had given the go-ahead for thousands of acres of natural habitat to be destroyed, so now we had more kangaroos on our property than ever. When we first moved in, it was rare you would count more than sixty at a time; now there was barely a day you couldn't count double that. They stripped the leaves off our vines, giving the hungry birds that came late in the season easier pickings of the lovely, sweet, juicy fruit. In all, the season was pretty much doomed from the start … and that was without the threat of bushfire.

One of the more astonishing symptoms of the drought around us was the visible impact on native plants. At various spots on our property, fifty- to one-hundred-year-old eucalyptus trees started dying. In a desperate effort to conserve what little moisture they had left, whole patches of trees started letting all of their green leaves die, and big dry areas of brown, dying trees soon emerged all over the Hunter Valley. Everything was fighting for whatever water was left in the ground, and no one was winning the war. Then, our olive trees started turning brown.

We saw the possibility of our thousand trees dying off as utterly heartbreaking, but with only enough water in the dam to get the grapes through the hot, dry summer, and knowing the olives had only produced one year in the last seven, we had no other choice but to let them go. That lovely grove, so beautiful and inviting, the first hint at some of the magic that Block Eight reveals would soon be an open field of dry dead grass … and we would have to spend money, time and energy to fell a thousand dead olive trees.

* * *

Despite such obvious signs of drought, our business continued on. A litre of water costs us almost half a cent. That doesn't sound like a lot, but on average, a typical stay can use up to five hundred litres. And when you have five villas, across the year, that can be well over five grand in fresh water. City folk have no idea how lucky they are to just turn on the mains and pay a few hundred bucks a year. When people are on holidays in the country, very few of them give a rat's clacker about the scarcity of the stuff, nor how much it costs. Guests have countless spa baths or run dishwashers with only a handful of plates inside.

Once we even had a guest who was utterly flabbergasted at my resistance to her request for thirty-six bath towels … for a two-night stay. Why anyone would drive all the way to the Hunter Valley to take thirty-six showers is beyond me. But when she checked out, it was the two kilograms of cooked meat in the fridge that frustrated me the most – it all ended up in the bin.

I did get a little bit of 'can't help myself' revenge during her stay though.

She texted, *I can see the ironing board but you don't seem to have an iron?*

To which I replied, *Yes we do. You'll find it behind your mountain of towels in the laundry.*

Fourteen

Full Circle

'So Block Eight is becoming a hotel?' Jeff asked one night as we sat drinking wine, trying to decide our future.

'We have to work with what we've got, and whatever we've got has to appeal to as many customers as possible. And dammit, if anyone can evolve and thrive in any environment, it's you and me. I mean, look at us. When we got here we didn't even know where water came from. We didn't know a grape cane from a node. You barely even knew a white from a red wine –'

'That's not bloody true!'

'Well, you know what I mean. I just think we still have work to do here. Do we really want to surrender this so easily?'

'I just don't know,' he said and poured us another glass of wine.

It was our 2014 Reserve Semillon, the first one we ever produced. Five years on it was subtle, butterscotchy and utterly delicious. Sitting on the back deck of the house the night we moved in back in 2012, drinking the 2006 Brokenwood wine made from our very own grapes, felt like several lifetimes ago. Our 2014 Reserve was now nearly as old as that had been, and in our opinion it was even better.

'I'm just saying that if we move fifty minutes out of Cessnock in some remote backwater we may not have an offering that would bring in enough customers,' I said.

'Do you still like living here?' he asked quietly.

'I still think Block Eight is one of the most stunning properties in the entire Hunter Valley wine region,' I said earnestly. In all my days driving the bus I'd seen so many and still, coming home was incomparable. 'And besides,' I added, 'our animals are happy here. I know we didn't buy Block Eight to build accommodation for a fly-in/fly-out "just here for a wedding" clientele, but we also didn't come here to lose, or surrender.'

* * *

I did some serious competitor analysis and while it showed that we were competitively priced when any prospective customer took into account all that we provided, it was also increasingly difficult for people to compare apples with apples. On comparison booking sites, which drove about eighty per cent of our bookings, our list price appeared expensive compared to an almost-endless supply of other options. It led to many sleepless nights and hours of teeth clenching for me, and a number of 'what if' conversations between Jeff and me, but eventually we came to the conclusion that what we offered still made us proud and remarkable, and the only way to secure more bookings was to lower our pricing, which we did by twenty to thirty per cent. It felt dire and drastic but it also felt like our last ditch effort to keep the business afloat.

After lowering our villa, wine and tour prices, the bookings and sales almost instantly flooded in and it seemed that we had found our sweet spot. Yes, we were working harder for every dollar but we were still profitable (though slightly less so) and the income gave us a little bit of breathing space. We knew we would have been busy anyway, but it was undeniable that our new pricing strategy was working. Still, at night I felt deflated that for every room we let, every tour I drove, and every bottle of wine we sold, we were earning less profit than we had before.

That we were doing the right thing though, was reinforced by a conversation I had with Linda at the local laundry, where we get our linen for the villas. Linda had been seeing a lot more of us in the weeks following our price drop.

'You guys must be the busiest people in the Valley,' she said.

'We are so flat chat,' I agreed with her. 'You know things were so quiet for us in March that we lowered our prices, by a lot, and things just turned around straight away.'

'Well you're doing something right,' Nikki, another staff member, joined in and the conversation continued. 'I was talking to a guy yesterday and he's been running his accommodation for over ten years; it's very similar to what you guys do. He said this month has been the worst he's ever seen.'

'It's just Block Eight and the big hotels that are busy,' Linda said. 'Good for you guys.'

'I can't tell you how happy I am to hear that,' I said to them both. 'Not for everyone else, obviously. We just wondered whether we'd still be getting all these bookings if our prices were higher, but you've answered that for me today.'

'An empty room is pointless,' Linda said. 'If people don't want to change to meet the demand, then they'll suffer.'

I raced home to relay the conversation to Jeff.

'We've definitely done the right thing,' he said. 'Even I wasn't sure at first, Toddy, but it's obvious now. And don't discount the impact of your book. We never expected it, but you can't deny how many people have stayed and mentioned how much they loved reading it.'

We hear so many other local business owners lament falling traffic and sales and yet so few of them seem brave enough to make a real shake-up of their offering. When we give wine tastings now, people get one flat price across all of our wines, sometimes as low as fifty per cent off retail, and it's working. We are selling more in gross sales.

Ironically, the additional busyness means I have never cleaned more toilets in my life and my grand plan to have the bus's turnover relieve me of that chore is firming up as more and more laughable.

This crazy time in our business also came with the realisation that Block Eight is not what we dreamed it would be. There had been talk of us selling up, moving further out, and starting all over.

'So if we're relying on the Hunter for income, and that income is being paid to us by millennials, or bridal parties and their guests, then it's about time we sucked it up and acknowledged that in order to survive this life, we may have to accept some of the side effects of the change in customer,' I said.

'In what way?'

'Well, in general, we've noticed customers want a high-level offering for a mid-range price ...'

'And if we aren't willing to accept any of that?'

'Then we are in the wrong place, and we should sell Block Eight. But setting up another business somewhere else in the Hunter Valley probably isn't going to work, because the customer is still going to be the same, more or less.'

Our plan, its name, our logo and every aspect of our branding was designed to represent a luxury, high-end offering. Our customers were meant to be wine-obsessed couples that loved spoiling themselves and spending big on weekend escapes and enjoying the finer things in life. But those customers, if they were still coming to the Hunter Valley, weren't staying with us very often any more.

It was never really part of our business plan, but driving wine tours, in many ways, saved our hides. Because the Hunter gets so hot and most people prefer to spend their breaks at the beach, January and February are always our quietest months for the accommodation side of our business. Some people do still visit the Valley and we advertised our luxury air-conditioned bus widely, so we managed to get a few bookings from across the local area. Having that extra few grand coming in was a godsend. We'd prepared to cushion summer's blow by offering our past customers a stay three/pay two deal and it helped bring in some extra bookings, but at the same time it kind of masked what was really happening – that we'd become a less profitable, discount hotel.

The summer of 2018/2019 was the hottest we'd experienced since moving to the Hunter Valley. It started, unusually, with several high thirty-degree days in November and confidently carried over into December. The Christmas period is usually bustling for us, with nomads and non-celebrators clambering to get out of the city. But they probably chose beaches instead of the bush that year because of how hot it was. And the bills kept coming in, especially now the bank had reverted our loan back to principal and interest, and we had two shiny new vehicles to pay off, and more animals to care for.

Without our special deal, January and February would have been over fifteen per cent down on previous years and as part of that deal we were also giving away six packs of our wine, so in all, we lost those months too. But March was the real kick to the guts we hadn't been expecting. Usually it heralds the end of summer, with our bookings taking a steep upward tick, but the heat was so bad that people stayed away in droves. A run of seven or so forty-degree days did nothing to encourage people to visit the Valley. Then came an election that generated a lot of economic uncertainty, so if people were spending on travel, it wasn't to Block Eight.

Of course, we weren't alone in the Hunter Valley – our friends at cellar doors could not believe how quiet it was.

Restaurants became ghost towns and the few concerts in the area that usually drove accommodation bookings were only moderately successful, but were an absolute logistics debacle, so people just wanted to get home rather than spend money on wine and food. By the end of the month, we were a gob-smacking forty-four per cent down on the previous year and, were it not for the bus bookings that came through in dribs and drabs, we would not have been able to make ends meet – though maybe if we'd got rid of the bus altogether the costs and income would have evened themselves out, or resulted in more spare cash for us.

When you're in the throes of a major challenge to everything your business stands for, sometimes you're just too blind to see a way out. You hope the bad times will pass, you know you're not the only one suffering, and you hope the coming winter (your busiest months) will be kind to you. But all in all, it became patently clear to Jeff and me that things had to change.

We considered removing all of the complimentary add-ons we provide our guests – breakfast, wine, treats ...

'But that's everything Block Eight stands for. That's what sets you apart,' my friends Belinda, Pet and Mel all responded. It was hard to argue against them.

Over a period of a few weeks, Jeff and I went through every minute line item in our costs, and slowly and carefully removed some of the more expensive ones – things that our guests wouldn't really notice, offerings that no one really seemed to use – so our business could become more profitable. But still, would the bookings come? And how did we really feel about taking away a chunk of Block Eight's soul?

With all of those drought warning signs, Jeff and I also felt we needed to make more of a stance for the planet. Mother Nature may have been one of our arch-nemeses, but we still felt a kinship with her. We spoke with a lot of our friends about whether they thought it was a bad move to provide our guests with vegan food during their stay. Jeff and I had come to the conclusion that, while it was great for the planet (and our health) that we had gone vegan, our business consumed more animal products than we ever would in our lifetime. We ummed and ahhed about the decision for weeks, but in the end felt it was just the right thing to do. Besides, we weren't militant about the foods we chose to provide – in most cases if we did it intelligently, most of our guests would barely notice or, if they did, would appreciate the quality of what we gave and so wouldn't think twice about it.

'Jeez, that's risky,' Vicky said on one of my visits to Brisbane.

'We know it is, but it's one we're prepared to take.'

'Bloody vegans,' her sister Sarah chimed in. After fifteen years in the family, I was used to these kinds of jibes from them.

'I know, right,' I agreed.

'I can handle vegans. It's your bloody gluten frees I can't stand,' Vicky said. 'Such a pain in the arse!'

'I know! I mean, what are they trying to do, exactly? Save all the world's wheat plants?' I asked, giving Lucy and Charlie the giggles.

Ninety-nine per cent of our guests have embraced the change we've made to our menus at Block Eight. Some have remarked over the delicious 'butter' and asked for more, most have commented on the generous amount of food we provide, others keep asking for certain recipes. My coconut, vanilla and maple cupcakes, a recipe I've refined over time, have replaced the oat and vanilla cookies we used to leave as a welcome for all of our guests. They're moist in the middle and crunchy on top, just as they should be. In place of bacon, we give hash browns, tomatoes, baked beans and mushrooms. We still give eggs, some from Stevie and Nicks, and others we source from local open-range farms.

During her seven-week stay with us, even Millie went completely vegan. Jeff's mum never once complained about the food we cooked, though she wasn't too afraid to tell us she thought the texture of tofu was absolutely disgusting! Every night she would rate the evening meal and, dammit, no matter how hard I tried, she always rated Jeff's meals better than mine. Jeff might be better than me at building, but a chef de cuisine he ain't! Every night I'd tease her to try to get her to say mine was better.

'But weren't Jeff's nachos too spicy, Millie? Weren't those corn chips too crunchy?'

'No,' she'd chime in that singsong, full Brummie accent of hers.

'But you have to admit this lasagna is pretty good …'

'It's a very close second to Jeffy's meal last night,' she'd insist and that only made me love her all the more.

Even 'meat and three veg' Dad was forced to go vegan whenever he and Mum came over for dinner. I made them pizza, my unbeatable herb bread, and served him pudding and ice cream for dessert.

'See Dad, it's not so hard eating vegan is it? Every single thing you had tonight was vegan.'

'What, the mushrooms?'

'Yes, Dad.'

'Not the potatoes? They're not vegan too, are they?'

And I think that kind of sums up how the knee-jerk reaction to a plant-based diet is based mostly on misinformation. Dad doesn't even realise he gets soymilk in his cuppa when he's here.

* * *

We were having a few wines one evening with Erin and Jarrod, helping them get their converted barn ready for accommodation rental, when the topic of eggs came up. Erin and Jarrod are so incredibly generous with their time, focus and resources, saving native and domesticated animals wherever they can. For our part, we felt the absolute least we could do was to give them something back, by offering suggestions for how to get their place ready sooner. Over wine, I mentioned that we were eager to get more chooks so we could ensure the eggs we provided our guests were ethically the best possible.

'How many chickens will you keep?' Jarrod asked us.

'Enough to keep our guests in eggs,' Jeff said. 'So maybe around fifteen.'

'There's a group who save chickens from egg farms,' Erin said. 'I'll send you their details.'

Whether caged, free-range or open-range, it's a little known fact that the majority of egg farms routinely have three barbaric policies: all cocks are murdered at birth (their little bodies are fed into a large metal meat grinder while they're still alive), all hens have their beaks cut back with a hot soldering iron, and all hens are gassed to death at around the age of eighteen months (after that age, their egg laying is irregular and unpredictable, so they become more of a liability than an asset).

'You just put your order in with the group and the next time they go to a farm on gas day, they will save that many chooks for you.'

'That's amazing,' I said.

'They can never guarantee they'll lay eggs every day, but the ones we've rescued generally do,' Erin said.

'But surely that's just a bonus. I mean, we don't even know where our open-range chickens, Stevie and Nicks, lay at the moment. We rarely get any of their eggs.'

'Exactly.'

Building a new henhouse is up near the top of our list of to-dos. I know we have more pressing issues at Block Eight, projects that will actually return us money (more than we currently spend in buying eggs), but I also have a feeling that at some point I might approach Jeff with an 'I wonder if we shouldn't prioritise ...' conversation and get those rescued girls higher up that list.

* * *

By the time we (and by 'we' I mean Jeff) were close to having our fifth villa finished, we started to feel like it wasn't a home for us. We'd originally rented out our three-bedroom home on the property to make ends meet. It was always meant to be a temporary situation, until we'd realised how much money it gave us, after which we chose not to move back in at all. The original idea had been for us to live in the fifth villa, but after spending a week in the house during a quiet time in bookings, we finally decided that it was time for us to return to our home, even if this meant a fall in income.

During the completion of the fifth villa, I'd had to endure a number of cushion parades from an excited Jeff, who showed them off like a mum does her toddler at a beauty pageant. It reminded me that he would never be getting over his little obsession. Indeed, I watched his whole demeanour come alive as he finished building and designing the villa, and it made me wonder what he would move onto next, and what role cushions would play there.

At the end of the 2017/2018 financial year, our business had turned a profit for the first time. Sure, it was only a few hundred dollars but it was the first time we'd officially been in the black. By the end of June 2019, our profit had jumped to tens of thousands of dollars. We had thought that 2019 would be catastrophic, but our determination to fight the fall in luxury travellers saved us from a significant loss. We still had no money in the bank, but surely this was a sign that we'd finally, indisputably, made it ... and this whole tree change shebang was starting to pay us dividends.

* * *

A few weeks after she left us, I called Shelly the real estate agent to let her know we'd made our decision. We would work through everything on the list of to-dos, and when that was done, *whenever* that was done, I would call her to take stock of the situation, consider the market, and ponder our feelings.

But within a few weeks both Jeff and I knew that our work here at Block Eight was far from over. It still wasn't perfect, but whoever believed there was such a thing as perfection anyway?

Six years and ten months after we moved to Block Eight, and about six years after we'd moved out of our home on the property to rent it out to tourists to help us make ends meet, we finally moved back in to the house. No longer would I be living through a renovation site with no running water, electricity or flushing toilet. And now that we were moving out of a villa, there would finally be a separation between our lives and our business. There was even foolish talk of a holiday.

It wasn't until we'd decided to move back into the house that I began to fully appreciate how much our family and friends have put up with over the years. I've lost count of the times Lucy and Charlie have had to 'camp out' with us on makeshift beds, with little heating or cooling, all of us crammed into one room as though we were on a permanent caravan trek through our own property. Not once did either of them complain about a lack of creature comforts, privacy or that our guests lived in luxury while they made do with a portaloo. They weren't the only ones. Glen and James slept in a tent inside an unfinished villa one forty-degree

Christmas, forcing James to masterfully hang a cheap fan upside down from the ceiling to circulate as much air as possible … and it wasn't until weeks after they left that Jeff realised the rotting cabbage smell inside the villa was due to a sewage pipe that hadn't been sealed.

Our friends Mel and Hamish flew out from Kuala Lumpur and didn't flinch at the prospect of sleeping on a still-in-plastic mattress on the floor inside our unfinished villa while our other friend Tash slept on the daybed in the same room, like a school camp forcing strangers to become instant friends sharing all meals and bodily functions within earshot. And if it's not Mel, Jesus, Sophia and Amelie cramming with us into a villa meant for two then it's Vicky bringing the kids down for school holiday fun when she could be living it large on the cruise ships that she often takes them on. But these sacrifices our friends have made only spur us on to get things finished faster, to make temporary beds for them or buy furniture or mattresses long before we actually need them. And it amazes Jeff and me that no one ever grimaces when they're shown their sleeping quarters, or are told they can't bathe during their stay and have to use the outside portaloo during freezing winter nights. But then, that's exactly what true friends do for one another isn't it?

The night we moved back into the house, just as we had on our first night on 22 September 2012, we cracked open a bottle of 2006 Brokenwood Belford Block Eight, the one they'd made using our own grapes. Only this time, it was our last bottle instead of our first.

'To coming full circle,' Jeff said, and raised his glass in a toast, Leroy purring away contentedly on his lap.

We were both facing the dam and the vineyard, just as we had that first night we moved in.

'To never losing faith in each other, or in this,' I said, and waved my glass to the surrounds.

'And to a bigger, brighter future.' We chinked glasses.

The wine – so breathtakingly delicious when we'd first tried it, the liquid to blame for us becoming farmers – was even more sublime. It had mellowed further; it was rich and velvety, vibrant and comforting.

'I'm going to build you the most amazing window seat inside the living room,' Jeff said after we'd marvelled aloud at the wine. 'And when you sit in it, you'll be surrounded by every one of your cookbooks, Toddy, just like you've always wanted.'

'I cannot wait,' I said and took another sip. 'But I just can't get it out of my head ...'

'What?'

'How perfect that spot in front of the olives is for building our dream home.'

'Are you serious?' he asked, his voice nervous but with an undeniable tinge of excitement.

'Just think of all the cushions you'd need to buy.'

Everything that has happened to us at Block Eight has prompted the thought that perhaps it's time for a rebrand, or even a renaming. But for now, we remain those two city boys who risked everything to give the rural life a go by turning their backs on every aspect of their lives. We never intended to be grape and olive farmers, or make wine and oil from them. We had never wanted to rent out our home to make extra money; never thought we'd have need of a stupidly expensive tractor; hadn't thought that I would fall head over heels in love with farm animals, become a bus driver or write down some of our crazy tales for people to read; nor that we would end up running what is more or less a hotel.

We had some more work to do and when that was done, it was probably time for us to move on … To lead a simpler life where we weren't so at the mercy of forces beyond our control.

Fifteen

Catastrophic

I never really thought it was going to happen. I don't think any of us in the local area did. It was Tuesday, 12 November 2019 and the Rural Fire Service had forecast catastrophic fire conditions across the state of NSW.

It's a very big state, I thought. *What are the chances anything is going to happen to us?* We didn't even have a fire evacuation plan, that's how seriously we were taking things.

On extreme, blistering, blustery days, the hot wind on our property is like stepping inside a fan-forced oven. Jeff and I, operating in our 'business as usual' attitude, began the morning by weeding our vegetable garden. It was sweaty uncomfortable work and by mid-morning the temperature was in the high thirties. The wind was so strong it went through us, seemed to knock my brain about my skull, and before long a headache started thumping behind my eyes.

'Bugger me, this is stupid,' I said to Jeff with a sigh. 'I don't know about you, but I think I'm done for the day.'

It was only eleven. There were still nine hours of working light left … but not today.

'Why don't we go inside and watch a movie?' he suggested. I didn't need asking twice. Truth be told, I've always been easily corrupted.

Our accommodation guests were all off the property, out exploring the wine region for the day. It's a guilty pleasure when we down tools, knowing so much work needs to be done. There is always work to be done – the list is unending.

By early afternoon the movie was nearly over when my phone rang. It was Mum.

'Gidday love,' I said chirpily – my usual greeting for Mum. 'I bet you're loving this heat!' She has been known, on the odd occasion, to make statements about her imminent death during hotter weather.

'Is that smoke anywhere near you?' she asked, her voice full of concern.

'Nope! No smoke near us! Don't worry, darl'. We're inside, safe as houses.'

I didn't even bother looking outside. Nope, not even when the Rural Fire Service predicts catastrophic fire conditions and your mother, who lives a few kilometres away, asks whether the massive fire she can see is anywhere near you.

'I'll call you a bit later on,' she said.

I hung up the phone then looked out the window. Off in the distance to the west of us I could see smoke billowing into the air. It was thick and menacing. I immediately opened the Fires Near Me app on my phone.

Fire. Out of Control. Whittingham. That's fifteen kilometres from us, as the crow flies.

Bush fire. Out of Control. Rothbury. Three kilometres from us. Rothbury also backs onto a national park, and that national park borders our property.

Grass fire. Out of Control. Old North Road. Five kilometres from us, and one of our routes for possible escape.

Fire. Out of Control. Sweetwater Road. Three kilometres from us. Our only road out.

I stared at the app for a few minutes, struggling to accept the information. I refreshed the screen three times, hoping it would update and the fires close to us would miraculously disappear. But they weren't going anywhere. Another look into the horizon showed me that the smoke billowing into the air was only getting thicker and blacker.

'Fuck!' I said to Jeff. 'I don't believe it. Look at this. We're completely surrounded.'

My body instantly went into panic mode and the adrenaline pumped hard through my veins.

'Why are you shaking?' Jeff asked.

'I have no idea,' I said with a shrug. 'Because I'm scared shitless?'

I called our neighbour Derice. She and her husband, Ross, have lived on Sweetwater Road for the best part of twenty years. *Surely they've seen this before. They'll know not to panic.*

'Hi Derice, how are you?'

'Yeah …' she said forlornly, 'not too great today actually.'

The adrenaline was still pumping and I knew I couldn't engage in small talk. I jumped straight in. 'Have you looked out your window? There's a big fire in Whittingham and the app says there's another one on Sweetwater, one on Old North and another in Rothbury. It's looking pretty grim.'

'Shit,' she said. 'Let me call Ross. Let's stay in touch.'

And though we had a handful of neighbours we knew, in that moment I felt like Jeff and I were utterly alone.

My body wouldn't stop trembling.

'Can you drive down to Sweetwater and see what you can see?' I asked Jeff. 'But just be really careful, okay?'

I went down to see the animals while Jeff was away. There was no reason for it; I just needed to see them, to be close to them. They were of course none the wiser, trying to avoid the heat and the wind. My phone was buzzing constantly with messages from people who all seemed to be glued to the Fires Near Me app.

There's one on Sweetwater. Are you boys okay? asked our friend Verity.

From Mel in Sydney, *Are you checking the app?*

But most were from Derice. *Thomas just drove past Old North Road and said there was no fire there. I'm waiting for Ross to get back from Sweetwater. Keep you posted.*

The warning icon over Rothbury turned red in the app, which meant the fire there was now very dangerous. Shortly after, so did the one in Whittingham. Our friend Jenny, who lives thirty minutes away in Broke, texted, *You and your animals have a place to stay if you need one. Stay safe boys.*

Jeff finally returned after what felt like an hour, though it must have only been ten minutes or so. 'I couldn't see a thing,' he said. 'And I drove all the way to Wine Country Drive.'

I texted Derice, *Jeff saw nothing at Sweetwater. Ross?*

Nothing, she texted back. *Now both it and Old North have gone from the app.*

Two down, two to go.

The Rural Fire Service texted us all, *TOO LATE TO LEAVE.* But now we knew there was a safe path out down Sweetwater, then down Old North Road to the west, and cutting south down Hermitage Road ... so long as the fire in Whittingham hadn't spread too quickly.

By now two sets of our guests had returned, and Jeff and I decided it was best to evacuate them; we couldn't risk it. I went to knock on one door, then another. Both sets of guests were ashen, shaken.

Gayle had read my *Helga* book, contacted me on Facebook to tell me how much she related to it and then booked one of our villas for a five-night stay with her sister. It was her first holiday in years. I tried my best to keep my shakes hidden, hands firmly in pockets. I struggled to keep the quaver out of my voice.

'We're not concerned at all,' I said calmly. *LIAR!* my inner voice screamed. *It's Armageddon!* 'But your safety is our primary focus at the moment and we are requesting you leave the property until we know it's safe for you to return.'

I explained the route out, told them a safe place to congregate in the town of Cessnock.

'But what about you guys?' Gayle asked sweetly. 'What about Helga?'

'It's a wait and see at this stage,' I said, and for the briefest of moments I thought I might burst into tears.

With the property emptied of guests, that howling hot wind still ripping shreds off us, and the unmistakable smell of fire and smoke in the air, Jeff and I looked around our property, at everything we'd worked so hard for, the fears and tears, blood and mud, our much-loved animals so helpless in a situation like this. But then weren't we all?

We were now stuck in an excruciating game of 'wait and see how desperate the situation becomes'. Jeff and I stood on the back deck of the house and watched the smoke get thicker behind our grapevines. It was impossible to know just how far away the bushfire was, or how close it was getting.

'Do you think it will get over the vineyard?' Jeff asked.

'It's the wind that's the problem. It could blow the embers so far in front of the fire all those trees around our villas would go up in minutes.'

We watched the water-bombing helicopter circle over our land and head back into the fore. The sky around us had taken on an eerie smoke-tainted glow. The wind was still so strong – the perfect accomplice to the fire's determination to destroy.

'I just can't stand here and do nothing,' I said, still in disbelief. 'I'm going to drive the bus down to The Farm and have it ready, just in case.'

We'd worked out our evacuation plan. Jeff would drive Leroy and a handful of our possessions in Dawyl the ute. I was going on a wine tour of an entirely different kind to what our bus was intended – Helga would be shoved into the back storage area, while our six goats and two sheep would be in the passenger area. If I could catch any of

261

the ducks I would. An ark through fire instead of water. It was sure to be a journey I wouldn't forget in a hurry. I left the keys in the door compartment and walked slowly back to the house, watching the helicopter water bomb again.

The wind was fierce, but it was blowing directly towards the fire – a godsend for us, at least. The land between the fire and our property is around two hundred hectares of national park and one small rural housing development. If Mother Nature decided to change the direction of the wind, there was no way we would get out of this okay. We were banking on the fact that she would finally be on our side and Jeff kept checking his weather app to make sure the wind wasn't forecast to change.

I checked the Fires Near Me app again. A new major fire had developed in Greta, my parents' suburb. It was time to call Mum.

'Gidday love,' she answered. Behind her were the tell-tale chimes of poker machines.

'Have you looked at the news?' I asked, redundantly.

'No, what?'

'Mum ... there are fires all around us. One in Whittingham, one in Rothbury and now one in Greta. There's so much smoke in the air ... Haven't you seen?'

'No, I've been here since lunch.'

'Where's Dad?'

'At the shops in Branxton.' Her nonchalance struck fury in me.

'Mum, I don't think you have any idea how serious this is. Call Dad and tell him to come and get you. Go home now and sit and wait until you hear from me next. You might have to evacuate.'

'But –'

'Mum! Just do it! I'll call you back soon.'

I walked back to Jeff and complained about their cluelessness. As usual, he tried to help me keep things in perspective. One thing was becoming pretty clear: old Toddy doesn't deal with emergencies too well.

We went for a drive up the back of the property to see if the smoke or smell of fire was more intense there. Being told not to leave, knowing we still could, and having absolutely no idea how big the fire in Rothbury was, how much it had spread, and how imminent the risk was for our animals and us ... just had us feeling so out of touch. It was weird, in some ways, that both Jeff and I had resigned ourselves to losing all of our material possessions. We'd agreed we'd only take a handful of things in the ute and hadn't even bothered to pack them yet. Despite how hard we'd worked to make Block Eight our home and thriving business, it also became blatantly obvious that physical things simply did not matter.

Back at the house, we tuned in to the news. We saw familiar Rothbury streets ablaze. I fielded calls from my dad, and from Aunty Hazel, who was checking in to see if Mum and Dad were all right (bizarrely and frustratingly, neither of them were answering their phones). More texts came in from countless people, checking in to see if we were okay. But we were sitting ducks – nothing more, nothing less.

'When's the right time to flee?' we both wondered aloud.

'I guess when we see flames behind the grapes?' I offered.

'I guess ...' Jeff agreed, and then we turned to face the news on the television once again.

It went on for hours. One blaze in the app disappeared and then reappeared. Colours changed in the app from 'not to worry', to bright scary red. Another fire popped up, then disappeared. I called Mum and apologised for snapping at her – they were both clearly stressed at the situation and my highfalutin drama wasn't doing much to calm them. I arranged for two of our guests to stay at hotels in Cessnock – the last thing we needed was to worry about trying to wake people in the middle of the night – but I couldn't get hold of our third set of guests.

Just as the sun set, they returned from a pleasant day of wine tasting. Was I overreacting, or were they ignorant and blissfully unaware?

'Oh we don't want to evacuate,' Chuck said. 'We'd much rather stay here.'

'We don't think that's wise,' I urged. 'We are strongly advising you to leave the property.'

'But I don't want to travel back on myself tomorrow when we head down the coast ...'

'Okay, so if you stay in Cessnock tonight it's on your way.'

'But Cessnock? What is there to do in Cessnock?'

'We could find a hotel for you in Sydney.'

'But then I'd have to fight the city traffic tomorrow. I think I'll just drive to the motorway at Branxton and carry on down to the coast tonight.'

'I don't think you fully understand. There's a fire on the way to Branxton. The roads are closed. You can't get through.'

'Then I think we should stay here.'

I turned to his wife to gauge whether she would be more rational. 'I can put you up in a hotel in any town between here and Nowra; you just need to pick one.'

'I think we should leave, darling,' she urged her husband, and this set off a minor marital meltdown.

After forty minutes of conversation, they finally agreed to leave. I found them an oceanfront room in Terrigal that cost us four hundred dollars. In a display of humbling support, several weeks later, Expedia (the guest's original booking platform) agreed to cover the full cost. Other platforms weren't quite so generous.

That night, we went to bed still on edge. We took it in turns to set our alarms each hour, to wake up and refresh the Fires Near Me app and scroll through the latest news stories. Finally, a little after dawn, both the Rothbury and Whittingham fires were removed from the app. It appeared we'd narrowly escaped with just a few headaches. I couldn't believe how lucky we were.

Over the following months, we watched huge chunks of Australia burn. We watched entire communities get decimated, sat with horror as the death toll rose, and lost our breath at the sheer magnitude of the loss of wildlife. Like many, I had to look away at the news images of burnt and burning animals. It was too painful to watch. Smouldering koalas haunted my dreams. Everywhere we drove, I silently gauged the size of the bushland around us, saw the drought-crisp trees and undergrowth and knew it would take precious little to send the whole lot up in smoke.

In our area, Broke copped it worst. Multiple fires raged in the region for weeks and we checked in with Jenny regularly. She went to bed at night watching orange embers glowing on the ridges of the mountains surrounding her. The media magnified the scale of our local crisis and before long Jeff's family and friends in the UK had heard that all of the Hunter Valley was on fire and feared the worst for us. Guests started cancelling their stays with us. Some feared for their safety, others cited respiratory issues that meant they wouldn't be able to stand the amount of smoke in the sky. In all, over ten thousand dollars in bookings were cancelled, but we still considered ourselves the lucky few, when so many others experienced such heartbreaking devastation.

Most of the Hunter Valley vineyards lost their crops. When there is enough smoke in the atmosphere it can penetrate the skin of grapes and taint the taste of the fruit, and therefore the wine. I don't believe anybody in Broke picked any grapes but we were far enough away from the later fires to remain relatively protected from the worst of the smoke. We'd agreed way back in October to sell our entire Semillon crop to a local buyer for the price of fifteen hundred dollars a tonne. Though our yield was reduced because of the drought, we still expected around five or so tonnes and that money was the perfect amount to counterbalance the number of bushfire-related accommodation cancellations we'd received.

'How much did I say I'd pay you?' the buyer asked alarmingly when it was close to harvest.

'Fifteen hundred,' Jeff reminded him.

'Bit worried about this smoke taint,' the buyer said. 'We'll have to take a sample.'

A few bunches of grapes were picked and fermented into wine. After a while, Jeff got a text. *There's smoke taint. We will pay $800 a tonne.*

So we sent our grapes off for professional analysis. The results showed readings of normal on every single one of the ten factors, bar one. I called Dan, our winemaker, and explained the situation.

'Mate, you just have to ferment under refrigeration,' Dan said. (The buyer had made two bottles and left both at room temperature in forty-degree days.) 'Pick the fruit and we will go halves so you don't have to pay me winemaking costs.'

'Looks like we're making wine this year after all,' I relayed to Jeff. 'And to be honest, I'd prefer to see every grape fall to the ground than sell it for eight hundred.' I may have thrown a few extra choice words into the conversation. Really, we should have been charging a premium for usable fruit in a scarce market.

But at least we got some fruit, and were able to make a bit of wine out of it – one of the few Hunter Semillons from the 2020 vintage, and it's utterly delicious.

Though the dual hiccups of cancelled bookings and a reneging grape buyer added some strain on our business, compared to the previous summer, we actually did remarkably well. With so many accommodation providers complaining of the worst summer ever, somehow, some way, Jeff and I managed to clamber through one of the most challenging seasons on record.

When you watch your property – your whole way of life – under direct threat, it helps put things into perspective. Good old Mother Nature can come along whenever she chooses and rip it all away from you in an instant. Well, we may have spoken about throwing in the towel more times than we could count but, truth be told, we aren't ready to surrender.

Like most farmers, we lived to fight another day. And that's probably just as well, because lurking just around the corner was COVID-19. On its way to us was a battle that would require every ounce of our stamina just to survive. In comparison, everything else had been a stroll through an olive grove.

Epilogue

The End of the Beginning

I wouldn't say that drought, bushfires, heat waves, industry pressures and Mother Nature herself were a cinch to beat in battle. But that's just life on the land. You learn to leap each hurdle as it approaches, sometimes working out your tactics on the fly and simply doing the best you can to make it through. At Block Eight we'd weathered our fair share of storms and made it to the other side, still sane, profitable, and willing and able to face more. Then Mother Nature threw a real doozy our way. As the R.E.M. song goes, it was the end of the world, and boy did she make sure we knew it.

Within two weeks of COVID-19 heating up, over $80,000 worth of our accommodation bookings had been cancelled. I spent the best part of two weeks working in what amounted to a call centre, fielding cancellations and begging people to accept credits instead of refunds.

Thankfully, all bar two agreed, and those two unleashed a tirade of anger the likes of which I'd never seen before. People were scared. And our income dried up faster than a bar at the end of a buck's night.

Like most of the world, Jeff and I went into a blind panic due to the sheer mass of uncertainty surrounding every component of our future. We put our mortgage on hold, we put our credit card payments on hold, we negotiated discounts with as many of our suppliers as we could. A lot of other people were a lot worse off than us, so we kept reminding ourselves not to complain, and just hoped that we'd get past this hurdle like all the rest. Our beautiful friends and past guests banded together and bought some of the wine we put on sale in April, and their generosity kept us afloat. Still, we had no idea what the future would hold, and our cash cushion could get us through four months, tops. After that, we didn't know what we would do.

At the same time, we couldn't deny that having no guests on the property and no neighbours next door (they moved back in with their parents) returned us to a simpler, more serene time – much like when we had first moved in to Block Eight all those years ago. Of course, it's not in Jeff's and my natures to just enjoy the peace and quiet, so we used our two and a half months of downtime to start ticking off all the jobs we'd never had a chance to do because preparing the villas for check-in had always been the priority. Without even realising it, we were gradually completing all those things Shelly had suggested we needed to do to prepare Block Eight for market. By the time the New South Wales restrictions were lifted, Block Eight was a gleaming gem and it had never looked better.

I returned to the Block Eight call centre as our bookings went haywire. Once the restrictions lifted in June, our occupancy across all villas across all nights was one hundred per cent. July was pretty much the same, then August and September followed suit, and October became the most successful month in the history of Block Eight. We were overwhelmed with relief. We'd never been busier, and had never worked harder but the adrenaline was something we both grew to thrive on. The only real negative in all of this was that I was so busy I had very little time to spend down at The Farm, usually no more than ten or fifteen minutes a day. I missed it more than I thought was possible.

At the same time, economic uncertainty was doing strange things to the property market. Sydney prices might have fallen but as the wisdom of shares, city property and other investment strategies became questionable, those whose finances were otherwise untouched by COVID-19 looked to focus on rural land banking. Two properties on our street sold for *well* over what Shelly's business partner, Cain, expected. In fact, like Block Eight, the local estate agents couldn't believe how busy they were. And we weren't alone: cellar doors, restaurants, tour buses, you name it, the entire Hunter Valley was abuzz with business, the likes of which no one could remember experiencing. Some suspected that it wouldn't last, that it was a side effect of state and international border closures, but whatever the cause, we were making wine while the tourist dollar shined!

We knew Cain well. He was the agent who'd shown us Block Eight in the first place, when we'd made a last-minute decision to inspect it one weekend. But we'd stayed in touch with Cain and, after hearing of his success selling two of our neighbours' properties, I made a mental note to call him later that afternoon. But Cain beat me to it.

'Congratulations,' I said upon answering the phone. 'And thanks for turning our street into the Golden Mile!'

'Mate,' he said, 'I have never seen anything like this. A few years ago you said to me, "If ever there's a time we should be selling, please call and tell me." Well I'm telling you, that time is now.'

'I think maybe you had better come and convince us then,' I said and then went into the house to find Jeff.

Jeff and I spoke for six hours straight. Block Eight was looking its absolute best. Our income looked better than ever thanks to our full bookings post-restrictions. We had a modest sum in the bank (finally!) that – *if* we were to put the place on the market – we could put to good use painting the house and shed roofs. (And it wouldn't be me this time, thanks to whichever gods for my official pardon!)

We had achieved our ten-year goal of opening the Hunter Valley's best accommodation and, judging by its occupancy, had achieved it two years ahead of schedule. Sure I hadn't become the Hunter Valley's version of Maggie Beer, but after all of our hard work over those COVID months, we had overhauled Block Eight into one of the more stunning properties in the Hunter – and with not a single net curtain in sight!

In the end, what felt right, in our hearts, was to go out on a high – to hand over Block Eight to the next custodian and let them fall in love with it just as much as we had. A few hours after we signed the sales agreement with Cain, we received a booking from James, the first guest to have ever stayed in one of our villas. Then, the following day, I got a call out of the blue from one of the tour drivers around town asking if I would consider selling him our bus, as if he knew what we'd just decided. He bought it from us the following week. Our neighbour and friend Derice has taught me how to be open to signs from the Universe, and even I couldn't ignore this one. Things were coming full circle indeed.

Jeff rushed out and bought lots of nice new cushions to stage the house for sale. Give him his due, that boy sure does know how to zhoosh up a space. The final piece of the puzzle had now fallen into place; our home was polished and it too was shining bright.

There was sadness, nostalgia and pride, but a small tinge of relief also peppered our mood in those following days. We absolutely knew the timing was right. This was the end of the Block Eight part of our journey, but the beginning of what will undoubtedly turn out to be a long-term tree (or sea!) change. (We could never return to the hustle and bustle of the city and besides, we had one pig, six goats, two sheep, five ducks, two chooks, the peafowl and one very spoilt cat to consider.)

As is our way, we started looking at properties before Block Eight was even officially on the market. We were still on the hunt for something more private than Block Eight, but hopefully something with as much beauty. We had no idea what we were going to do next, and hadn't ruled out anything: accommodation, farming, winemaking, house renovating. We dreamt that we would finally build that house on the hill after all … just on another hill.

'Oh look at this,' Jeff said, and turned the computer around for me to see.

The property he was looking at was not far from Block Eight. It was nice and quiet, and very, *very* big.

'Jeff, it's huge. It's *nine times* the size of Block Eight!'

'Yeah … and?'

'I love it, but …'

'Come on, Toddy,' he said with that gleam in his eyes, 'how hard can it be?'

Recipes

Larger

Individual Mushroom, Tarragon and Lemon Pies

Serves 4

Make a batch of these in advance and keep in the freezer to re-heat when you want something fast and delicious. Serve as an entrée or a tasty lunch. You could even have these as part of a special breakfast or make smaller versions for canapés or high tea. I think the tarragon is a must but if you can't find it, substitute thyme, rosemary or one your favourite herbs.

Ingredients
4 tbsp vegan butter
4 sheets vegan shortcrust pastry
2 leeks, trimmed, peeled and thoroughly washed, then sliced
3 cloves garlic, crushed
3 tbsp fresh tarragon, finely chopped (or 1 tbsp dried)
4 preserved lemon quarters, peel only, finely diced (if you can't find preserved lemons, the finely grated zest of 1 lemon)
800g button mushrooms, thinly sliced
2 tbsp vegan stock powder
200ml white wine (I use Semillon)
2 tbsp cornflour
1 sheet vegan puff pastry
olive oil spray
ground paprika

Special equipment

Four individual pie cases – you could use metal or foil – or if you don't have these, use small ovenproof bowls or large cappuccino mugs.

Method

1. Pre-heat oven to 180 degrees Celsius.
2. Generously grease the pie cases with 2 tbsp of the vegan butter.
3. Place a sheet of shortcrust pastry into each pie case and trim to fit. Prick liberally with a fork.
4. Bake for 10–15 minutes until golden, then remove to cool but leave the oven on.
5. Melt the remaining 2 tbsp vegan butter in a large saucepan.
6. Add the leek, garlic, tarragon and lemon and cook, stirring, for 2 minutes, until the leek is tender.
7. Add the mushrooms and vegan stock powder and stir well. Cook for 5 minutes, stirring occasionally, until the mushrooms are tender.
8. Add the wine and bring to the boil, allowing to bubble for 2–3 minutes to let the alcohol burn off.
9. In a separate bowl, combine the cornflour with enough water to form a runny paste, ensuring there are no lumps.
10. Pour the cornflour paste in with the mushrooms and stir until the mixture thickens. Remove from the heat and allow to cool.
11. Once cool, divide the mushroom mixture evenly between the four pie cases, then top each with a piece of puff pastry large enough to cover the whole pie.
12. Dust each pie with paprika then bake in the oven for 10–15 minutes, until the puff pastry is golden and crunchy.

Sweet and Salty Pea-nutty Cauliflower

Serves 2–6

The combination of these flavours works well on lots of different types of vegetables (try it with mushrooms, eggplant and zucchini, for example) but especially cauliflower. Serve this as a main meal with a side salad, as a side to another dish or be really decadent and coat the cauliflower pieces in breadcrumbs and deep fry for a delicious canapé.

Ingredients
½ cup natural coconut yoghurt
1 tbsp soy sauce
1 tbsp sugar-free crunchy peanut butter
2 tbsp maple syrup
1 clove garlic, crushed
1 whole cauliflower, broken into florets, about the size of a golfball
FOR THE DEEP-FRYING OPTION
1 cup hummus
1 cup gluten-free breadcrumbs
1 tbsp vegan stock powder
1 cup canola oil

Method
1. Pre-heat oven to 180 degrees Celsius.
2. Mix all of the liquid ingredients and garlic together in a bowl until well combined.
3. Add the cauliflower and toss until each piece is well coated in the sauce.
4. Spread out on a lined baking tray and bake in the oven for 15–20 minutes, until golden brown and tender.
5. Serve hot.

For deep frying
1. Follow the above method then allow the cauliflower to cool to room temperature.
2. Pre-heat oven to 120 degrees Celsius.
3. Toss the cauliflower in a bowl with the hummus until each piece is well coated.
4. Combine the breadcrumbs with the stock powder in a separate bowl.
5. Toss individual pieces of the cauliflower in the breadcrumbs and place aside in a single layer.
6. Heat the oil in a deep-frying pan until it's steaming.
7. Deep fry 5–6 pieces of the cauliflower at a time until brown and crunchy – remove from the oil and place on paper towel in the oven to keep warm.
8. Once all the cauliflower is fried, serve immediately.

Couscous with Roasted Vegetables, Macadamia Nuts and Mustard Vinaigrette

Serves 4 for lunch or 2 for dinner

The most time-consuming part of this dish is waiting for the vegetables to roast. Next time you're making a roast dinner, cook extra vegetables and use them in this dish the following day.

Ingredients

1 bunch baby carrots, unpeeled (or 4 large carrots, quartered lengthways)
4 zucchinis, quartered lengthways
1 eggplant, cut into sixths, lengthways
250g button mushrooms
1 bunch spring (green) onions, ends trimmed
1 red capsicum, deseeded, cut into quarters, lengthways
5 tbsp olive oil
sea salt
1 sprig rosemary
1 cup couscous
1 tbsp vegetable stock powder
1 cup boiling water
¼ cup olive oil, extra
juice of 1 lemon
1 tbsp Dijon mustard
2 tbsp fresh dill, chopped
1 cup macadamia nuts, chopped

Method

1. Pre-heat oven to 180 degrees Celsius.
2. In a large baking tray, toss all of the vegetables with 2 tablespoons of the oil, and sea salt and rosemary.
3. Bake for 30–40 minutes, until all the vegetables are tender.
4. In a large serving bowl, combine the dry couscous with the vegan stock powder then pour over the boiling water.
5. Cover the bowl with cling film then leave to sit for five minutes.
6. While the couscous sits, put the remaining 3 tablespoons of oil, and lemon juice, mustard and dill in a bowl and whisk until well combined to make the vinaigrette dressing.
7. Pour the roasted vegetables, macadamia nuts and vinaigrette over the couscous and mix until well combined.
8. You can leave this to sit for up to one hour to let the flavours really soak in, or serve immediately.

Carrot, Ginger and Coriander Soup

Serves 4-8

In 2019 I had a bumper yield of carrots and I wanted to create a dish that showcased their amazing flavour. The secret to this soup is to roast the unpeeled carrots first for even more flavour, and add the ginger and coriander just prior to serving.

Ingredients
1 kg carrots, unpeeled and cut into chunks (reserve a handful of carrot top greens, to garnish (optional))
1 tbsp olive oil
2 tsp sea salt
1 tbsp sesame oil
2 large brown onions, roughly chopped
1 litre vegan stock
8cm knob of ginger, peeled and grated
½ bunch of coriander, finely chopped
sea salt, to taste
freshly ground black pepper, to taste

Special equipment
A hand-held blender or a large bench-top blender.

Method
1. Pre-heat oven to 180 degrees Celsius.
2. Toss the carrot chunks with the olive oil and sea salt and place on a large baking tray lined with baking paper.
3. Bake the carrots for around 30 minutes, until tender.
4. In a saucepan, heat the sesame oil for one minute, then add the onions and cook for 3–5 minutes, until they're soft.
5. (If you want a less fragrant soup, add the ginger and coriander now, and cook for another 2 minutes.)
6. In a large saucepan, add the carrots, onions and stock and cook for 10–15 minutes to allow the flavours to infuse.
7. Just before serving, add the ginger and coriander (if not added earlier) and then whizz all the ingredients with a blender until it reaches your desired consistency (I prefer my soup a little chunky).
8. Taste for salt and pepper before serving in individual soup bowls.
9. Sprinkle over some carrot top greens, if using.

Whole Roasted Fennel with Verjuice, Raisins and Pine Nuts

Serves 4

We often include fennel when we make a whole tray of roasted vegetables and it's usually my favourite, so I thought about making roasted fennel the hero of its own dish. Including roasted leek really lifts this dish so don't substitute onions or shallots. Serve as a filling lunch dish, or a main meal over a bed of plain pasta.

Ingredients
4 fennel bulbs, each cut in half
2 leeks, trimmed, washed and sliced down the middle
2 tbsp olive oil
1 tbsp sea salt
½ cup verjuice (or white wine if you can't find it – it's usually in the vinegar section of the supermarket)
1 cup raisins (yellow if you can find them)
½ cup pine nuts

Method
1. Pre-heat oven to 180 degrees Celsius.
2. Combine the fennel, leeks, oil, salt, verjuice (or wine) and raisins in a deep baking dish and toss to mix well.
3. Bake for 25–30 minutes, until the leeks and fennel are completely tender (test the core at the centre of the fennel to make sure it's tender).
4. Heat a saucepan and add the pine nuts – stir constantly until they are toasted and brown.
5. When the fennel and leeks are tender, sprinkle over the toasted pine nuts and serve.

Larger

Quick Asian Stir-fry with Noodles

Serves 2

Once you've chopped the vegetables, this will take about 6–7 minutes to make. It's full of flavour and crunch, and is super-low in calories thanks to the soybean noodles. You have the option of adding tofu for more protein (though more calories). Fast food at its best.

Ingredients
1 tbsp salt
200g soybean noodles
1 tbsp sesame oil
4 spring (green) onions, sliced
2 cloves garlic, crushed
1 red chilli, finely sliced (include seeds for extra heat)
5cm knob of ginger, peeled and grated
1 zucchini, sliced
2 carrots, thinly sliced
6 mushrooms, thinly sliced
1 capsicum, de-seeded and sliced
1 cup green beans, trimmed and cut into 2cm lengths
2 cups greens (spinach or a mix of Asian greens)
1 tbsp soy sauce
2 tbsp sweet soy sauce (kecap manis)
1 tbsp sweet chilli sauce
1 tbsp tomato sauce
2 tbsp sesame seeds

Method
1. Bring a kettle of water to the boil, then pour into a saucepan with the salt.
2. Once boiling rapidly, add the noodles and cook for 2–3 minutes, until tender.
3. Drain the noodles and set aside.
4. In a large frying pan or wok, heat the sesame oil then add the spring onions, garlic, ginger and chilli. Cook, stirring constantly, for 1 minute.
5. Add all of the vegetables and cook for 3 minutes, stirring regularly, until all vegetables are just tender.
6. Add all of the sauces and stir for 1 minute.
7. Add the noodles and stir for 1 more minute until well mixed.
8. Spoon into bowls, sprinkle over sesame seeds and serve immediately.

Edamame Spaghetti with Tomato, Chilli, Lemon and Rocket

Serves 4

I was browsing the health food section of the supermarket one day and came across edamame spaghetti. I've tried other low calorie / non-wheat versions of pasta but nothing quite stacks up to the taste and texture of the real thing ... until now. This has become a staple in our home – we eat it at least once a week.

Ingredients

1 tbsp salt
1 packet edamame spaghetti
1 tbsp olive oil (use a quick spray of olive oil instead if you want lower calories)
2 small red chillies (include seeds for extra heat, or replace with one long red chilli without seeds for less heat)
2 tbsp finely diced preserved lemon peel (if you can't find a jar of preserved lemons in your supermarket, just zest a lemon instead)
2 cloves garlic, crushed
1 punnet cherry tomatoes, each cut in half
½ cup white wine
1 tbsp nutritional yeast (optional)
1 bunch or bag rocket, roughly chopped
4 tbsp chopped flat leaf parsley
your favourite bread and vegan butter, to serve

Method

1. Bring a kettle of water to the boil.
2. Pour the water into a pasta pot / large saucepan with the salt, and bring to a rapid boil then add the spaghetti.
3. Cook for 2–3 minutes, until tender. Drain and set aside.
4. In the pasta pot / saucepan, heat the oil, then add the chilli, lemon and garlic. Cook, stirring, for 1 minute.
5. Add the tomato and cook, stirring for 2 minutes, until the tomatoes begin to soften.
6. Pour in the white wine and nutritional yeast (if using) and cook for 2 more minutes.
7. Add the chopped rocket and cook for 1 minute.
8. Pour the drained spaghetti back into the pot and using a fork, work the sauce through the spaghetti to make sure each strand is well coated.
9. Spoon into a large serving bowl and top with chopped parsley.
10. Get your guests to help themselves and serve with crunchy bread and lashings of vegan butter.

Spaghetti with Tofu-naise Sauce

Serves 4

This is it – my one (small) concession to something plant-based almost pretending to be something else. I don't add the tofu for flavour but rather to give the sauce a bit more of a bite. The tofu in this Bolognaise sauce is grated and added toward the end of cooking so it gives the sauce a mince-like texture. I served it to the kids once and they had no idea it was vegan.

Ingredients
1 tbsp olive oil
1 clove garlic, crushed
2 medium onions, finely diced
1 tbsp dried oregano
250g mushrooms, roughly chopped
4 tbsp tomato paste
400ml Shiraz red wine
1 x 400g can chopped tomatoes
375g firm tofu, grated
1 tbsp salt
400g dry spaghetti

Method
1. In a large saucepan, place the oil, garlic, onions and oregano and stir fry for 2 minutes.
2. Add the mushrooms and cook for 3–5 minutes, until they are tender.
3. Add the tomato paste and cook for 2 minutes, stirring often to keep it from burning.
4. Add the red wine and bring to the boil, then turn down the heat, add the canned tomatoes and let simmer for at least 15 minutes to let the flavours develop. Do this for as much time as you have, up to 1 hour for a deep, rich tomato sauce.
5. Add the tofu and leave to simmer while you prepare the spaghetti.
6. Bring a large saucepan of water and the salt to the boil, then add the spaghetti and cook it for 5–8 minutes until the spaghetti is ready (the best way of testing is to eat a strand).
7. Drain the spaghetti and pour onto a serving plate. Pour over the sauce and place in the middle of the table so your guests can help themselves.

Miso Eggplant with Ginger Fried Rice

Serves 4

When most of us think of eggplant, we probably think of squeaky spongy stuff without much flavour! Eggplant is a bit like meat, in that it needs to be prepared and cooked properly in order for it to be its best. For me, eggplant and miso are a match made in heaven and this dish is salty and sweet, tender and bitey – it will transform the way you think of eggplant.

Ingredients
FOR THE MISO EGGPLANT
1 large eggplant, cut in half lengthways
½ cup miso paste (you should find this in the Asian or health food section of your supermarket)
1 clove garlic, crushed
1 tbsp sea salt
1 tsp sesame oil
FOR THE FRIED RICE
1 tsp sesame oil, extra
1 clove garlic, crushed, extra
8cm knob of ginger, peeled and grated
1 packet microwave white rice
1 cup frozen peas
3 spring onions, sliced
1 x 200g tin corn kernels
4 tbsp soy sauce

Method
For the miso eggplant
1. Pre-heat oven to 180 degrees Celsius.
2. Score each eggplant half, diagonally. (Using a knife cut diagonal lines into eggplant about 1cm deep, making sure you don't cut all the way through. Turn the eggplant and cut across the diagonal with more lines, so that you're making diamond patterns.)
3. In a bowl, mix the miso, 1 clove crushed garlic, salt and 1 tsp sesame oil.
4. Smother each eggplant half with the miso mix and leave to marinade for at least 30 minutes.
5. Bake in the oven for 20–30 minutes until the flesh of the eggplant is soft.

For the fried rice
1. Heat the sesame oil in a frying pan or wok.
2. Add the garlic and ginger and stir fry for 2 minutes.
3. Add the remaining ingredients and stir fry a further 5 minutes.

Four-serve Minestrone

Serves 4

I never really thought soup made a hearty enough meal until my neighbour Derice served us a version of this dish – it was simple yet one of the most delicious and filling things I've ever eaten.

Ingredients
4 tbsp olive oil
1 brown onion, sliced
2 cloves garlic
2 tsp sea salt
2 tsp black pepper
1 tbsp vegan stock powder
3 tbsp tomato paste
2 zucchinis, sliced
2 carrots, peeled and sliced
8–10 mushrooms, sliced
1 head broccoli, chopped into chunks (including the stem – it's delicious)
250g vegan penne
1 x 400g chickpeas, not drained
1 x 400g tin chopped tomatoes
1 bunch chopped parsley
crusty bread, to serve

Method
1. Heat the oil in a large stock pot (it seems a lot but trust me, you need that much to coat all the vegetables).
2. Stir fry the onion for 3–4 minutes, until soft.
3. Add the garlic and stir fry another 1 minute.
4. Add the salt, pepper, stock powder and tomato paste and cook for 1 more minute.
5. Add all of the vegetables and pasta and stir fry for 3 minutes, until they're all coated in the oily mixture.
6. Add the chickpeas and tinned tomatoes and cook until the pasta and vegetables are tender.
7. Before serving, taste for salt and pepper and add more if required, then stir though the parsley.
8. Served piping hot with fresh crusty bread.

Sweeter

Coconut, Vanilla and Maple Cupcakes
Makes 24

I've struggled to find a vegan cake that was moist, tasty and light in texture. The secret to these is the desiccated coconut, and the coconut oil in the batter helps give the cakes a crunchy golden top. I love that when you make the batter, it 'sings' to you with a lovely crackle and pop sound. These are delicious without the icing, decadent with.

Ingredients
DRY INGREDIENTS
3½ cups plain flour
2 cups sugar
2 cups desiccated coconut
2 tbsp baking powder
2 tsp salt
WET INGREDIENTS
1½ cups coconut milk
½ cup olive oil

½ cup water
½ cup apple sauce
2 tbsp coconut oil (solidified)
1 tbsp vanilla extract
FOR THE ICING
¼ cup pure maple syrup
¼ cup coconut milk
2 cups soft icing mixture
2 tbsp shredded coconut to garnish

Special equipment
A 12-cupcake baking tin and cupcake patties.

Method
For the cupcakes
1. Pre-heat oven to 180 degrees Celsius.
2. In a large bowl, mix together all the dry ingredients.
3. In another large bowl, mix together all the wet ingredients.
4. Pour the wet ingredients into the dry ingredients and mix well with a wooden spoon or spatula, making sure all the dry ingredients are incorporated into the wet.
5. Using a dessert spoon, place 2 heaped spoonfuls of the mixture into each cupcake patty.
6. Bake for around 15 minutes, until each cake is lightly browned and firm to the touch.
7. Remove from the oven and allow to cool completely.

For the icing
1. Combine the maple syrup and coconut milk in a bowl and microwave for around 3 minutes, until it starts to boil.
2. Combine the icing sugar with enough of the maple syrup mixture to form a thick toothpaste-like consistency.
3. Spread 2 tsp of the icing onto each cupcake.
4. Sprinkle each cupcake with a little shredded coconut.

Macerated Strawberries with Golden Coconut Cream

Serves 4

The strawberries are super-fast and easy. You need to prepare the coconut cream in advance by leaving the can in the fridge for at least 24 hours so that it solidifies.

Ingredients
FOR THE STRAWBERRIES

1 cup of rosé wine

½ cup sugar

1 tbsp vanilla extract (or for a much better taste, the seeds from one vanilla pod)

¼ tsp freshly ground black pepper (sounds very strange but it brings out the strawberry flavour beautifully)

2 punnets of strawberries, halved and ends removed

FOR THE GOLDEN COCONUT CREAM

1 x 400g can coconut cream, refrigerated for at least 24 hours

3 tbsp golden syrup

2 tbsp chopped macadamia nuts

mint sprigs, to serve (optional)

Method
For the strawberries
1. Place the wine, sugar, vanilla and pepper in a saucepan and heat until it is just boiling.
2. Add the strawberries and remove from the heat – the strawberries will soften in the warm liquid in about 5 minutes.

For the cream
1. Remove the can of cream from the fridge, open it and carefully spoon out the set cream, separating it from the milky liquid.
2. Working quickly, stir through the golden syrup and the nuts and place back in the fridge until ready to serve.

To serve
1. Spoon the strawberries and some of the liquid into individual serving bowls. Place a dollop of golden coconut cream on top. Garnish with the mint sprigs, if using.

White Chocolate, Almond and Cranberry Balls

Makes 12 (approximately)

If I don't have anything sweet on hand for an after-dinner treat, I whip up a batch of these to satisfy my sweet-tooth cravings. They're fast, easy and 'sugar free'.

Ingredients
120g vegan white chocolate, melted in the microwave
1 cup almonds
½ cup almond meal
½ cup dried cranberries
¼ cup maple syrup or (if you can find it) coconut condensed milk
½ cup shredded coconut
¼ tsp salt
½ cup desiccated coconut, for rolling

Special equipment
A table-top blender.

Method
1. Put all of the ingredients, except the desiccated coconut, into a blender and blitz for 2–3 minutes, until the mixture forms into a ball.
2. Roll slightly smaller than golfball chunks of the mixture in the palm of your hand, then roll in the desiccated coconut.
3. Place in the fridge for at least 15 minutes to help them firm up a little, then serve.

Char-grilled Pineapple with Lime, Mint and Jalapeño Raspberry Ice

Serves 8

Sometimes after dinner I just want something light and fresh, with a hint of sugar and a nice little kick. This does the trick.

Ingredients
2 bags frozen raspberries
2 limes, juiced
handful chopped fresh mint
1 fresh (do not use jarred) jalapeño chilli, finely chopped (remove seeds for less heat)
4 tbsp icing sugar
1 pineapple, peeled and cut into 8 slices
¼ cup brown sugar (approximately)

Method
For the raspberry ice
1. Place the raspberries, lime juice, mint, chilli and icing sugar into a large metal bowl and mix with a fork, breaking up the raspberries a little.
2. Place back in the freezer until ready to serve.

For the pineapple
1. Pre-heat a grill plate or barbecue until very hot, about 5 minutes.
2. Sprinkle one side of each slice of pineapple with a little brown sugar and place sugar-side down on the grill.
3. Grill for around 3–5 minutes, until that side of the pineapple is nice and brown and softened.
4. Sprinkle the top side with a little more sugar and flip.
5. Cook for another 3–5 minutes on the second side.

To serve
1. Place a piece of grilled pineapple on each serving plate and spoon a heap of the raspberry ice to the side.

Baklava

Serves 8

Super easy to make, this is even better than the real thing because of the caramel / coffee-like taste the maple syrup gives.

Ingredients
4 cups walnuts, finely chopped
1 cup brown sugar
½ cup dairy free butter
1 packet of vegan filo pastry, defrosted in the fridge overnight
200ml maple syrup

Method
1. Pre-heat oven to 180 degrees Celsius.
2. Mix together the nuts and sugar.
3. Melt the butter in the microwave.
4. Using a pastry brush, brush some of the melted butter on the base and sides of a rectangular baking dish (about 20cm x 30cm).
5. Working carefully, remove a sheet of the pastry and place in the bottom of the dish (it's okay to fold it a little if you need to).
6. Brush the pastry generously with melted butter and place another sheet on top, butter the next sheet then place another sheet on top of that, then butter that.
7. Pour over a few handfuls of nut mixture then repeat until all the pastry and nuts are used up. (So, it's three layers of buttered pastry sheets, one layer of nuts, repeated.)
8. Bake in the oven for around 25–30 minutes, until lightly browned all over.
9. Remove from the oven and, while hot, cut into your desired shapes while leaving it all in the dish.
10. Heat the maple syrup in the microwave for 2–3 minutes, until steaming hot, then pour evenly over the baklava.
11. Leave to cool completely in the dish for around 2 hours before serving.

Acknowledgements

I think there comes a point in some writers' careers when they feel as though they're frauds. The Universe conspires to make you feel what you've created is not worthy of publication, and will not be embraced by readers. For me, that very low point came in the winter of 2019 and I was drifting out to sea wondering if I would ever write again.

Two women came to my rescue. Jane Novak – you are one of the most generous and genuine people I know, and one hell of an agent. Mary Rennie, the publisher of this book – you are a priceless gift. Thank you both.

Thank you to the legendary and inimitable Di Morrissey.

Thank you to Nick Cubbin (www.nickcubbin.com) for permission to use his lovely photo of us with Wilma and the chooks. And thank you to Jurds (www.jurds.com.au) for permission to use the photo of our vineyard. Other beautiful photography in this book was very generously provided by Work of Heart Photographic Studios (www.workofheart.com.au).

Thank you Mum (Judy Alexander) for being my proofreader. Any errors or typos in this book are entirely her fault so please forward any complaints directly to my mum. (I'm kidding.)

To the Kevin Costner of my *Big Chill* cast, Lisa Burston aka Bust-up, sorry you ended up on the cutting room floor … again.

My new home at HarperCollins Australia fits like a glove. Thank you Hazel Lam for the beautifully poignant and witty cover (and your patience), Belinda Yuille for driving the project, Shannon Kelly for another 'you read my mind' copy edit, and Georgia Williams for booking first-class travel for my goats and helping us all get this out to more readers. To the rest of the team, I can't wait to work with you all.

For every single reader who took the time to write to me, or came to one of my events, expressing your appreciation for my work, and how much you related to our little lives here in the Hunter – it means more to me than you'll ever know.

To the booksellers who have embraced my work and helped get these words in the hands (and minds) of readers – I am humbled and indebted. I dream of an evening every single one of you can come to Block Eight for a night of books, booze and banter.

Last of all, just as he is in the pecking order of mammals at Block Eight, thank you Jeff. You never quite knew what you were getting yourself into sixteen years ago but look how far we've come. And look how high we're yet to soar.

* * *

2020 was probably the most challenging year many of us has ever faced. I was frequently buoyed by the indifference our animals showed to the chaos. When I was at my wit's end, I'd lay my head against the top of Helga's head, or run my hands through Wilma's long mane or close my eyes to the soft motor purrs of Leroy. These are the images that will last with me longest from a year most of us would sooner forget. Thousands more animals need rescuing, though I think in truth it is us they rescue in the end. www.adoptapet.com.au